COMBINING and CREATING

SENTENCE COMBINING AND GENERATIVE RHETORIC

WILLIAM L. STULL

University of Hartford

Holt, Rinehart and Winston, Inc.

Fort Worth Chicago San Francisco Philadelphia
Montreal Toronto London Sydney Tokyo

Library of Congress Cataloging in Publication Data
Stull, William L.
Combining and creating.
Includes index.
1. English language—Rhetoric. 2. English language—Sentences. 3. English language—Grammar, Generative.
I. Title.
PE1408.S774 1983 808.042 82-15401
ISBN 0-03-057054-9

Address Editorial correspondence to:
301 Commerce
Fort Worth, TX 76102

Printed in the United States of America
9012 090 9 8 7 6 5 4 3
Holt, Rinehart and Winston, Inc.
The Dryden Press
Saunders College Publishing

Acknowledgments

Walter Van Tilburg Clark. Excerpts from *The Ox-Bow Incident* by permission of Random House, Inc. **Clarence Day.** Excerpts from *The Best of Clarence Day* by permission of Alfred A. Knopf, Inc. **Joan Didion.** Excerpts from *Slouching Towards Bethlehem* by Joan Didion. Copyright © 1966, 1967, 1968 by Joan Didion. Reprinted by permission of Farrar, Straus and Giroux, Inc. **Theodore Dreiser.** Excerpts from "The Lost Phoebe" from *Best Stories of Theodore Dreiser* by permission of The Dreiser Trust, Harold J. Dies, Trustee. **Kai T. Erikson.** Excerpts from review of *Laying Waste: The Poisoning of America by Toxic Chemicals, New York Times Book Review,* May 18, 1980. Copyright © 1980 by The New York Times Company. Reprinted by permission. **F. Scott Fitzgerald.** Excerpts from *The Great Gatsby.* Copyright 1925 Charles Scribner's Sons; copyright renewed. Reprinted with the permission of Charles Scribner's Sons. **Ernest Hemingway.** Excerpts from *The Short Stories of Ernest Hemingway.* Copyright 1938 Ernest Hemingway; copyright renewed 1966 Mary Hemingway. Reprinted with the permission of Charles Scribner's Sons. **Anne Morrow Lindbergh.** Excerpts from *Gift from the Sea* by permission of Pantheon Books. **Carl Sagan.** Excerpts from *The Dragons of Eden: Speculations on the Evolution of Human Intelligence* by permission of Random House, Inc. **David St. John.** Four lines from "Until the Sea is Dead," *The New Yorker,* July 7, 1980. From *The Shore* (Houghton Mifflin). Reprinted by permission. © 1980 The New Yorker Magazine, Inc. **Mary Jo Salter.** Excerpts from "Annie, Don't Get Your Gun," *The Atlantic Monthly,* June, 1980. Copyright © 1980 by The Atlantic Monthly Company, Boston, Mass. Reprinted with permission. **Irwin Shaw.** Excerpt from "The Eighty-Yard Run" reprinted by permission of Irwin Shaw. Copyright © 1955, 1961 by Irwin Shaw. **Lewis Thomas.** Excerpts from *The Lives of a Cell: Notes of a Biology Watcher* by Lewis Thomas. Copyright © 1974 by Lewis Thomas. All of the essays in this book were originally published in *The New England Journal of Medicine.* Copyright © 1971, 1972, 1973 by Massachusetts Medical Society. Reprinted by permission of Viking Penguin, Inc. **John Updike.** "Beer Can" from *Assorted Prose.* Copyright © 1964 by John Updike. First appeared in *The New Yorker.* Reprinted from *Assorted Prose* by John Updike by permission of Alfred A. Knopf, Inc. Excerpts from "Hub Fans Bid Kid Adieu" from *Assorted Prose* by permission of Alfred A. Knopf, Inc. **E. B. White.** Excerpts from *Essays of E. B. White.* Copyright © 1977 by E. B. White. Excerpts from *One Man's Meat* by E. B. White. Copyright 1939, 1940 by E. B. White. Reprinted by permission of Harper & Row, Publishers, Inc.

Cover and chapter opening designs: Mike Quon Design Office
Text design: Barbara Bert/North 7 Atelier Ltd.

PREFACE
To the Instructor

Combining and Creating brings together two of the most effective strategies English teachers have yet devised for improving students' writing: sentence combining and the once "new" generative rhetoric devised by the late Francis Christensen. Both methods have been rigorously tested in the classroom and found to enhance not only the fluency of students' writing but also—and far more important—the overall *quality* of their writing.[1]

While a few years ago sentence combining and generative rhetoric were cast as competing rather than complementary teaching methods, recent essays have suggested that the two strategies share common assumptions, methods, and goals.[2] These similarities notwithstanding, the two methods used together have distinct advantages over either one used alone. Sentence combining can improve students' writing even without formal grammar instruction. It helps them translate into writing the grammar they intuitively know as speakers of English. To do this, sentence-combining exercises ask students to combine simple sentences into more mature (i.e., more deeply embedded) sentences that establish explicit relationships among ideas. The generative rhetoric likewise fosters maturity in writing, but maturity of a different sort. As Christensen himself wrote, "We need a rhetoric of the sentence that will do more than combine the ideas of primer sentences. We need one that will generate ideas."[3] Toward this end, Christensen undertook a long inductive study of modern prose, both fiction and nonfiction, seeking the essential principles of good writing. In the course of this study, he isolated what *Combining and Creating* introduces in Chapter 6 as "The Four Elements of Style": addition, direction of movement, levels of structure, and texture. Furthermore, he discovered that one hallmark of a mature style is the non-restrictive or "free" modifier added to a short base clause, thereby creating a "cumulative" sentence. By its very structure, Christensen argued, the cumulative sentence generates ideas, since it encourages writers to pursue, shape, and further develop their

[1] See Donald A. Daiker, Andrew Kerek, and Max Morenberg, "Sentence Combining at the College Level: An Experimental Study," *Research in the Teaching of English,* 12 (October 1978), 245–56; and Lester L. Faigley, "The Influence of Generative Rhetoric on the Syntactic Maturity and Writing Effectiveness of College Freshmen," *Research in the Teaching of English,* 13 (October 1979), 197–205.

[2] On sentence combining and generative rhetoric as competing strategies, see the paired articles "Sentence Combining: Back to Basics and Beyond" by William Strong and "The Sentence-Combining Myth" by Robert Marzano, both in *The English Journal,* 65 (February 1976), 56–64. For an attempt to reconcile the debate that began here, see my own essay "Sentence Combining: Full Speed Ahead!" *The Leaflet,* 79 (Spring 1980), 25–30.

[3] "A Generative Rhetoric of the Sentence," in *Notes Toward a New Rhetoric: Nine Essays for Teachers* (New York: Harper & Row, 1978), p. 26.

thoughts. Thus, where sentence combining enhances students' fluency in writing, the generative rhetoric enhances their sense of style. To invoke a homely analogy, sentence combining is a starter motor for good original writing. It gets writers moving. Generative rhetoric, on the other hand, is a steering system—and a brake. It gives writers control over their speed and direction. Together, the two systems enable writers to get where they want to go under their own power.

Bringing sentence combining and generative rhetoric together makes sense in developmental terms as well. In her 1980 dissertation, "Sentence-Combining and Developmental Psycholinguistics," Janice Kleen proposed that for sentence combining to be used most effectively, it should follow the natural order of language acquisition. As youngsters grow up speaking English, they progress from using simple sentences to coordinating independent clauses and thence to creating complex sentences containing adjective, adverb, and noun clauses. The phrasal modifiers—verbals, appositives, and absolutes—which are the building blocks of Christensen's cumulative sentences, are, in comparison, late developments. While professional writers do indeed cultivate these late-blooming structures, few student writers ever use them without instruction.[4]

Combining and Creating follows this natural sequence of language development. In the first few chapters, students review strategies of coordination and subordination as they create compound and complex sentences. It is only after they have been introduced to Christensen's four elements of style that they begin concentrating on the "free" modifiers and cumulative sentences that characterize professional writing. Then, in the closing chapters, they study and practice such relatively sophisticated structures and strategies as noun substitutes and recombining patterns.

Perhaps the greatest common denominator of sentence combining and generative rhetoric is that they both teach writing *from the inside out.* All the examples in *Combining and Creating* come from professional or student writing, and all of the sentence-combining exercises derive from such writing. When students study the structures and strategies discussed in the chapter introductions, they learn how other writers have managed the language. Then, when they do the combining and creating exercises and compare their versions with the originals and with their classmates' versions, they learn not merely from admiring the masters, but from writing along with them.

Another assumption underlying *Combining and Creating* has to do with the place of grammatical and stylistic analysis in the composition classroom. Fifty years of educational research have revealed no direct connec-

[4] Janice Kleen, "Sentence-Combining and Developmental Psycholinguistics: A Critique of Seven Sentence-Combining Textbooks," Diss. Purdue University 1980. See also Kellogg W. Hunt, "Early Blooming and Late Blooming Syntactic Structures," in *Evaluating Writing: Describing, Measuring, Judging,* eds. Charles R. Cooper and Lee Odell (Urbana, IL: National Council of Teachers of English, 1977), pp. 91–104.

tion between grammar instruction and good writing. Yet English teachers are rightly loath to abandon stylistic analysis as a teaching tactic. Fortunately, while sentence combining provides teachers with a potentially "grammar free" method of enhancing fluency in writing, the generative rhetoric reaffirms the importance of stylistic analysis. As Christensen noted, "Grammar maps out the possible; rhetoric narrows down the possible to the desirable or effective."[5] For this reason, each chapter in *Combining and Creating* presents one major structure of English in both grammatical and rhetorical terms; that is, in terms of style.

But while the principal goal of *Combining and Creating* is to foster effective writing, the book should enhance students' reading power as well. Again, the approach is *from the inside out.* In the introductory material to each chapter, students learn how to read professional writing closely. Then, when the students re-combine the "de-written" passages in the exercises, they face the same semantic and syntactic challenges that the original authors faced. Finally, when they re-read their versions and compare them with each other's and with the original, they discover how different syntactic choices produce different stylistic effects. In other words, they learn to appreciate firsthand the interrelationship of grammar, style, and meaning.[6]

Like the chapter introductions, the exercises in *Combining and Creating* are all a means to a single end: fluent original writing. Toward this end, the book contains exercises of five sorts, each geared to teach a particular skill. Although many exercises urge students to practice a single structure or strategy, most of the exercises follow an open, unsignaled format that invites more than one "right" answer. In every case, the student can compare his or her exercise with a student or professional writer's version in the Appendix.

The short sentence-combining exercises are of three sorts. The "Combinations" exercises ask students to try out a particular structure or strategy they have studied in the chapter introduction. The "Creations" exercises call on the students to *invent* an appropriate structure and add it to a given sentence. The "Sentence Acrobatics" exercises are syntactic muscle-stretchers, extended verbal addition problems for students to solve in the most inventive ways they can think of. The phrase "sentence acrobatics" comes from Christensen, who said of his own students, "I want them to become sentence acrobats, to dazzle by their syntactic dexterity."[7] Naturally, such dazzlements become merely flashy when overcultivated, but most students' writing is so underdeveloped that this is hardly a danger. As

[5] "The Problem of Defining a Mature Prose Style," in *Notes Toward a New Rhetoric,* p. 134

[6] On the relationship between sentence combining and reading, see Marilyn Sternglass, "Sentence-Combining and the Reading of Sentences," *College Composition and Communication,* 31 (October 1980), 325–328.

[7] "A Generative Rhetoric of the Sentence," p. 36.

James Moffett observed, "Sentences must grow rank before they can be trimmed."[8]

Each chapter also contains four extended sentence-combining exercises, ranging from short paragraphs (about twenty simple sentences) to substantial essays (about one hundred simple sentences). These exercises vary in mode, from personal narrative and literary description to scientific exposition and political argumentation. About 10 percent of the exercises are derived from my own students' writing, while the rest come from the work of professionals. These master writers include novelists like Steinbeck, Hemingway, and Faulkner, as well as essayists like Joan Didion, Lewis Thomas, and Walter Lippmann. All in all, 237 professional writers are represented.

Finally, each extended sentence-combining exercise is followed by two "Writing Suggestions." These assignments, which students may do in class or at home, are based on the topics raised in the exercises. Typically, one of the suggestions calls for personal writing, writing that draws on the students' own experiences, opinions, or imagination. The second suggestion usually calls for objective writing based on analysis, imitation, or research. It is the "Writing Suggestions" that connect sentence combining and generative rhetoric with *original composition*—the real test of *Combining and Creating.*

Many people—students, teachers, editors, and reviewers—contributed much to *Combining and Creating.* My students, first at UCLA and more recently at the University of Hartford, have diligently worked through the exercises and helped me test the assumptions upon which the book rests. To them, especially to the many students whose work appears in these pages, my debt is great. My colleagues at the University of Hartford, particularly Sherry Horton, Charles Lipka, Robert A. Logan, Leo Rockas, Margaret Rundle, and Joan Shapiro, cheered me on through long hours of writing, revision, and proofreading. To Susan Goldberg, my research assistant during 1980–1981, my thanks are deep.

The indefatigable Richard S. Beal read and re-read drafts of the manuscript, offering invaluable advice born of long experience, always with encouragement and tact.

In the final stages of its composition, *Combining and Creating* profited from reviews by the following scholars: Raymond Brebach, Drexel University; Donald A. Daiker, Miami University, Ohio; Tom Davis, Ulster County

[8] James Moffett, *Teaching the Universe of Discourse* (Boston: Houghton Mifflin, 1968), p. 172. See also Douglas R. Butturff, "Sentence Combining, Style, and the Psychology of Composition," in *Sentence Combining and the Teaching of Writing,* eds. Donald A. Daiker, Andrew Kerek, and Max Morenberg, Studies in Contemporary Language No. 3 (Conway AR: L & S Books, 1979), pp. 39–42.

Community College; Thomas E. Gaston, Purdue University; Joan Garcia Kotker, Bellevue Community College; Walter E. Meyers, North Carolina State University; Michael Moore, University of California, Los Angeles; James W. Ney, Arizona State University; John J. Ruszkiewicz, University of Texas at Austin; Pauline G. Woodward, Lesley College.

Kenney Withers initially took on this project for Holt, Rinehart and Winston, and Anne Boynton-Trigg saw it through to completion. I owe special thanks to Pamela Forcey for shepherding the book through the press.

W. L. S.

Authors Quoted in the Text

All of the examples and exercises in *Combining and Creating* are derived from actual writing by students and professionals. While roughly 10 percent of the material comes from student writers, the greater part of the examples and exercises comes from the 237 professional writers listed here.

Alice Adams
James Agee
Conrad Aiken
William Allen
Woody Allen
A. Alvarez
Kingsley Amis
Sherwood Anderson
Peter Andrews
Roger Angell
John Ashbery
Isaac Asimov
Margaret Atwood
Jane Austen

Shaul Bakhash
James Baldwin
Bill Barich
Walter Jackson Bate
Bennett H. Beach
Ann Beattie
Robert Benchley
Arnold Bennett
Sally Benson
Bruno Bettelheim
Louis Bogan
Paul Bowles
Kay Boyle
Anthony Brandt
Richard Brautigan
Joseph Brodsky
John Brooks
Holly Brubach
Kenneth A. Bruffee
Eugene Burdick
William S. Burroughs
Elizabeth Burton

Erskine Caldwell
Truman Capote
Rachel Carson
Bruce Catton
John Cheever
Francis Christensen
Robert Claiborne
Walter Van Tilburg Clark
Eldridge Cleaver
Walter Clemons
Jay Cocks
John Collier
James Conaway
Joseph Conrad
Norman Cousins
Harvey Cox
W. Bowman Cutter

Clarence Day
Edwin J. Delattre
Agnes de Mille
Robert L. Dial
Joan Didion
Annie Dillard
Margaret Drabble
Theodore Dreiser
Elizabeth Drew

Phillip Edwards
Gretel Ehrlich
Loren Eiseley
Peter Elbow
Niles Eldredge
Alexander Eliot
Ralph Ellison
Kai T. Erikson
John Erskine
Howard Ensign Evans

William Faulkner
F. Scott Fitzgerald
Robert Fitzgerald
Edward Howe Forbush
Daniel Ford
E. M. Forster
Jerome D. Frank
Victor E. Frankl
Erich Fromm

John Kenneth Galbraith
Wolcott Gibbs
Brendan Gill
Penelope Gilliatt
Ralph J. Gleason
Harry Golden
William Golding
Emma Goldman
Barbara L. Goldsmith
June Goodfield
Donald Greene

Emily Hahn
Nancy Hale
Donald Hall
Garrett Hardin
S. I. Hayakawa
Harold Hayes
Mark Helprin
Ernest Hemingway
Michael Herr
John Hersey
Eric Hoffer
John Holt
Robert Hughes
Aldous Huxley
Ada Louise Huxtable

Christopher Isherwood

Henry James
Martin Joos
James Joyce

Pauline Kael
Nikos Kazantzakis
Kenneth Keniston
Nicholas Kenyon
Jack Kerouac

Michael Kinsley
Jerome Klein
John Knowles
Arthur Kober
Herbert Kohl
Lucy Komisar
Hans Koning
Jerzy Kosinski
Joseph Kraft
Joseph Wood Krutch

Jeri Laber
R. D. Laing
John Langan
Christopher Lasch
Andrea Lee
Ursula K. LeGuin
Alan Lelchuk
Michael A. Lerner
Simon O. Lesser
A. J. Liebling
Anne Morrow Lindbergh
Walter Lippmann
Katinka Loeser
Paul A. London

Janet Malcolm
Bobbie Ann Mason
W. Somerset Maugham
Daniel Menaker
Henry Miller
Yukio Mishima
Christopher Morley
Desmond Morris
Jan Morris
Toni Morrison
Mohammed Mrabet

Judith Nadell

Kenzaburo Oë
John O'Hara
Jane O'Reilly
George Orwell

Thomas Paine
Mollie Panter-Downes
David Plante
J. H. Plumb
Edgar Allan Poe

Carin C. Quinn

Anatol Rapoport
Carter Ratcliff
Rex Reed
Charles Rembar
Paul Reps
Tom Robbins
Elizabeth Madox Roberts
Theodore Roethke
Harold Rosenberg
Leo Rosten
Bertrand Russell

Abram Leon Sachar
Carl Sagan
David St. John
Saki (H. H. Munro)
J. D. Salinger
Mary Jo Salter
Stanley Sanders
Winthrop Sargeant
Mark Schorer
Delmore Schwartz
Allan Seager
Richard Selzer
Victor Serge
Robert Shaplen
Irwin Shaw
Max Shulman
Hugh Sidey
Judith S. Siegel
Isaac Bashevis Singer
William Smart
Robert Sommer
John Steinbeck
James Stevenson
Thomas Szasz

Paul Theroux
Dylan Thomas
Lewis Thomas
Lowell Thomas
Hunter S. Thompson
James Thurber
Lester C. Thurow
Lionel Tiger
Alvin Toffler
Calvin Tomkins
H. M. Tomlinson
Stephen Toulmin
TRB (Richard L. Strout)
Calvin Trillin
Frank Trippett
Barbara W. Tuchman

Fred Uhlman
Sanford J. Ungar
John Updike

Gore Vidal

Loudon Wainwright
George Wald
Robert Penn Warren
Edward Weeks
Eudora Welty
E. B. White
Norbert Wiener
Elie Wiesel
Oscar Wilde
Roger Wilkins
George F. Will
Edmund Wilson
Larry Woiwode
Tom Wolfe
Virginia Woolf
Richard Wright

William Butler Yeats
John V. Young

Karen Zelan
Leane Zugsmith

Contents

Writing is an act of faith, not a trick of grammar.

E. B. White, *The Elements of Style*

Grossbooted draymen rolled barrels dullthudding out of Prince's stores and bumped them up on the brewery float. On the brewery float bumped dullthudding barrels rolled by grossbooted draymen out of Prince's stores.

James Joyce, *Ulysses*

If one wishes to better the world, one must, paradoxically enough, withdraw and spend more and more time fashioning one's sentences to perfection in solitude.

Virginia Woolf

INTRODUCTION

To the Student

If you have just thumbed through *Combining and Creating,* you may well feel puzzled. For one thing, much of the book is taken up with long lists of simple-sounding sentences like these:

I walked far down the beach.
I was soothed by the rhythm of the waves.
The sun was on my bare back and legs.
The wind and mist from the spray were on my hair.

At first glance, this looks like a prize story from a second-grader's Dick and Jane book. It certainly seems out of place in a college text. Any bright ten-year-old can write better sentences than those.

And what about the last third of the book? It's nothing but a collection of quotations from various writers, some of whom you may recognize—John Steinbeck, Ernest Hemingway, George Orwell, and so forth. But the sentences and paragraphs aren't in any obvious order. In fact, they don't seem connected at all, unless you consider it a connection that they are all by professional writers. And if you look closely, you will find many student writers quoted there, too.

Clearly, *Combining and Creating* is an unusual book. It brings together writing by novelists, scientists, and newspaper columnists; it brings together writing by professionals and by students. Writing is the common denominator of the book, but the approach to writing is different from the approach you may have taken up to now.

Combining and Creating is different from most English textbooks because it approaches writing—professional writing, student writing, your writing—*from the inside out.* Instead of asking you to take writing apart, this book asks you to put writing together. Instead of telling you what you don't know about good writing, it reminds you that as a speaker of English you know more about the language than you may suspect. It assumes, in a word, that you are competent in English, even if your writing has not been what you would like it to be.

If you have ever wondered how professional writers manage the dazzling things they do with such seeming ease, you will find *Combining and Creating* a revealing book. In fact, if you have ever wished you could do a few dazzling things on paper yourself, you will get your chance here. Although *Combining and Creating* is not a workbook, it continually asks you to try out the things you study.

To help you master writing from the inside out, *Combining and Creating* brings together two proven strategies: sentence combining and generative rhetoric. Sentence combining is a way of improving writing without formal grammar instruction. It will help you translate into writing the grammar you already know as a speaker of English. It works by asking you to combine simple Dick-and-Jane sentences into more mature ones that establish close relationships among ideas. Generative rhetoric, on the other hand, is an approach to style, an approach based on actual professional writing, not "made-up" examples. The word *generative* suggests the word *generator*: a source of energy. Generative rhetoric introduces you to four principles of energetic writing and then asks you to *generate,* or *create,* writing of your own based on those principles. Thus, sentence combining is a starter motor for your own writing. It will get you moving. Generative rhetoric, on the other hand, offers you a generator and steering system to keep you moving in the right direction.

All the exercises in *Combining and Creating* come from professional or student writing that has been "de-written." That is, the writing has been taken apart, disassembled, reduced to its barest bones. It's your job, once you have studied the principles and examples set forth in each chapter, to put the writing back together again, to restore its muscle, to make it live. Naturally, you may not do exactly what the original author did. In some cases, you may feel that you have actually done a *better* job than the professional. But what's important is not whose version is best, but rather how the versions you and your classmates write are similar to, and different from, each other's and from the original author's. In other words, *Combining and Creating* puts you on an equal footing with the masters. And you will be surprised at how quickly your writing begins to stand up to theirs.

But all this combining and creating would be pointless if you never did any original writing yourself. Therefore, every sentence-combining exercise is followed by writing suggestions, assignments based on the topics you have begun thinking about in doing the exercise. In this way, the exercises are all springboards for original writing—and original writing is the real test of any writer's skills. As with the combining exercises, you will learn most if you compare your original writing with your classmates' work, seeking their reactions as well as your instructor's comments.

Sometimes your instructor will ask you to do the combining exercises in class and your original writing at home, sometimes just the opposite. But before you begin reading *Combining and Creating,* you should understand a few things about how the exercises work. "Combinations" exercises ask you to practice one structure or strategy that you have studied in the chapter introduction. "Creations" ask you to *invent* a particular structure and add it to a given sentence. "Sentence Acrobatics" are verbal free-for-alls, chances for you to experiment with *any* combinations that seem right to you. Each chapter also contains four paragraph- or essay-length sentence-combining exercises like this one:

Home on the Range

Combine the sentences below into an effective paragraph. You can compare your paragraph with a professional or student writer's version in the Appendix.

1. The Crow, Shoshone, Arapaho, Cheyenne, and Sioux roamed the intermountain West.
2. They roamed two hundred years ago.
3. They orchestrated their movements according to hunger.
4. They orchestrated their movements according to season.
5. They orchestrated their movements according to warfare.

6. They acquired horses.
7. They traversed the spines of all the big Wyoming ranges.
8. They traversed the Absarokas, the Wind Rivers, the Tetons, and the Big Horns.
9. They wintered on the unprotected plains.
10. The plains fan out from the ranges.

11. Space was life.
12. The world was their home.

First, notice that the twelve sentences here are subdivided into three groups, with each group separated from the last and from the next by a blank space. These spaces suggest where you might end one sentence and begin another, but the divisions are suggestions only. You may further subdivide a group, or you may ignore a division. Second, while professional writers do, on the average, write sentences that are longer than those by nonprofessionals, no successful writer stretches every sentence to the breaking point. Sometimes a short sentence is more effective than a long one in a particular exercise. Therefore, *not to combine sentences* is always one of your options. Finally, while you will surely eliminate repeated words when you combine sentences, feel free to add words—especially *connective* words—as well.

The best way to do a sentence-combining exercise is as an experiment in which you try out several versions of a sentence before settling on one. Use your voice as well as your hand when you write, saying each combination softly, and testing it with your ear. With these things in mind, try writing a version of *Home on the Range* in your notebook.

Once you've finished your version, you'll want to see how other writers handled the material. (After this, all other versions are in the Appendix.) Here, then, are three versions of *Home on the Range* for comparison with yours. Two are by students; one is by a professional writer:

1. The Crow, Shoshone, Arapaho, Cheyenne, and Sioux roamed the intermountain West two hundred years ago. They orchestrated their movements according to hunger, season, and warfare. They acquired horses and traversed the spines of all the big Wyoming ranges. They traversed the Absarokas, the Wind Rivers, the Tetons, and the Big Horns. They wintered on the unprotected plains which fan out from the ranges. Space was life, and the world was their home.

2. Because space was life, the world was their home. When the Crow, Shoshone, Arapaho, Cheyenne, and Sioux roamed the intermountain West two hundred years ago, they orchestrated their movements according not only to hunger and season, but according to warfare. They acquired horses, traversed the spines of all the big Wyoming ranges (which include the Absarokas, the Wind Rivers, the Tetons, and the Big Horns), and wintered on the unprotected plains fanning out from the ranges.

3. Two hundred years ago, the Crow, Shoshone, Arapaho, Cheyenne, and Sioux roamed the intermountain West, orchestrating their movements according to hunger, season, and warfare. Once they acquired horses, they traversed the spines of all the big Wyoming ranges—the Absarokas, the Wind Rivers, the Tetons, the Big Horns—and wintered on the unprotected plains that fan out from them. Space was life. The world was their home.

Before you make any comments on the versions, you should be sure to read them carefully, both silently and aloud, listening to the *voice* that speaks in each. First, notice that all three versions are grammatically acceptable and contain approximately the same information. But you will notice, too, that each version is somehow different from the others. Explore that difference by asking questions: Which version is most efficient? What parts of the exercise does each version emphasize? How does each writer handle the material? the rhythm? the punctuation? Which versions sound authoritative? Why so?

Once you have written out *Home on the Range,* the next step is to compare your version with the other versions. Let us begin by examining version 1. Here the writer has not so much combined the sentences as added them up mechanically, using *and* as an all-purpose connection. This gets the story told, but it hardly creates a plot. Notice, too, that four of the six sentences here begin with the word *they*. In fact, this version is so steady, balanced, and repetitive that it threatens to lull the reader to sleep.

Not version 2. It starts out with a surprise that catches our attention at once. The writer has boldly shifted the last two sentences in the exercise to the very beginning of the paragraph. What effect does this create? In fact, this writer is willing to take chances and experiment not only with the order of the exercise but also with the theme. Perhaps you thought *Home on the Range* was about wide-open spaces. Not writer 2. Notice how this version focuses on *warfare* in the second sentence. How does this shift in emphasis affect our perception of the Indians? Is the emphasis here consistent with the theme of the exercise at large? Notice, too, how this writer has used the connective word *because* to suggest cause-and-result and the word *when* to establish a time relationship. All in all, the writer of 2 has imposed a plot on the basic story. Whether or not you agree with the writer's interpretation of the data, this consistently experimental version of the exercise demands a reasoned response. And while you may feel out of breath at the end of the marathon-length sentence that ends this version, you have to admire the writer's stamina. In fact, although version 2 is less steady than version 1, it's far more interesting and original.

Version 3 is considerably different from both the others. Like 1, it's steady and balanced, but it's hardly dull. In fact, it's the shortest version of the three. Does this make it the most efficient? Like 2, version 3 moves quickly and establishes relationships among ideas. Unlike 2, it doesn't surge ahead and trip over itself. Notice how the long second sentence carries its thirty-five words lightly, almost effortlessly. And finally, notice that the writer of 3 chose *not* to combine the last two sentences. What effect does this choice have on the theme of the passage?

Which version is the best? Don't forget to consider your own. Certainly, versions 2 and 3 both have much to be said in their favor. As you work your way through the exercises in *Combining and Creating,* you will gain more and more ideas about what makes good writing work. As it happens, versions 1 and 2 of *Home on the Range* are by student writers. Version 3, which was the basis for the exercise, comes from an essay entitled "Wyoming: The Solace of Open Spaces" by Gretel Ehrlich, an author and occasional ranch hand. But whichever version you think best, notice how the sentence-combining exercise put you and the other student writers on an equal footing with the author. That is, you learned about good writing *from the inside out.*

That's how *Combining and Creating* works. But after doing a sentence-combining exercise, you should always do some original writing. The writing suggestion below will allow you to compose yourself before you move on to Chapter 1.

Writing Suggestion: Reflect back over your own history as a writer and compose a short autobiography of yourself as an author. How has your writing developed over the years? What do you feel you do well on paper? What still gives you trouble? How would you like your writing to change in the future?

COMBINING AND CREATING SENTENCES

Shreve was coming up the walk, shambling, fatly earnest, his glasses glinting beneath the running leaves like little pools.

WILLIAM FAULKNER, ***The Sound and the Fury***

Even when he describes nothing more than a character's progress down a tree-lined walkway, William Faulkner commands the reader's attention—and the writer's respect. What is it that gives professional writing such authority? Surely a part of the effect lies in the vivid images Faulkner has created: the shambling figure, the glinting glasses, the running leaves. Another striking feature is the steady addition of specifics. We begin with a general statement—*Shreve was coming up the walk*—and gradually learn the specifics that bring the character into sharp focus: *shambling, fatly earnest, his glasses glinting beneath the running leaves like little pools.*

As vivid and telling as these specific images are, however, they cannot fully account for the rich texture of Faulkner's writing. This richness lies not in any one word or image. Instead, the texture results from the whole process by which Faulkner *combined* the specifics he *created.* Writing well thus involves two processes, combining and creating. The advice and exercises in *Combining and Creating* should help you master both these processes.

COMBINING SENTENCES

Let us begin by considering some of the basic ways in which writers put their ideas together into sentences. For example, we can isolate five constituent parts within Faulkner's sentence. There is, first, the general image:

Shreve was coming up the walk.

Faulkner next notes a *detail* about Shreve's way of walking:

He was shambling.

The writer also adds a *quality* about the man himself:

He was fatly earnest.

Finally, Faulkner focuses in on a single part of the picture, Shreve's glasses:

His glasses were glinting beneath the running leaves.

To clarify this image still further, Faulkner makes a *comparison:*

They were like little pools.

The result of this analysis is a sentence-combining exercise with five parts:

Shreve was coming up the walk.
He was shambling.
He was fatly earnest.
His glasses were glinting beneath the running leaves.
They were like little pools.

In later chapters, you will learn how to create vivid details, qualities, and comparisons in your own writing. For now, however, let us consider how writers combine their material into different kinds of sentences. We can do this by trying several versions of the exercise above.

Simple Sentences

When William Faulkner wrote the sentence we are considering, he combined all five parts of the exercise. We might, on the other hand, choose to combine none of them:

VERSION 1

Shreve was coming up the walk. He was shambling. He was fatly earnest. His glasses were glinting beneath the running leaves. They were like little pools.

Childish as this version sounds, it is grammatically acceptable. Each part of the sentence-combining exercise is capable of standing on its own, and here we have merely set the parts next to each other.

The reason why each part of the original exercise can stand alone is that each part is a ***simple sentence.*** A simple sentence has a **subject** (like *Shreve*) and a **predicate** (like *was coming up the walk*). Note that the predicate consists of two parts: **the verb** (*was coming*) and the **complement** (*up the walk*). The complement "completes" the meaning of the verb. As a look at the five sentences reveals, not all simple sentences contain complements, but all contain subjects, predicates, and verbs:

Simple Sentences

Subject	***Predicate***	
	Verb	***Complement***
Shreve	was coming	up the walk.
He	was shambling.	———
He	was	fatly earnest.
His glasses	were glinting	beneath the running leaves.
They	were	like little pools.

Any construction that has a subject and predicate is called a **clause**. Because a simple sentence has a subject and predicate and can stand alone, it is also called an **independent clause**.

Compound Sentences

When you do a sentence-combining exercise, then, you are free *not* to combine the parts—to use simple sentences. But when we analyzed Faulkner's sentence, we found that certain parts seemed to go together logically. The first three simple sentences present Shreve at large:

> Shreve was coming up the walk.
> He was shambling.
> He was fatly earnest.

The last two focus in on Shreve's glasses:

> His glasses were glinting beneath the running leaves.
> His glasses were like little pools.

If we wish to preserve this grouping, we might combine the five sentences into two:

> **VERSION 2**
>
> Shreve was fatly earnest, **and** he came shambling up the walk. His glasses were glinting beneath the running leaves, **so** they were like little pools.

Here, the five simple sentences have been combined into two ***compound sentences,*** one devoted to Shreve, one devoted to his glasses. A compound sentence, as its name suggests, is a combination of two or more simple sentences linked together by a **coordinator** (like *and, but, for, so,* etc.) or by a colon or semicolon. Note that each of the two compound sentences in this version of the exercise contains two independent clauses linked by a coordinating connective:

Compound Sentences

Independent Clause	***Coordinator***	***Independent Clause***
Shreve was fatly earnest,	**and**	he came shambling up the walk.
His glasses were glinting beneath the running leaves,	**so**	they were like little pools.

Compound sentences are common in our speech and in our writing, too. They work well, so long as the things we link together go together logically, as they do in the sentences above.

Complex Sentences

The connections in a compound sentence are relatively loose. By combining the five sentences in a different way, we can create a much tighter statement:

> **VERSION 3**
>
> **As** Shreve, **who** was fatly earnest, came shambling up the walk, his glasses were like little pools **because they were glinting beneath the running leaves.**

Here the five simple sentences have been combined into one ***complex sentence.*** A complex sentence has one independent clause and one or more **dependent clauses.** A clause is called dependent when it cannot stand by itself. Which of the following four clauses is the independent clause and which are dependent?

> **As** Shreve came shambling up the walk . . .
> . . . **who** was fatly earnest . . .
> his glasses were like little pools . . .
> . . . **because** they were glinting beneath the running leaves.

When the clauses are separated this way, you can easily tell that only the third can stand alone. The rest are said to be *dependent* on the third clause. The words **as, who,** and **because** indicate this dependence. We may, therefore, call the independent clause in such a construction the **base clause** of the sentence because it supports the other clauses.

Note that dependent clauses, like independent clauses, have subjects and predicates:

Complex Sentence

	Dependent Clauses		*Independent Clause*	
	Subject	***Predicate***	***Subject***	***Predicate***
As	Shreve	came shambling up the walk,		
	who	was fatly earnest,		
			his glasses	were like little pools
because	they	were glinting beneath the running leaves.		

A glance at the analysis above tells you not only which clauses are dependent but also why they are dependent. The first and last clauses are each preceded by a **subordinator**—*as* and *because,* respectively. Each of these words establishes a close relationship between the clause it precedes and the base clause. In fact, the subordinator establishes such a close relationship that the **subordinate clause** depends on the base and cannot stand without it. On the other hand, in the second dependent clause the word *who* stands in for the subject, *Shreve.* Words like *who, that,* and *which* are called **relatives,** since they are closely related to other words in the sentence and therefore depend upon them. A relative like *who* eliminates needless repetition of *Shreve,* but it also makes the **relative clause** it introduces dependent, hence unable to stand alone. Because a complex sentence contains at least one dependent clause linked to an independent clause, it gives an impression of close logical coherence.

Cumulative Sentences

In the next few chapters, we shall study how to combine simple sentences into compound and complex sentences that include coordinating connectives like *and,* subordinators like *as,* and relatives like *who.* But before we leave Faulkner's sentence, we should consider one more version of our sentence-combining exercise:

> **VERSION 4**
> Shreve was coming up the walk, shambling, fatly earnest, his glasses glinting beneath the running leaves like little pools.

This is, of course, the very sentence that William Faulkner originally wrote. The sentence is not compound, since it has but one independent clause: *Shreve was coming up the walk.* At the same time, the sentence is not complex, since it includes neither a subordinator nor a relative. We must therefore conclude that Faulkner's sentence is simple in its structure, although it is far from simple in its effect.

To grasp just how Faulkner's artfully simple sentence works, let us reconsider the exercise with which our study of sentence combining began:

Shreve was coming up the walk.
He was shambling.
He was fatly earnest.
His glasses were glinting beneath the running leaves.
They were like little pools.

How did Faulkner manage the combination? Because the first simple sentence gives a general image of the scene, Faulkner used it as the **base clause**:

Shreve was coming up the walk . . .

Then, to bring the image into focus, Faulkner *added* information from the next four sentences to the base clause. This process of addition involved two steps. First, Faulkner reduced each of the four sentences to a **phrase,** a word or group of words that functions as a unit but lacks a complete subject and predicate:

Sentence	*Phrase*
He was shambling.	shambling
He was fatly earnest.	fatly earnest
His glasses were glinting beneath the running leaves.	his glasses glinting beneath the running leaves
They were like little pools.	like little pools

Notice how this process eliminates repeated words like *he was.* In later chapters of this book, you will learn exactly how phrases like these are formed and how they can enliven your writing.

Next, having reduced the sentences to phrases, Faulkner simply added the phrases after the base clause:

Cumulative Sentence

Base Clause	*Modifiers*
Shreve was coming up the walk,	shambling, fatly earnest, his glasses glinting beneath the running leaves like little pools.

That is, Faulkner used the phrases as **modifiers** of the base clause. A modifier is a word or group of words that explains, clarifies, or defines another word or group of words elsewhere in the sentence. Notice that the modifiers in Faulkner's sentence are of two basic sorts. First, three modifiers of the base are set off by punctuation: *shambling, fatly earnest, his glasses glinting beneath the running leaves like little pools.* Because these modifiers are set off by punctuation, they are called **free modifiers.** On the other hand, some of the modifiers within these phrases are not set off by punctuation. For instance, in the phrase *like little pools,* the word *little* modifies the word *pools.* Furthermore, the entire phrase *like little pools* modifies the verb *glinting.* Because these modifiers are not set off by punctuation, they are called **bound modifiers.** In later chapters, you will learn how to distinguish between free and bound modifiers of a word, phrase, or clause.

Faulkner's sentence is thus a simple sentence made up of a base clause to which free and bound modifiers have been added. Because such a sentence develops by accumulation, it is called a ***cumulative sentence*** (from the Latin verb *cumulare,* "to heap up"). In a cumulative sentence, the main idea comes first, in the base clause, with modifiers added after the base in order to bring the idea into sharp focus. Because the cumulative sentence may seem unusual to you, you should try creating one for yourself. Try combining these four sentences into one cumulative sentence:

> Woods and Ricketts work for Michael and T. Hudson Margraves.
> Michael and T. Hudson Margraves are two brothers.
> They are in partnership.
> They live in Cookstown.

Write your version here:

____

____

____

If you used the first sentence as the base clause and then turned the next three into free modifiers, your version is probably something like this:

> Woods and Ricketts work for Michael and T. Hudson Margraves, two brothers, in partnership, who live in Cookstown.
>
> JAMES AGEE, *Let Us Now Praise Famous Men*

Naturally, other combinations are possible. Still, the cumulative version has a simple elegance that's worth cultivating, as we saw in the example by William Faulkner. To help you grasp this, here are three more examples of cumulative sentences. The first comes from a personal reminiscence, the second from an essay on ballet, and the third from a furniture advertisement:

> Mrs. Fennemore's husband had a place in the background—Burt, slow, gray, and stolid, a diabetic, on a pension after a life in "building," a dim figure rarely seen, though his bike stood in the hall.
>
> ROBERT FITZGERALD, "The Third Kind of Knowledge"

In 1912, Vaslav Nijinsky made for Diaghilev's Ballets Russes the first of several ballets on modern themes—his *Jeux,* a three-way tennis match that turns into a love triangle.

HOLLY BRUBACH, "Designer Dancing"

Our furniture is inspired by the simplicity of Shaker design, with a delicate insinuation of contemporary; constructed with pride; and executed by hand, individually, restoring a relationship between man and his practical art.

THOS. MOSER, Cabinet Maker

Notice how in each instance the cumulative sentence includes a base clause and several bound and free modifiers that add up to a telling statement.

PULLING IT ALL TOGETHER

Sentence combining is thus a matter of *choices.* When you do a sentence-combining exercise, you have to choose whether a simple sentence, a compound sentence, a complex sentence, or a cumulative sentence creates the effect you seek. As we saw, some exercises can be combined in any of the four ways we have studied:

Exercise: Combine these sentences into one or more effective sentences.

Shreve was coming up the walk.
He was shambling.
He was fatly earnest.
His glasses were glinting beneath the running leaves.
They were like little pools.

VERSION 1: SIMPLE SENTENCES

Shreve was coming up the walk. He was shambling. He was fatly earnest. His glasses were glinting beneath the running leaves like little pools.

VERSION 2: COMPOUND SENTENCES

Shreve was fatly earnest, **and** he came shambling up the walk. His glasses were glinting beneath the running leaves, **so** they were like little pools.

VERSION 3: COMPLEX SENTENCE

As Shreve, **who** was fatly earnest, came shambling up the walk, his glasses were like little pools **because** they were glinting beneath the running leaves.

VERSION 4: CUMULATIVE SENTENCE

Shreve was coming up the walk, shambling, fatly earnest, his glasses glinting beneath the running leaves like little pools.

For his purposes in *The Sound and the Fury,* William Faulkner chose the last combination. For another purpose, subject, and audience, Faulkner might have chosen differently. What's important to realize is that good writers know their options. Indeed, it's not unusual for a professional writer to try out many combinations of a single sentence before settling on a final version.

For instance, an interviewer once asked Ernest Hemingway about how much rewriting he did. Hemingway replied, "It depends. I rewrote the ending of *Farewell to Arms,* the last page of it, thirty-nine times before I was satisfied." Perplexed by this answer, the interviewer pressed Hemingway on the issue. "What was it that had stumped you?" The novelist replied with a phrase: "Getting the words right." Sentence combining is the best method teachers have yet discovered for helping students faced with Hemingway's problem: getting the words right.

Combining and Creating Sentences: Combinations

Combine each set of simple sentences below into one effective compound, complex, or cumulative sentence. Try writing several versions of each exercise so that you get a feel for different combinations. You can compare your combinations with professional or student writers' versions in the Appendix.

SAMPLE EXERCISE

Stephen stood at his post.
He gazed over the calm sea towards the headland.

VERSION 1: COMPOUND SENTENCE

Stephen stood at his post, **and** he gazed over the calm sea towards the headland.

VERSION 2: COMPLEX SENTENCE

Stephen, **who** stood at his post, gazed over the calm sea towards the headland.

or

As Stephen stood at his post, he gazed over the calm sea towards the headland.

VERSION 3: CUMULATIVE SENTENCE

Stephen stood at his post, gazing over the calm sea towards the headland.

JAMES JOYCE, *Ulysses*

1. A man has decided to murder another.
   He does not play to the gallery.
2. On the farms the hens brooded.
   No chicks hatched.
3. All four brothers were lively by nature.
   They were athletic men.
   They were red-haired men.
4. He got out quietly.
   Some mischief had been done him.
   He had his dignity to remember.
5. They walked along.
   They were two continents of experience.
   They were two continents of feeling.
   They were unable to communicate.
6. It was eight in the evening.
   My husband would be studying.
   My daughter would be in bed.
   I'd be drinking my third glass of rosé.
7. A trade union can break an opposition.
   The union breaks an opposition by mass action.
   The mass action is in a strike.
   The union official can negotiate an agreement.
8. One is free.
   One is like the hermit crab.
   One can change one's shell.
9. It was early afternoon.
   The grounds were deserted.
   The buildings were deserted.
   Everyone was at sports.
10. She was drinking.
    She held the cup in both hands.
    She began to make the sound again.
11. People had gone to bed Thursday night.
    They went to bed in their habitual state of uncertainty.

The governmental crisis was still the chief subject of preoccupation.
The governmental crisis was in London.
The governmental crisis was bringing Winston Churchill to power.

12. Young men and women sat everywhere.
They sat on a bench.
They sat on the floor.
They were smoking.
They were trying to be heard above the general din.

13. Our current problems are allowed to persist.
They persist for the next ten to twenty years.
They will destroy our standard of living.
They will threaten our international alliances.
They will jeopardize our domestic tranquility.

14. A school of minnows swam by.
Each minnow had its shadow.
Its shadow was small.
Its shadow was individual.
The shadows doubled the attendance.
The shadows were so clear and sharp in the sunlight.

15. Multiple regression is a shotgun.
All the variables in the predictor set affect each other.
All the variables in the predictor set affect the criterion.
Path analysis is a rifle.
Path analysis designates lines of influence.
The lines are inexorable.
The lines are assumed to be causal.

Milton Barker

Combine the sentences below into a paragraph that contains both bound and free modifiers. You can compare your paragraph with a professional or student writer's version in the Appendix.

1. Milton Barker stood at the window.
2. Milton Barker was the car checker.
3. He looked out at the freight yard.

4. It was mid-April.

5. A thin rain was blowing in from New York Harbor.
6. The rain blew in little gusts and showers.
7. The rain filled the melancholy of the yard with further desolation.
8. The melancholy was usual.

9. The dirt and cinders had turned to mud.
10. The dirt and cinders were between the ties.
11. The mud was gray.

12. The smoke from a switching engine was flattened down.
13. The engine was idle.
14. The engine was in one of the leads.
15. The rain flattened down the smoke.
16. The smoke trailed off along the ground.

17. The steel towers stood up against the sky.
18. The towers were intricate.
19. The towers stood up dimly.
20. The towers held the machinery.
21. The machinery was for handling the car floats.

22. Ben Rederson went by.
23. Ben Rederson was the switchman.
24. The switchman was old.
25. He had a lantern.
26. The lantern was lighted.
27. It was only three o'clock in the afternoon.

Writing Suggestion 1: Milton Barker works in a freight yard—grimy, smoky, and filled with dim machinery. Write a paragraph describing one of the places where you have worked. Try to enliven your description by adding bound and free modifiers to your sentences.

Writing Suggestion 2: Once you have completed this exercise, continue the story. Use your imagination as well as hints in the exercise to develop the plot and characters.

Salao

Combine the sentences below into a paragraph that contains both bound and free modifiers. You can compare your paragraph with a professional or student writer's version in the Appendix.

1. He was an old man.
2. He fished alone in a skiff.
3. The skiff was in the Gulf Stream.

4. He had gone eighty-four days now.
5. He had not taken a fish.

6. A boy had been with him.
7. This was in the first forty days.

8. The boy's parents had told him something.
9. This was after forty days without a fish.
10. The old man was now definitely and finally *salao.*
11. *Salao* is the worst form of unlucky.

12. The boy had gone in another boat.
13. He went at his parents' orders.
14. The boat caught three good fish the first week.

15. The boy saw the old man come in each day.
16. His skiff was empty.
17. This made the boy sad.

18. He always went down to help him.
19. He helped him carry either the lines or the gaff and harpoon and the sail.
20. The lines were coiled.
21. The sail was furled around the mast.

22. The sail was patched with flower sacks.
23. The sail was furled.
24. It looked like the flag of defeat.
25. The defeat was permanent.

Writing Suggestion 1: The exercise above deals with bad luck. Do you consider luck to be a real force in our lives or merely a myth? Write a short essay explaining your beliefs, using details and examples to support your opinions.

Writing Suggestion 2: Write a short essay analyzing the attitudes that youngsters and young adults have toward older people in our culture.

Meditation on a Camel Pack

Combine the sentences below into several paragraphs that contain both bound and free modifiers. You can compare your paragraphs with a professional or student writer's version in the Appendix.

1. Three of the four elements are shared.
2. All creatures share them.
3. Fire was a gift to humans alone.

4. We smoke cigarettes.
5. This is as intimate as we can become with fire without excruciation.*
6. The excruciation is immediate.

**excruciation:* intense pain, torture

7. Every smoker is an embodiment of Prometheus.*
8. Every smoker steals fire from the gods.
9. Every smoker brings it on back home.

10. We smoke to capture the power of the sun.
11. We smoke to pacify Hell.
12. We smoke to identify with the spark.
13. The spark is primordial.†
14. We smoke to feed on the marrow of the volcano.

15. We are not after the tobacco.
16. We are after the fire.

17. We smoke.
18. We are performing a version of the fire dance.
19. The fire dance is a ritual.
20. The ritual is as ancient as lightning.

21. Does that mean something?
22. Chain smokers are fanatics.
23. The fanatics are religious.

24. You must admit this.
25. There's a similarity.

26. The lung of the smoker is a virgin.
27. The virgin is naked.
28. The virgin is thrown into the god-fire.
29. The virgin is thrown as a sacrifice.

Writing Suggestion 1: This "meditation" offers an imaginative explanation for a commonplace habit. Do you find the explanation persuasive? farfetched? both? Write a paragraph in which you analyze and evaluate the *Meditation on a Camel Pack.* Using specific evidence from the exercise, explain why you find the meditation persuasive, farfetched, or both at once.

Writing Suggestion 2: Using *Meditation on a Camel Pack* as a model, write a similar meditation on another everyday habit. For example, you might explain why businessmen wear ties, why some women wear lipstick, or why new acquaintances shake hands. Whatever your topic, imitate the exercise as closely as you can.

**Prometheus:* in Greek mythology, a Titan who stole fire from the gods and passed it on to mankind; for this he was punished by Zeus, who chained Prometheus to a rock where a vulture came each day to gnaw his liver, which Zeus renewed each night.

†*primordial:* existing from the beginning of time, original

Brown Paper Bag

Combine the sentences below into a paragraph that contains both bound and free modifiers. You can compare your paragraph with a professional or student writer's version in the Appendix.

1. He crossed the road slowly.
2. The road was sandy.
3. He shuffled along.
4. He shook his head.
5. He muttered to himself.

6. He carried a brown paper bag.
7. The bag was wrinkled.
8. The bag fit the shape of a bottle.

9. The scruff on his face made him look ageless.
10. The scruff was gray.
11. He was in the predawn light.
12. He could have been twenty.
13. He could have been sixty.

14. He reached the other side of the road.
15. The smell of the saltwater filled his nostrils.
16. The cries of the seagulls were loud in his ears.

17. He stood.
18. He stared at the ocean.
19. He raised the bag to his lips.
20. The raising was awkward.
21. He watched the gray-green waves.
22. The waves slapped the shore.

23. Suddenly, it was as if he saw something in the fog.
24. He took a half-step forward.
25. He stepped into the water.
26. The water swirled from the last wave.

27. But the cold water seemed to startle him.
28. The cold water gripped his shoe.
29. His shoe was worn out.

30. He stepped back to the shore.
31. His step was weary.
32. His step was unsteady.
33. On the shore he bent down.
34. He removed his shoe.
35. His shoe was wet.

36. He placed the shoe beside him.
37. He sat down.
38. He dried his foot.
39. He dried it with the inside of his coat.
40. His coat was tattered.

41. He sat for a long while.
42. He was motionless.
43. He clutched the brown paper bag.
44. He stared out at the sea.

Writing Suggestion 1: You don't have to be a professional writer to tell someone's story vividly. As William Faulkner observed, "It begins with a character, usually, and once he stands up on his feet and begins to move, all I do is trot along behind him with a paper and pencil trying to keep up long enough to put down what he says and does." Observe someone closely, noting every detail, quality, and comparison that occurs to you. Then write a paragraph or two telling the person's story as faithfully as you can render it.

Writing Suggestion 2: Alcoholism is one of the most serious problems affecting our society. Go to the library and learn what alcoholism is and how many people it affects in the United States. Then write a short essay analyzing the problem and suggesting possible solutions to it.

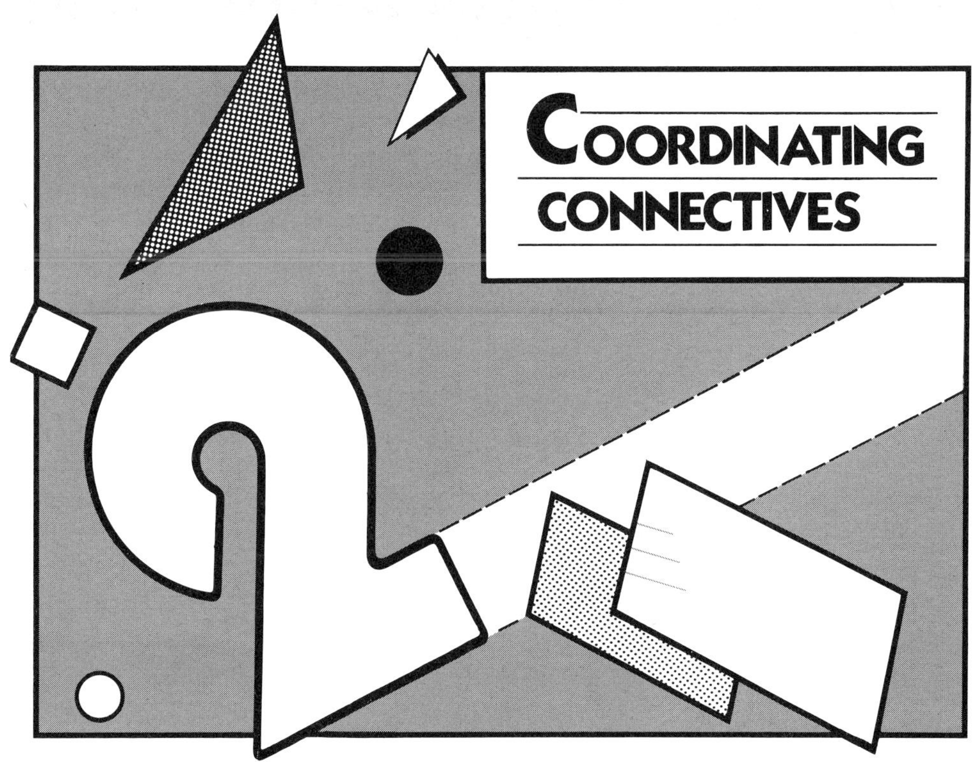

> ***In the orchard bush they found a herd of impala, and leaving the car they stalked one old ram with long, wide-spreading horns and Macomber killed it with a very creditable shot that knocked the buck down at a good two hundred yards and sent the herd off bounding wildly and leaping over one another's backs in long, leg-drawn-up leaps as unbelievable and as floating as those one makes sometimes in dreams.***
>
> **ERNEST HEMINGWAY, "The Short Happy Life of Francis Macomber"**

Ernest Hemingway's sentence moves as gracefully as the animals it describes, and thus it captures the dreamlike feeling of the hunt. Hemingway tells the story in time order. First, there is the discovery of the prey:

> In the orchard bush they found a herd of impala.

Next comes the actual hunt:

> Leaving the car they stalked one old ram with long, wide-spreading horns.

Finally comes the kill and its aftermath:

> Macomber killed it with a very creditable shot that knocked the buck down at a good two hundred yards and sent the herd off bounding wildly and leaping over one another's backs in long, leg-drawn-up leaps as unbelievable and as floating as those one makes sometimes in dreams.

Understandably, as the episode unfolds and gradually reaches its climax, the writer adds more and more details, qualities, and comparisons. But, significantly, all these additions are bound modifiers linked directly to each base clause. An analysis of the actual *compound* sentence reveals the essential equality among the three independent clauses:

> In the orchard bush they found a herd of impala,
>
> **and**
>
> leaving the car they stalked one old ram with long, wide-spreading horns
>
> **and**
>
> Macomber killed it with a very creditable shot that knocked the buck down at a good two hundred yards and sent the herd off bounding wildly and leaping over one another's backs in long, leg-drawn-up leaps as unbelievable and as floating as those one makes sometimes in dreams.

By connecting the three base clauses with **and**—here a sign of simple linear sequence—Hemingway asserted the *equal* importance of the three parts of his narrative.

USING COORDINATING CONNECTIVES

The all-purpose connective in Hemingway's sentence—and in our everyday speech—is **and.** In fact, this little word appears five times in Hemingway's sentence. As we saw, it links the three base clauses into a simple time sequence: beginning, middle, and end. Secondly, it twice connects paired verb phrases within the final base: Macomber's shot "*knocked* the buck down at two hundred yards **and** *sent* the herd off *bounding* wildly **and** *leaping*. . . ." Finally, **and** serves as the pivot in a double comparison, "as unbelievable **and** as floating." Indeed, it is no exaggeration to say that **and** holds Hemingway's long, loose sentence together.

Little words like **and,** paired constructions like "**either . . . or,**" and logical linking words like **thus** and **therefore** are all ***coordinating connectives.*** The term "coordinating" comes from the Latin prefix *co-* ("equal") added to the verb *ordinare* ("to set or place"). The process of ***coordination*** thus sets words, phrases, or clauses *in equal rank,* either in pairs or in series.

Coordinating connectives are so much a part of our everyday speech and writing as to be taken for granted. For this reason, a systematic review of them is in order. As the discussion below will reveal, coordinating connectives fall into three classes: coordinators, correlatives, and conjunctive adverbs.

Coordinators

Coordinators are little words. They are few in number, but they have immense importance in our writing:

and	nor	so
but	or	yet
for		

The common trait among all these little words is that any one of them preceded by a comma may connect two independent clauses:

> The task was not to be assumed lightly, **for** it was men as well as starfish that we sought to save.
>
> LOREN EISELEY, *The Immense Journey*

> The morning air was chilly, **so** most of the spectators soon closed their windows and went back to bed.
>
> A. J. LIEBLING, "The Knockdown: Paris Postscript," *The Road Back to Paris*

In these examples, the coordinators link independent clauses. With the exception of **for** and **so,** all the coordinators can also join words and phrases together.

Correlatives

Correlatives are two-part structures that are separated by other words:

both . . . and	not . . . but
either . . . or	not . . . nor
neither . . . nor	not only . . . but (also)
never . . . nor	whether . . . or

Correlatives may link paired words, phrases, or clauses:

> A young man in his early thirties, **neither** *short* **nor** *tall,* came into the room.
>
> J. D. SALINGER, "Just Before the War with the Eskimos"

> The stones look **not** *like natural stones* **but** *like the rubble* of some unmentioned upheaval.
>
> JOAN DIDION, "Some Dreamers of the Golden Dream"

> ***Either*** *the world is too slack* **or** *I am not taut enough.*
>
> HENRY MILLER, *Black Spring*

In Salinger's sentence, a correlative links two words; in Didion's, two prepositional phrases; and in Miller's, two independent clauses. The only peril in using such constructions arises when **either . . . or** or **neither . . . nor** connects two sentence subjects, both of which are singular in number:

> But **neither** *woman* **nor** *man* are likely to be fed by another relationship which seems easier because it is in an earlier stage.
>
> ANNE MORROW LINDBERGH, *Gift from the Sea*

Since *man,* like *woman,* is singular, Lindbergh's main verb should be *is,* not *are.* The same would be true if the correlative were **either . . . or.** As you can see, even professional authors have to proofread their work carefully.

Conjunctive Adverbs

Conjunctive adverbs are sometimes called "signpost" words. These "signposts" tell the reader which way the discussion is heading:

accordingly	however	next
afterward(s)	incidentally	otherwise
also	indeed	similarly
besides	instead	still
consequently	later	then
earlier	likewise	therefore
furthermore	moreover	thus
hence	nevertheless	

Unlike coordinators and correlatives, conjunctive adverbs can join independent clauses *only,* never just words or phrases. Nevertheless, these words are important indeed, since they serve as signposts for your readers by pointing out key relationships among your main ideas.

But while a coordinator like **and,** preceded by a comma, may join two complete sentences, conjunctive adverbs call for stronger punctuation. You have two choices, the semicolon or the period, depending on whether you wish to connect the sentences or separate them. Whichever you choose, you may place a conjunctive adverb at the beginning of the second sentence or, for a subtler emphasis, somewhere *within* the second sentence:

> A finite world can support only a finite population**; therefore,** population growth must eventually equal zero.
>
> GARRETT HARDIN, "The Tragedy of the Commons"

> Hers was a cruel, heartless punishment**. Moreover,** it was a punishment imposed by herself.
>
> YUKIO MISHIMA, *Thirst for Love*

> On Friday she lay quiet and unlike herself in her room attended by Katherine**.** By Saturday**, however,** she was joking and nudging her doctor while telling him some mischievous story.
>
> CLARENCE DAY, "Mother's Last Home"

Conjunctive adverbs are thus among the most mobile and expressive parts of speech. Note that in the three sample sentences above, commas either follow or surround the conjunctive adverbs. Follow this practice when you hear a distinct pause in reading the sentence. On the other hand, where no pause occurs, no commas are necessary.

WHAT COORDINATING CONNECTIVES ADD TO YOUR WRITING

Whether you're doing sentence-combining exercises or original writing, you can use coordinating connectives to perform six important functions:

1. Adding details or emphasis
2. Indicating time relationships
3. Proposing alternatives
4. Revealing cause and result
5. Stating conditions
6. Making contrasts or comparisons

You have been using coordinators like **and, but,** and **or** to establish some of these relationships between clauses ever since you first began to speak English. Nevertheless, some of the correlatives and conjunctive adverbs may not be as familiar to you as they should be. Therefore, all the coordinating connectives are presented below, classified by their functions. Each category includes at least one illustration from a professional or student writer's work.

1. Adding Details or Emphasis

Writing is basically a process of *addition*. Indeed, one of the first sentence combinations that youngsters master is the linking of clauses with **and.** You should note, however, that all three kinds of coordinating connectives can add details or emphasis:

also	indeed
and	incidentally
besides	moreover
both . . . and	not only . . . but (also)
furthermore	

While most of the connectives in this group indicate simple additions of detail, words like **furthermore, indeed,** and **moreover** indicate emphasis, not just addition:

> Love of the theater is a very special perversion, **and** you have to think of ways to support your habit.
>
> JAMES STEVENSON, "A Moment"

> **For** the problem of the multiplicity of life **not only** confronts the American woman, **but also** the American man.
>
> ANNE MORROW LINDBERGH, *Gift from the Sea*

> Behind all this I sensed the desires of the gadgeteer to see the wheels go round. **Moreover,** the whole idea of push-button warfare has an enormous temptation for those who are confident of their power of invention and have a deep distrust of human beings.
>
> NORBERT WIENER, *I Am a Mathematician*

Notice that the second sentence above begins with the word **for.** Such an example should dismiss the common superstition that no respectable writer ever begins a sentence with a coordinator. In the light of Lindbergh's example, how might you connect these two sentences?

> What determines the quality of civilization is the use made of power. That use cannot be controlled at the source.

Write your version here:

____

____

____

As usual, more than one "correct" combination is possible. The political commentator Walter Lippmann put the material together this way in *The Good Society:*

> What determines the quality of civilization is the use made of power. **And** that use cannot be controlled at the source.

Like Anne Morrow Lindbergh, Lippmann chose to begin a sentence with **and.** Indeed, far from seeming informal, the coordinator beginning Lippmann's sentence underscores the importance of the information it adds to the first statement. That is, it adds emphasis as well as information.

2. Indicating Time Relationships

All the connectives in this category are conjunctive adverbs:

afterward(s)	later	next
earlier	meanwhile	then
henceforth		

When we speak, we use these words automatically. Using them on paper calls for some thought, however, since conjunctive adverbs require careful punctuation. To review this matter, select a word from the list above to indicate a time relationship between these two sentences:

> The only time I mind being alone is when something is funny.
> When I am laughing at something funny, I wish someone were around.

Write your version here:

____

____

____

If you chose the word **then** for the job, your version should look something like this:

> The only time I mind being alone is when something is funny; **then,** when I am laughing at something funny, I wish someone were around.
> ANNIE DILLARD, "Death of a Moth"

Notice that while Annie Dillard used **then** to indicate a time relationship between the sentences, she also used a semicolon to connect them. She could also have separated them with a period:

> The only time I mind being alone is when something is funny. **Then,** when I am laughing at something funny, I wish someone were around.

Whether the sentences are joined or separated, **then** clearly indicates a time relationship between them.

3. Proposing Alternatives

Whereas the last category included conjunctive adverbs only, this category includes no conjunctive adverbs at all. Rather, it consists of coordinators and correlatives only. Notice that these connectives can propose alternatives that are positive, negative, or neutral:

Positive	***Negative***	***Neutral***
either . . . or	neither . . . nor	whether . . . or
or	never . . . nor	
	nor	
	not . . . but	
	not . . . nor	

To practice using these connectives logically, try combining the paired sentences below to propose alternatives:

A. Competitive display no longer crosses class lines.
It crosses them much less readily than before.

B. The suit she wore was not severe.
The suit she wore was not flashy.

Write your versions here:

____

____

____

____

____

____

You can compare your versions with these:

A. Competitive display no longer crosses class lines, **or** it crosses them much less readily than before.

JOHN BROOKS, *Showing Off in America*

B. The suit she wore was **neither** severe **nor** flashy.

STUDENT WRITER

In the first case, John Brooks has proposed positive alternatives by means of a coordinator, **or.** In the second case, the student writer has proposed a negative pair of alternatives by means of the correlative **neither . . . nor.**

4. Revealing Cause and Result

Not all coordinating connectives simply add information. As we have seen, some of the connectives create relationships between the words or sentences they join. This is very much the case with the following words, which reveal cause-and-result relationships:

accordingly	hence
(and)	so
consequently	therefore
for	thus

Note that this group includes no correlatives, just coordinators and conjunctive adverbs. How might you use a word from the list to reveal a cause-and-result relationship between the following two sentences?

Every substance that has ever been found in an organism displays thereby the finite probability of its occurrence.
Given time, it should arise spontaneously.

Write your version here:

____

____

____

The first of these two sentences is already long and complex. Therefore, when the scientist George Wald put the sentences together in his essay "The Origin of Life," he chose *not* to combine them. Instead, Wald established a cause-and-result connection between the sentences by means of a conjunctive adverb:

> Every substance that has ever been found in an organism displays thereby the finite probability of its occurrence**. Hence,** given time, it should arise spontaneously.
>
> GEORGE WALD, "The Origin of Life"

Even though the sentences remain separate, the word **hence** reveals a close connection between them.

Earlier, we saw how the coordinator **and** can add details or emphasis to writing. Sometimes, particularly in informal writing, **and** can also suggest cause and result:

> My money did not last long**, and** I soon found myself on skid row.
>
> ERIC HOFFER, "What America Means to Me"

If he had chosen to write more formally, Hoffer would likely have used another word from the list above, perhaps **so** or **thus,** to make the cause-and-result relationship more explicit.

5. Stating Conditions

This category includes all three kinds of connectives:

either . . . or	or else
or	otherwise

When two sentences are combined into a conditional relationship, one becomes the logical consequence of the other. To grasp this, use one of the connectives above to combine these two sentences:

> We had to pay the rent on the first of every month.
> We were liable for a twenty-dollar surcharge.

Write your version here:

____

____

____

Any one of the connectives in this category can express the conditional relationship between these two ideas. A student writer used **or else** to state the conditions of the agreement:

> We had to pay the rent on the first of every month, **or else** we were liable for a twenty-dollar surcharge.

Notice the rigorous logic implied by the conditional connectives. If the rent is paid on time, then the surcharge is voided. If the payment is late, the surcharge applies. The conditional relationship is an **or else** relationship, as the student writer clearly suggested.

6. Making Contrasts or Comparisons

As we saw, coordinating connectives can propose alternatives. They can also make contrasts and comparisons as well. This sixth category of connectives includes no correlatives:

but	nonetheless
however	otherwise
instead	similarly
likewise	still
nevertheless	yet

Like all the coordinating connectives, these words establish relationships not just between words but between ideas. Therefore, the sentences they connect may or may not be joined by punctuation:

> He was impatient of hard work and humdrum restrictions**, yet** expression was the need of his soul.
>
> E. B. WHITE, "Don Marquis"

> Wearily obedient, the choir huddled into line and stood there swaying in the sun. **Nonetheless,** some began to protest faintly.
>
> WILLIAM GOLDING, *Lord of the Flies*

Both E. B. White and William Golding used coordinating connectives to make contrasts. But where White used a coordinator, **yet,** and a comma to join two clauses, Golding separated his clauses with a period, using only the conjunctive adverb **nonetheless** to make the contrast.

There are only two coordinating connectives that make comparisons rather than contrasts. Review the list above to find likely connectives for joining these two sentences:

> Marchers carried "Ban the Bomb" placards during the 1960s.
> Protesters carry "No Nukes Is Good News" signs today.

Write your version here:

____

____

____

The words for making comparisons are **likewise** and **similarly,** both conjunctive adverbs. A student writer used **likewise** and a semicolon to connect the two sentences:

> Marchers carried "Ban the Bomb" placards during the 1960s**; likewise,** protesters carry "No Nukes Is Good News" signs today.

Here the conjunctive adverb **likewise** appropriately makes a comparison between the sentences it connects. Notice that the semicolon joining the clauses creates a steady balance between them as well. But whether or not the clauses are actually joined by punctuation, the coordinating connective between them makes the likeness clear.

PARALLEL STRUCTURE

Coordinating connectives thus perform a very wide range of functions. There is, however, a common characteristic here, an effect so subtle and pervasive that we take it for granted until a lapse in speech or writing upsets our expectation. That common characteristic is **parallel structure,** our long habit of putting similar ideas in similar forms. Naturally, since coordination always implies a relationship between or among equals (words, phrases, or clauses), it invites parallel structure. Indeed, nearly every sample sentence in this chapter exhibits parallel structure of one sort or another, whether it contains a pair of balanced clauses, two correlative phrases, or a series of single words. Writers strive for parallel structure because it creates a physical and intellectual impression of order and authority. In a word, parallels are persuasive. Consider the effects of the following sentences:

> The impression one gets from campaign oratory is that the sun revolves around the earth, the earth revolves around the United States, and the United States revolves around whichever city the speaker happens to be in at the moment.
>
> E. B. WHITE, "Sootfall and Fallout"

> The environment is complex. Man's political capacity is simple.
>
> WALTER LIPPMANN, *The Phantom Public*

> The shape of my life is, of course, determined by many other things; my background and childhood, my mind and its education, my conscience and its pressures, my heart and its desires.
>
> ANNE MORROW LINDBERGH, *Gift from the Sea*

Balance is the keynote in each case, balance of various sorts. Step by step and clause by clause, White's wry sentence parodies the simple-minded order it describes. On the other hand, Lippmann uses two short sentences to make a blunt contrast or *antithesis* (from a Greek word meaning "placed against"). He uses no connectives at all, just parallel structure. Finally, Anne Morrow Lindbergh's sentence creates an impression of unruffled composure with its carefully balanced pairs.

With study and practice, you can achieve similar effects in your own writing. The trick is to put like ideas in like structures, whether these structures be words, phrases, or clauses. Consider, for example, how you might combine each set of sentences below into one sentence with parallel structure:

A. Kushner wants his art to have wit.
Kushner wants his art to be vivid.
Kushner wants his art to be easy of access.

B. Jessie was fair-skinned.
Jessie had green eyes.
Jessie spoke softly.

Write your versions here:

____

____

____

____

____

____

Note that, as written, each set includes several kinds of structures modifying the subjects *Kushner* and *Jessie*. Since these modifiers are presumably of equal importance, they should be cast in equivalent forms. Here's how two authors, one a professional, one a student, managed the problem:

A. Kushner wants his art to be *witty, vivid,* and *accessible.*

CARTER RATCLIFF, "Art Stars for the Eighties"

B. Jessie was *fair-skinned, with green eyes,* and *spoke softly.*

STUDENT WRITER

By creating a series of three adjectival words, Carter Ratcliff created an effective parallel structure. The student writer, however, tried to combine an *adjectival word* ("fair-skinned") with a *prepositional phrase* ("with green eyes") and a *verb phrase* ("spoke softly"). These structures are neither equivalent nor parallel. A more effective version of the series would recast the modifiers in the following way:

Jessie was *fair-skinned, green-eyed,* and *soft-spoken.*

Written as three adjectival words, the modifiers are in equivalent form. The series is brisk, economical, and emphatic, thanks to its parallel structure.

ADDING AND DELETING CONNECTIVES

A typical series is thus made up of parallel structures separated by commas, with a coordinator linking the last two items. Still, you can achieve striking effects by varying the pattern. For instance, you can place a coordinator next to *each* item in the series:

It was a hot day **and** the sky was very bright **and** blue **and** the road was white **and** dusty.

ERNEST HEMINGWAY, *A Farewell to Arms*

This construction slows down the series and draws it out. On the other hand, by deleting *all* coordinators and linking the items with commas only, you create an opposite effect:

The goldfinch is on the dandelion**,** the goose is on the pond**,** the black fly is on the trout brook**,** the Northeast Airliner is on course for Rockland.

E. B. WHITE, "Coon Tree"

This strategy compresses the information and speeds up the action. It can create a sense of pressing urgency, as in Julius Caesar's famous pronouncement *I came, I saw, I conquered.* Finally, when you create a parallel structure, you can sometimes leave out repeated words:

Now the sun **was** golden, the air [**was**] keen blue, and the desert with its occasional rivers [**was**] a riot of sandy, hot space and sudden Biblical tree shade.

JACK KEROUAC, *On the Road*

Although Kerouac includes the linking verb **was** in his first clause only, it is understood in each of the two clauses that follow. By adding or deleting connective words like these, you can speed up or slow down the pace of your writing.

PULLING IT ALL TOGETHER

The coordinating connectives, then, are neither as plain nor as simple as they might seem to be at first. Indeed, they can express subtle relationships and emphasize important ideas. Furthermore, they regularly serve as signposts for the reader, pointing the way through difficult or unfamiliar material. For example, the Nobel-prize-winning biochemist George Wald once undertook to explain "The Origin of Life"—a challenging topic, to say the least—in *Scientific American,* a journal read by both scientists and laymen. At one point, Wald sought to explain why fermentation was not an adequate energy source for living organisms if they were to develop into higher forms. Having postulated that fermentation was indeed a step in the right direction, Wald then stated its limitations:

> Fermentation is an extraordinarily inefficient source of energy.
> It leaves most of the energy potential of organic compounds unexploited.

He next drew a conclusion:

> Huge amounts of organic material must be fermented to provide a modicum of energy.

This was not, however, the only problem. Wald added yet another caution:

> It produces various poisonous waste products—alcohol, lactic acid, acetic acid, formic acid and so on.

Finally, he closed the discussion with a significant contrast:

> In the sea such products are readily washed away.
> If organisms were ever to penetrate to the air and land, these products must prove a serious embarrassment.

Because Wald organized his material logically, his case seems clear even when stated in outline. Nevertheless, when he composed his essay for *Scientific American,* he carefully highlighted the relationships among his ideas by supplying appropriate coordinating connectives:

> Fermentation, **however,** is an extraordinarily inefficient source of energy. It leaves most of the energy potential of organic compounds unexploited; **consequently,** huge amounts of organic material must be fermented to provide a modicum of energy. It produces **also** various poisonous waste products—alcohol, lactic acid, acetic acid, formic acid

> and so on. In the sea such products are readily washed away, **but** if organisms were ever to penetrate to the air and land, these products must prove a serious embarrassment.

With these coordinating connectives serving as signposts, Wald's explanation seems not only logical but also persuasive. We move from one step of the argument to the next with assurance, confident of our direction. Whether you're taking us on an African safari or leading us toward the very origin of life, coordinating connectives help make our way smooth, clear, and direct.

Coordinating Connectives: Combinations

Combine each set of sentences below into one or more sentences that contain coordinating connectives and parallel structures. You can compare your combinations with professional or student writers' sentences in the Appendix.

SAMPLE EXERCISE

It was dark.
It was cloudy outside.
No one had lit the oil lamps.

PROFESSIONAL WRITER'S VERSION

It was dark**, for** it was cloudy outside**, and** no one had lit the oil lamps.
DONALD HALL, *String Too Short to Be Saved*

1. The Big Bang may be the beginning of the universe.
   It may be a discontinuity in which information about the earlier history of the universe was destroyed.

2. I think democracy a most precious thing.
   I think so not because any democratic state is perfect.
   I think so because it is perfectible.

3. All the other farmers had to contribute to these benefits by paying the processing taxes.
   A dairyman paid a tax on cotton, wheat, hogs, and corn.

4. I felt like shouting.
   I felt like running.
   Shouting was useless.
   There was no place to run.

5. It will not mean the end of nations.
   It will mean the true beginning of nations.

6. They made one another very happy.
   Finally they fell into a perfect sleep.

7. Magic in the sense of something "inciting wonder" is also here to stay.
   If it is not, man will have been vastly diminished by its loss.

8. The silence is not actually suppression.
   It is all there is.

9. But Paris was a very old city.
   We were young.
   Nothing was simple there.
   Not even poverty was simple.
   Sudden money was not simple.
   The moonlight was not simple.
   Right and wrong were not simple.
   The breathing of someone was not simple.
   Someone lay beside you in the moonlight.

10. The resources of a planet are limited.
    They are limited at each stage of the arts.
    There is only a limited space on a planet.

11. There was not time to consider moral issues.
    There was not time to consider ethical issues.
    There was not desire to consider moral issues.
    There was not desire to consider ethical issues.

12. Even Letitia Baldrige in 1978 pronounced the use of marijuana and hashish to be "marginally socially acceptable."
    Letitia Baldrige is the Establishment arbiter of etiquette.
    The street cost of all illegal drugs is sky-high.

13. He had a violent temper.
    He kept a hatchet at his bedside for burglars.
    He would knock a man down instead of going to law.
    Once I saw him hunt a party of men.
    He hunted them with a horsewhip.

14. They stood for democracy.
    They did not stand for it from any reasoned conclusion about the proper ordering of human society.
    They stood for it simply because they had grown up in the middle of democracy.
    They knew how it worked.

15. The artist knows he must be alone to create.
The writer knows he must be alone to work out his thoughts.
The musician knows he must be alone to compose.
The saint knows he must be alone to pray.

Petey's Predicament

Combine the sentences below into a paragraph that contains several coordinating connectives. You can compare your paragraph with a professional or student writer's version in the Appendix.

1. I sat down in a chair.
2. I pretended to read a book.
3. I kept watching Petey.
4. I watched him out of the corner of my eye.

5. He was a torn man.

6. First he looked at the coat.
7. He had the expression of a waif.
8. The waif was at a bakery window.

9. He turned away.
10. He set his jaw.
11. The setting was resolute.

12. He looked back at the coat.
13. He had even more longing in his face.

14. He turned away.
15. He had not so much resolution this time.

16. Back and forth his head swiveled.
17. Desire waxed.
18. Resolution waned.

19. Finally he didn't turn away at all.

20. He just stood there.
21. He stared at the coat.
22. He stared with mad lust.

Writing Suggestion 1: The exercise above describes a man caught in a quandary, a perplexing state of uncertainty, wherein he vacillates between desire and resolution. Write a paragraph describing someone (perhaps yourself) caught in a similar predicament between two alternatives. Which force won out in the end?

Writing Suggestion 2: One way of presenting two viewpoints on a single topic is by writing a dialogue. Choose a topic that is open for debate and then write a dialogue that examines the issues from two viewpoints. If no topic leaps to mind, you might consider one of these: Should the draft be reinstated? Is traditional marriage right for you? Does the violence on television encourage violent behavior? Are there any circumstances under which euthanasia (mercy killing) would be justifiable?

Inside Dope

Combine the sentences below into a paragraph that contains several coordinating connectives. You can compare your paragraph with a professional or student writer's version in the Appendix.

1. Drug use is no different from any other form of human behavior.
2. A great variety of distinct motives can cooperate to produce it.

3. The particular weight of each of these motives differs.
4. The way they are combined differs.
5. This is in each individual.

6. Drug use is affected by motives and forces.
7. The motives and forces are *within* the individual.
8. Drug use is affected by what is happening *outside* of him.
9. It is happening in his interpersonal environment.
10. It is happening in the wider social and political world.

11. Any effort to delineate "types" of motivations is bound to be an oversimplification.
12. The motivations enter into drug use.

13. For example, there are many individuals.
14. They share common characteristics with drug users.
15. They do not use drugs.
16. Drugs are not available on their campus.

17. There are individuals.
18. They have little in common with other drug users.
19. They use drugs.

Writing Suggestion 1: On the basis of your own reading and observation, write a paragraph supporting or refuting the argument made in the exercise above. Use specific examples to prove your case—and coordinating connectives to clinch it.

Writing Suggestion 2: Write a short essay in which you argue either for or against any of our current drug laws. You may focus on any drugs you wish, from alcohol to LSD. While you should use details and examples to make your case, be sure your logic is persuasive as well.

Coordinating Connectives: Creations

Create at least one kind of coordination in each sentence or pair of sentences below. While most of the exercises ask you to use coordinators that perform specific functions, some leave you free to use any coordinating connectives that seem appropriate. You can compare your creations with professional or student writers' sentences in the Appendix.

SAMPLE EXERCISES

A. Some people said I was a federal agent ____________ (alternative),

____________ (cause and result)

____________ (cause). [signaled format]

B. The press must be free. [open format]

PROFESSIONAL WRITERS' VERSIONS

A. Some people said I was a federal agent **or** *a fool,*

for

no reasonable man, they said, returns to Watts by choice.

STANLEY SANDERS, "I'll Never Escape the Ghetto"

B. The press must be free **not** *merely to express opinion* **but also** *to obtain information.*

CHARLES REMBAR, "For Sale: Freedom of Speech"

1. We are told that the enormous and expanding use of pesticides is necessary to maintain farm production.

____________ (contrast)

____________ (contrast)?

2. I must have been a chronically suspicious small boy.

3. Jack lifted his head ____________ (addition).

____________ (time)

he raised his spear ____________ (addition).

4. Possibly a war can be fought for democracy.

5. The young movie actress was ______________________
(alternatives—use correlative construction)
____.

6. I was an observer and a scientist.

______________________________,
(contrast—use conjunctive adverb)
____.
(contrast)

7. The environment was empty.

8. For the most part, blacks and whites differ profoundly in their ideas ______________________
(addition—use correlative construction)
____.

9. I would have to win a scholarship.

10. It is thought to be an unnecessary cruelty to deny the patient the most successful treatment for his condition.

______________________________,
(cause and result—use conjunctive adverb)
____.
(result)

The Stormy Season

Combine the sentences below into a paragraph that contains several coordinating connectives. You can compare your paragraph with a professional or student writer's version in the Appendix.

1. I have only to break into the tightness of a strawberry.
2. I see summer.
3. I see its dust.
4. I see its skies.
5. Its skies are lowering.
6. It remains for me a season of storms.
7. The days and nights are undistinguished in my mind.
8. The days were parched.
9. The nights were sticky.
10. But the storms frightened me.

11. The storms quenched me.
12. They were violent sudden storms.

13. But my memory is uncertain.

14. I recall a summer storm in the town.
15. We lived in the town.
16. I imagine a summer.
17. My mother knew the summer in 1929.

18. There was a tornado that year.
19. It blew away half of Lorain.
20. She said this.

21. I mix up her summer with my own.

22. I bite the strawberry.
23. I think of storms.
24. I see her.

25. She is a young girl in a crepe dress.
26. She is slim.
27. The dress is pink.

28. One hand is on her hip.
29. The other lolls about her thigh.
30. The other is waiting.

31. The wind swoops her up.
32. It swoops her high above the houses.
33. But she is still standing.
34. Her hand is on her hip.

35. She is smiling.

36. The anticipation and promise are not altered.
37. The anticipation and promise are in her hand.
38. Her hand is lolling.
39. The holocaust does not alter them.

40. My mother's hand is unextinguished.
41. This is in the summer tornado of 1929.

42. She is strong.
43. She is smiling.
44. She is relaxed.
45. The world falls down about her.

46. So much for memory.

47. Fact becomes reality.
48. The fact is public.
49. The reality is private.

50. The seasons of a town become the *Moirai** of our lives.
51. The town is Midwestern.
52. Our lives are small.

Writing Suggestion 1: Whether north, south, east, or west, every region has its season of storms. Write a paragraph reminiscing about the storms you have witnessed. As in the exercise above, develop your paragraph by association, freely, letting each recollection call forth the next.

Writing Suggestion 2: The exercise above refers to a local storm in 1929. The year 1929 was a stormy year in America at large, since it was in that year that the "crash" of the stock market occurred, ushering in the Great Depression. Go to the library and learn about the crash and the economic depression that followed it. Write a short essay on your research. Could the events of 1929 be repeated today?

Coordinating Connectives: Sentence Acrobatics

Combine each set of sentences below into one or more "acrobatic" sentences. See if you can use coordinating connectives as you do each exercise, but feel free to try out other constructions as well. Naturally, each problem invites more than one "correct" answer. Therefore, you must create original sentences that strike *you* as both correct and stylish.

You may enjoy comparing your combinations with the professional or student writers' versions in the Appendix. Look for both similarities and differences, but try to decide whose version is the more stylish—it may well be your own.

SAMPLE EXERCISE

They have only their labor to sell.
They are very few buyers of their labor.
They have only the choice.
They can truckle to the powerful.
They can perish.
They will perish heroically.
They will perish miserably.

STUDENT AND PROFESSIONAL WRITERS' VERSIONS

Since there are very few buyers of their labor, which is the only thing they have to sell, they have only one choice: **either** they can truckle to the powerful **or** they can perish—heroically **yet** miserably.

STUDENT WRITER

**Moirai:* Greek for the fates that shape our destinies

They have only their labor to sell, **and** there are very few buyers of their labor. **Therefore,** they have only the choice of truckling to the powerful **or** of perishing heroically **but** miserably.

WALTER LIPPMANN, "How Liberty Is Lost"

1. This was last year.
   Organized crime was directly responsible for more than one hundred murders.
   Mafiosi participated indirectly in several hundred more.
   The *mafiosi* lent the killers carfare.
   The *mafiosi* held their coats.

2. This is in short.
   Game theory is concerned with rules.
   It is concerned with rules only to the extent that the rules help define the choice situation.
   It is concerned with rules only to the extent that the rules help define the outcomes.
   The outcomes are associated with the choices.
   The rules of games play no other part in game theory.

3. The burden of being sued inhibits free expression.
   The burden is financial.
   The burden is the judgment.
   One might have to pay the judgment.
   The burden is the cost of the defense.
   The Supreme Court rewrote the law of libel.

4. A light falls from the window.
   The light is pale.
   The light is gray.
   The window is above us.
   We sit in the dimness.
   We are like wood lice.
   The lice are under a rock.

5. This is in the simplicity.
   The simplicity is sheltered.
   It is the simplicity of the first few days after a baby is born.
   One sees again the circle.
   The circle is magical.
   The circle is closed.
   One sees again the sense of two people.
   The sense is miraculous.
   The people are existing only for each other.
   One sees again the sky.
   The sky is tranquil.

The sky is reflected on the face of the mother.
The mother is nursing her child.
It is only a brief interlude.
It is not a substitute for the original relationship.
It is not a substitute for the complete relationship.

6. Dorothea Brooke absorbs the afternoon.
She is like a buried seed.
The seed absorbs the sunlight.
She is not consciously aware of the afternoon.
She is not mindful of the internal changes.
The afternoon is causing the changes.

7. Dora was having trouble.
The trouble was with her income tax.
She was entangled in that enigma.
The enigma is curious.
The enigma said the business was illegal.
Then the enigma taxed her for it.

8. It can be war.
It can be revolution.
They may fight under one flag.
They may fight under another.
It does not matter what their slogan is.
Their aim remains the same.
They aim to perpetrate evil.
They aim to cause pain.
They aim to shed blood.

9. He became conscious.
He was conscious of the weight of his clothes.
He kicked off his shoes.
The kicking was fierce.
He ripped off each stocking.
Each stocking had its elastic garter.
He ripped them off in a single movement.
He leapt back on the terrace.
He pulled off his shirt.
He stood there among the coconuts.
The coconuts were like skulls.
Green shadows slid over his skin.
The shadows were from the palms.
The shadows were from the forest.

10. They had challenged kings.
They had challenged them from here.

They had despoiled the Church.
They had departed for crusades.
They had died on crusades.
They had been condemned for crimes.
They had been excommunicated for crimes.
They had enlarged their domain.
The enlargement was progressive.
They had married royalty.
They had nurtured a pride.
The pride took for its battle cry *"Coucy à la merveille!"*

Playing Housewife

Combine the sentences below into a short essay that contains several coordinating connectives and parallel structures. You can compare your essay with a professional or student writer's version in the Appendix.

1. I played housewife for eight months.

2. I had worked five years as an RN.*
3. The work was full-time.
4. I looked forward to the chance.
5. I would be a homebody.

6. I'd worked days.
7. I'd worked evenings.
8. I'd worked nights.
9. I'd worked holidays.
10. I'd worked every birthday.

11. I'd mopped puddles of urine from the floor.
12. I'd wrestled with alcoholics.
13. I'd cuddled babies.
14. The babies were screaming.

15. I'd taken care of women, infants, and men.
16. The women had slit wrists.
17. The babies had birth defects.
18. The men had cancer.
19. The cancer ate away their manhood.

20. I awaited peace.
21. I awaited freedom.
22. I awaited time for myself.
23. My waiting was expectant.

**RN:* Registered Nurse

24. I made lists of the projects.
25. I would accomplish the projects.
26. I would paint the bedroom.
27. I would finish the needlepoint kit.
28. I would play with Jennifer. . . .

29. I stuck to my lists religiously.
30. This was for the first two months.

31. Soon I'd crossed off everything but "play with Jennifer."
32. She was always playing with the girl next door.
33. She was always playing with the boy down the street.

34. Life settled into a routine.

35. I fried eggs and squeezed juice for breakfast.
36. The breakfast was my husband's.
37. I packed a peanut butter and jelly lunch.
38. The lunch was for my daughter.
39. Then I went back to bed until eleven o'clock.

40. I had a bubblebath.
41. Then I watched "As the World Turns" and "The Edge of Night" until four.

42. By eight in the evening, my husband would be studying.
43. My daughter would be in bed.
44. I'd be drinking my third glass of rosé.

45. On Saturday mornings I did the ritual.
46. I vacuumed.
47. I dusted.
48. I cleaned the toilet bowl.
49. Jennifer watched cartoons.
50. Allen slept in.

51. Then I watched.
52. The dog shed hair on the carpet.
53. The dust resettled.
54. The Ty-D-bol man drowned.

55. I ran out of Ban Roll-on.
56. I had to ask my husband for the necessary $1.79.

57. I learned 369 ways to make hamburger into meals.
58. The meals were nutritious.
59. Sometimes they were even delicious.

60. Dinner at McDonald's was a treat.
61. The treat was infrequent.

62. We went only to Walt Disney movies.
63. We couldn't afford a sitter.

64. We went to a party.
65. I'd cringe in my dress.
66. My dress was two years old.

67. At first I tried to get into the conversation.
68. I shared such tidbits.
69. "Ellen is Dan's mother."
70. "Alex married his half sister."
71. "David is dying of cancer."
72. Then I ran out of current events.

73. I realized that sitting was easier.
74. I sat quietly.
75. I sat in the corner.

76. Our sex life should have been terrific.

77. I had twelve hours of sleep each day.
78. I had all afternoon to think up techniques.
79. The techniques were dazzling.
80. The techniques were new.

81. My husband will verify this.
82. Not once was I sheathed in Saran Wrap.
83. I met him at the door.

84. The event of my day occurred at 4:30.
85. The event was most exciting.
86. I decided something.
87. Would I have green beans or corn with dinner?

88. Frankly, neither one turned me on.

89. Anyway, all the couplings and gropings left me exhausted.
90. The couplings and gropings were on TV.

91. I found the housewife game lacking.
92. It lacked physical stimulation.
93. It lacked intellectual stimulation.
94. It lacked sexual stimulation.
95. It lacked monetary reward.

96. After eight months, I looked forward to bedpans.
97. I looked forward to bandages.
98. I looked forward to bottoms.

99. I didn't want to play anymore.

Writing Suggestion 1: In recent times, many women have found playing housewife to be a less-than-satisfying game. In the light of the exercise above and your own experience, write an essay on the housewife game. Should the rules be changed?

Writing Suggestion 2: While each of us has a private self, we have social selves as well. Our social selves are made up of the many roles we play in everyday society, from housewife to student to junior executive. Write an essay in which you analyze and classify your own social selves.

> ***They were solitary little girls whose loneliness was so profound it intoxicated them and sent them stumbling into Technicolored visions that always included a presence, a someone, who, quite like the dreamer, shared the delight of the dream.***
>
> **TONI MORRISON, *Sula***

Toni Morrison's account of the lonely little girls' dreams has impressive psychological depth. The first clause of the sentence broadly states the cause of the girls' fantasies:

> They were solitary little girls.

The author then delves into the effects of their loneliness:

> Their loneliness was so profound it intoxicated them and sent them stumbling into Technicolored visions.
> The visions always included a presence, a someone.
> The someone, quite like the dreamer, shared the delight of the dream.

When Morrison puts these ideas together, she simultaneously eliminates repetitions and relates each idea closely to the next. By turning her observations on the little girls into both bound and free modifiers, the author creates a penetrating analysis of the children's feelings:

> They were solitary little girls **whose** *loneliness was so profound it intoxicated them and sent them stumbling into Technicolored visions*

> **that** *always included a presence,* a someone, **who,** quite like the dreamer, *shared the delight of the dream.*

Toni Morrison achieves this effect of dense psychological texture smoothly. The connective words **whose, that,** and **who** relate the details into a pattern. Just what are these important words, and how can they work in your sentences?

RELATIVES AND RELATIVE CLAUSES

Connectives like **whose, that,** and **who** are called ***relatives.*** In Morrison's sentence, each of these relatives introduces a ***relative clause.*** Such structures are called "relative" because they add and *relate* information that modifies a noun, pronoun, or even a full clause elsewhere in the sentence. Consider, for example, how you might combine these three short sentences:

> Flanagan was a large man.
> Flanagan looked like a barkeeper.
> Flanagan's face was tough and belligerent.

Write your version here:

____

____

____

Obviously, the sentences contain a common denominator: Flanagan. You might replace this repeated name with **he** or **his,** then link the sentences together with **and:**

> Flanagan was a large man, **and he** looked like a barkeeper, **and his** face was tough and belligerent.

But this is hardly an improvement. The three short, linked clauses remain choppy. Worse yet, the details are not related together into a coherent picture of the whole man. The relative clause offers you a more effective way of pulling Flanagan together:

> Flanagan was a large man, **who** *looked like a barkeeper,* and **whose** *face was tough and belligerent.*

This is just what Clarence Day did when he wrote the sentence in his story "Father Tries to Make Mother Like Figures." Day's sentence contains two relative clauses. In the first, the relative **who** replaces the name *Flanagan.* In the second, the relative **whose** replaces the possessive form *Flanagan's.* In each case, the substitution makes for coherence and economy.

THE RELATIVES: *WHO, WHOM, WHOSE, THAT,* AND *WHICH*

Ever since early childhood, you have been creating relative clauses naturally. Nevertheless, you may not be using them as efficiently as possible in your writing. Choosing the right relative and correctly punctuating relative clauses can give even a mature writer some trouble. For these reasons, a conscious review of your "built-in" knowledge is in order.

As the sentences by Toni Morrison and Clarence Day showed, relatives replace key words that might otherwise be needlessly repeated. The basic relatives are five:

who	**that**	**which**
whom		
whose		

Except for **whose,** the **who** relatives modify only nouns that refer to people. **That** is the all-purpose relative, capable of modifying nouns that refer to people, animals, or things. Finally, **which** modifies only nouns that refer to animals and things—never nouns that refer to humans.

Who or *Whom*?

The choice between **who** and **whom** gives nearly everyone trouble. Fortunately, sentence-combining practice can help you learn to choose the right relative every time. To grasp this, consider how you might combine these paired sentences:

A. Andy Warhol is a businessman.
The businessman is by category an artist.

B. I escorted an actress from Prague.
I had known the actress a long time.

Write your versions here:

____

____

____

____

____

____

In each pair, the repeated noun refers to a human being: *businessman* in the first pair, *actress* in the second. But which relative, **who** or **whom,** should you use to combine each pair?

You can determine which relative to use by performing a simple substitution test using *he, she, they, him, her,* or *them.* First, substitute the appropriate word from this set for the word you want to replace with a relative:

A. **He** is by category an artist.
B. I had known **her** a long time.

Now you can select the correct relative by following a rule of thumb. If you replaced the word with *he, she,* or *they,* the relative should be **who.** If you replaced the word with *him, her,* or *them,* the relative should be **whom:**

Substitute	***Relative***
he she they	**who**
him her them	**whom**

If you perform this test when you combine the sample sentences, you'll get the results these writers got:

A. Andy Warhol is a businessman **who** is by category an artist.
BARBARA L. GOLDSMITH, "La Dolce Viva"

B. I escorted an actress from Prague, **whom** I had known a long time.
ISAAC BASHEVIS SINGER, "A Friend of Kafka"

Thanks to the substitution test, the **who–whom** distinction should give you little trouble. But notice another difference between the two sentences above: the punctuation. The relative clause in Singer's sentence is marked off by a comma, while the relative clause in Goldsmith's sentence is not. This brings us to a second major distinction you must understand if you are to master the relative clause, the distinction between **bound** and **free** modifiers.

WHO, WHOM, AND *WHOSE* AS BOUND AND FREE MODIFIERS

Depending on its relationship to the noun it modifies, a relative clause will either be bound directly to the noun (*my sister* **who** *sings*) or marked off by punctuation as a free modifier (*my sister***,** **who** *sings*). Since this distinction affects not only punctuation but meaning, we shall consider how it affects each of the relative pronouns.

As we saw, the **who** relatives change form, depending on the function of the words they replace. Each of these three—**who, whom,** and **whose**—can introduce either bound or free relative clauses. Consider first the relative **who**. Try combining each pair of sentences below into one sentence that includes a relative clause beginning with **who**:

A. One suspects that much of the praise of seriousness comes from people.
The people have a vital need for a façade of weight and dignity.

B. The Head Nurse pressed down a little lever.
The Head Nurse was standing by a switchboard at the other end of the room.

Write your versions here:

____

____

____

____

____

____

Two writers combined and punctuated the sentences in these ways:

A. One suspects that much of the praise of seriousness comes from people **who** *have a vital need for a façade of weight and dignity.*
ERIC HOFFER, *The Ordeal of Change*

B. The Head Nurse**, who** *was standing by a switchboard at the other end of the room***,** pressed down a little lever.
ALDOUS HUXLEY, *Brave New World*

Although both authors used **who** to combine their sentences, they punctuated their combinations differently. Eric Hoffer created a bound relative clause that defines *people who have a vital need for a façade of weight and dignity.* Without the relative clause, we would not know exactly which people Hoffer meant. The modifier adds grammatically essential information—a *definition.* Therefore, the relative clause is not set off by punctuation.

On the other hand, Aldous Huxley created a free relative clause that simply adds extra information about *the Head Nurse,* whose very title fully identifies her as an individual. The relative clause here, *who was standing by a switchboard at the other end of the room,* adds grammatically *nonessential* information—a *comment.* Hence, it is set off by punctuation.

Now consider the relative **whom.** Once again, try combining each pair of sentences below into one sentence that contains a relative clause. Remember the substitution test you learned earlier:

A. Lots of fellows had been named after their fathers without having such troubles.
I knew lots of fellows.

B. My father advised me against starting college right after high school.
I respected my father.

Write your versions here:

____

____

____

____

____

____

You can compare your combinations with these versions, one by a student, one by a professional writer:

A. Lots of fellows **whom** *I knew* had been named after their fathers without having such troubles.

CLARENCE DAY, "Father Opens My Mail"

B. My father, **whom** *I respected,* advised me against starting college right after high school.

STUDENT WRITER

When the sentences are combined, **whom** replaces a noun in the second sentence of each pair. Note again how the punctuation of the combined sentences depends on whether the newly created relative clause defines the word it modifies or merely comments on it. Day's bound modifier defines a specific group of "fellows"—"lots of **fellows whom I knew**." The student writer's free modifier, on the other hand, merely comments on a fully identified individual, "my father."

Finally, consider how the relative **whose** can replace a noun that ends in **'s** or **s'**—a possessive form. Unlike **who** and **whom,** which replace only nouns that refer to human beings, **whose** can replace *any* possessive noun. As before, combine the following pairs of sentences:

A. Most of them seemed to be people.
The people's families had always danced.

B. It was just one picture.
The picture's visualization took less than a second.

Write your versions here:

____

____

____

____

____

____

You can compare your combinations with these:

A. Most of them seemed to be people **whose** *families had always danced.*

CALVIN TRILLIN, "A Stag Oyster Eat Below the Canal"

B. It was just one picture, **whose** *visualization took less than a second.*

ERICH FROMM, *The Forgotten Language*

Notice that Calvin Trillin used **whose** to replace *the people's,* a possessive noun that refers to human beings. On the other hand, Erich Fromm used **whose** to replace *the picture's,* a possessive noun that refers to something nonhuman. Can you explain why Trillin's relative clause is a bound modifier, while Fromm's is a free modifier? Trillin's bound relative clause *defines* "people whose families had always danced." In contrast, Fromm's free modifier *comments* on "one picture," whose identity has already been established.

THAT: ALWAYS A BOUND MODIFIER

So much for **who, whom,** and **whose.** Although the next relative, **that,** can modify any noun, whether it refers to humans, animals, or things, **that** raises no punctuation problems. Unlike **who** and company, which can introduce either bound or free relative clauses, **that** introduces only bound modifiers—definitions. Use **that** to combine these paired sentences:

A. These are the times.
The times try men's souls.

B. He sported a skimpy juvenile moustache.
The army permitted him to grow the moustache.

Write your versions here:

____

____

____

____

____

____

Here are the original authors' combinations:

A. These are the times **that** *try men's souls.*

THOMAS PAINE, *Common Sense*

B. He sported a skimpy juvenile moustache **that** *the army permitted him to grow.*

LARRY WOIWODE, *Fathers and Sons*

Because both authors created relative clauses that present essential, defining information, neither sentence contains any punctuation between the relative and the noun that it modifies. Hence, the modifiers are bound rather than free. Such is always the case with the relative **that.**

WHICH: BOUND OR FREE?

The last relative we shall consider, **which,** presents a different set of options. While **which** can replace only nouns that refer to things or animals—never to humans—it can introduce either a bound or free relative clause. Try these combinations:

A. He lived in a static society.
The society could endure almost anything except change.

B. Low light from the east came through the trees.
The trees were full and dark green.

Write your versions here:

____

____

____

____

____

____

Here are versions by two professionals:

A. He lived in a static society **which** *could endure almost anything except change.*

BRUCE CATTON, "Grant and Lee: A Study in Contrasts"

B. Low light from the east came through the trees, **which** *were full and dark green.*

DONALD HALL, *String Too Short to Be Saved*

In Catton's sentence, the relative clause is essential. It defines *a static society* **which** *could endure almost anything except change.* Therefore, **which** is bound to the word it modifies: *society.* In Hall's sentence, the **which** clause is nonessential. It merely comments on the *trees,* which happened to be full and dark green. Therefore, the clause is a free modifier, set off by a comma.

While writers do indeed use **which** for bound and free modifiers alike, some stylists argue that **which** is best reserved for free modifiers only, for nonessential comments set off by commas. Since **that** is used only for bound modifiers, this argument makes sense. Surely the more imposing of the two words is **which.** As a general rule, reserve **which** for free modifiers—commentary. For essential, bound modifiers—for *information* **that** *we must grasp quickly*—**that**'s enough.

WHERE AND *WHEN* AS RELATIVES

If you recall the "substitution test" explained earlier, you'll have no trouble combining these two sentences by creating a relative clause:

One night we had a new waitress.
Mother had great hopes **of** her.

Write your version here:

Since the word *her,* not *she,* already appears in the second sentence, the correct relative will be **whom.** When the sentences are combined, the phrase **of whom** shifts from the end to the beginning of the newly created relative clause:

> One night we had a new waitress, **of whom** *Mother had great hopes.*
> CLARENCE DAY, "Mother and the Servant Problem"

You can follow much the same strategy when you combine these paired sentences:

A. Abe North was still **at** the Ritz bar.
He had been at the Ritz bar since nine in the morning.

B. The next day was one of those crisp late fall days.
On those crisp late fall days one feels so good that he wants to stay right in bed under the blankets all morning.

Write your versions here:

That is, you can create structures introduced by **at** and **on:**

A. Abe North was still at the Ritz bar, **at which** *he had been since nine in the morning.*

B. The next day was one of those crisp late fall days **on which** *one feels so good that he wants to stay right in bed under the blankets all morning.*

But there's another option. You can combine the sentences as their authors originally did:

A. Abe North was still at the Ritz bar, **where** *he had been since nine in the morning.*

F. SCOTT FITZGERALD, *Tender Is the Night*

B. The next day was one of those crisp late fall days **when** *one feels so good that he wants to stay right in bed under the blankets all morning.*

ROBERT BENCHLEY, "The Helping Hand"

This is a neat trick—and quite grammatical. In such combinations, **where** and **when** can replace **at which** and **on which,** respectively. That is, **where** and **when** can serve as relatives.

THE "BROAD-REFERENCE" RELATIVE CLAUSE

Finally, a "broad-reference" relative clause can modify an entire sentence, not just a single noun or pronoun. To grasp this, try to combine these two sentences:

Marriages are said to be made in heaven.
This must be why they don't work here on earth.

Write your version here:

____

____

____

In the second sentence above, *this* stands for the entire idea expressed by the first sentence—not just for one word. The second sentence is a broad general *comment* on the first, as the author's version reveals:

Marriages are said to be made in heaven, **which** *must be why they don't work here on earth.*

THOMAS SZASZ, *Heresies*

Here, the relative **which** refers not to just one noun in the base clause, but rather to the whole idea expressed in the base. A broad-reference clause like this adds information that is not grammatically essential. Therefore, it is always a free modifier, set off by punctuation.

As the above sentence proves, broad reference is not necessarily vague reference. Still, the broad-reference **which** can be confusing. Consider this sentence, which comes from a student writer's first draft:

We spent long hours talking about the finals, **which** *worried our coach.*

Was it the *finals* that worried the coach—or was it the *talking?* The **which** in this version is not so much broad as vague. Therefore, the student recombined the sentence to clarify the meaning:

It worried our coach that we spent long hours talking about the finals.

This recombination eliminates the broad reference **which**—and the confusion. If you suspect that a broad reference is *too* broad, that it is vague or ambiguous, try another combination.

PULLING IT ALL TOGETHER

The sentence that opened this chapter came from Toni Morrison's novel *Sula.* It illustrated how a master writer can combine several relative clauses to create a richly textured portrait. The exercises that follow will ask you to create just such sentences yourself. Imagine, for example, that you are writing a film review—a job that calls for detailed observation. You want to sum up Alan Bates's performance as Sergei Diaghilev in the movie *Nijinsky.* Here are four related perceptions that you hope to combine:

His is a lush, fruity, enjoyable performance.
His performance is in keeping with the tone of the movie.
The movie often seems enjoyable but excessive.
The movie is like a box of Godiva chocolates.

Very likely, if you've mastered the relative clause, your combination will look something like this version:

His is a lush, fruity, enjoyable performance **that** *is in keeping with the tone of the movie,* **which** *often seems enjoyable but excessive,* like a box of Godiva chocolates.

That's how Roger Angell pulled it all together in his review of *Nijinsky* for *The New Yorker.* Like Toni Morrison and the other writers you studied in this chapter, Angell combined related ideas by creating relative clauses.

The Relative Clause: Combinations

Combine each set of sentences below into one sentence that contains at least one relative clause. You can compare your combinations with professional or student writers' sentences in the Appendix.

SAMPLE EXERCISE

The sun's radiation contains ultraviolet components.
No living cell can tolerate the ultraviolet components.

PROFESSIONAL WRITER'S VERSION

The sun's radiation contains ultraviolet components **which** *no living cell can tolerate.*

GEORGE WALD, "The Origin of Life"

1. Mrs. Gaffney and Mrs. Betz nudged Mrs. Farrell.
   Mrs. Farrell left her mouth open to giggle quickly with them.
2. He was a sallow-faced man.
   His hair, moustache and sharply pointed beard were all tinged with gray.
3. He had expected that Yakichi would make them separate.
   This would have caused him little pain.
4. A strength surged through Rabbi Naphtali.
   The strength astounded him.
5. Few American industries have suffered so spectacular a decline as wrestling.
   Wrestling had its happiest days during the early years of the general depression.
6. We backed up to an old gray man.
   The man bore an absurd resemblance to John D. Rockefeller.
7. There was once a town in the heart of America.
   In this town all life seemed to live in harmony with its surroundings.
8. Everyone has a moment in history.
   The moment belongs particularly to him.
9. Renunciation is a luxury.
   All men cannot indulge in this luxury.
10. I recently met somebody.
    Somebody's eating memories of a childhood in Iowa are dominated by a barrel of oysters.
    The barrel of oysters was kept in the cellar.
11. I took along my son.
    My son had never had any fresh water up his nose.
    My son had seen lily pads only from train windows.
12. The store smelled of cheese.
    The Justice of the Peace's court was sitting in the store.

13. The following afternoon the maid told her that a man had come and fixed the radio.
    Irene returned to the apartment from a luncheon date the following afternoon.

14. But for the figure of his grandfather, he thought the world must be altogether empty.
    He was afraid he would never find the figure of his grandfather in the darkness.

15. There is a front porch with white wooden columns.
    The columns support a white wooden balcony.
    The balcony runs along the second floor.

Comrade Laski

Combine the sentences below into a paragraph that contains at least one relative clause. You can compare your paragraph with a professional or student writer's version in the Appendix.

1. Michael Laski is a young man.
2. He is also known as M. I. Laski.
3. He is relatively obscure.
4. He has deep fervent eyes.
5. He has a short beard.
6. He has a pallor.
7. The pallor seems particularly remarkable in Southern California.

8. His appearance is striking.
9. His diction is relentlessly ideological.
10. He looks precisely like the image.
11. He talks precisely like the image.
12. The image is popular.
13. The image is of a professional revolutionary.
14. He is in fact a professional revolutionary.

Writing Suggestion 1: Have you ever known a "revolutionary," someone who sought to overturn the status quo? Remember, not all revolutionaries are political like Comrade Laski. Someone can be a revolutionary in anything from education to personal grooming. Write a paragraph describing a revolutionary you have known or about whom you have read.

Writing Suggestion 2: The news is filled with accounts of political revolutions under way around the world, from Poland to El Salvador. Select one of these contemporary revolutions, gather information about it from the library, and write an essay explaining its significance.

Westerners

Combine the sentences below into a paragraph that contains at least one relative clause. You can compare your paragraph with a professional or student writer's version in the Appendix.

1. The solitude makes westerners quiet.
2. Westerners live in the solitude.

3. They telegraph thoughts.
4. They telegraph feelings.
5. They do this by the way they tilt their heads.
6. They do this by the way they listen.

7. They pull their Stetsons into a dive over their eyes.
8. The dive is steep.
9. Or they pigeon-toe one boot over the other.
10. They lean against a fence.
11. They have a fat wedge of snoose* beneath their lower lips.
12. They take the whole scene in.

13. These looks of amusement are sometimes cynical.
14. The looks are detached.
15. The amusement is quiet.
16. But the looks can also come from a humility.
17. The humility is dry-eyed.
18. The humility is as lucid as the air is clean.

Writing Suggestion 1: All too often, when we discuss a group like "westerners," we speak in stereotypes and clichés. In the exercise above, the added details bring what might have been a blurry set of generalizations into sharp focus. Select another regional group with which you are familiar—easterners, northerners, or southerners—and write a paragraph analyzing their distinctive traits in detail.

Writing Suggestion 2: Although the Civil War ended well over a century ago, on many important issues—energy, employment, and values, to name a few—America remains a divided nation. Write an essay analyzing one or more of the key issues on which the North, South, East, and West remain divided in the United States.

The Relative Clause: Creations

Create at least one relative clause in each sentence below. While most of the exercises ask you to create specific kinds of relative clauses, some leave you free to create any kind that seems appropriate. You can compare your creations with professional or student writers' sentences in the Appendix.

* *snoose:* a strong, moist snuff sometimes chewed by sheepherders

SAMPLE EXERCISES

A. Macon drummed his fingers on the steering wheel, ____________
(free modifier of **steering wheel**) ____________________. [signaled format]

B. It was one of those fantastically lush May days. [open format]

PROFESSIONAL WRITERS' VERSIONS

A. Macon drummed his fingers on the steering wheel, **which** *trembled a little as the car idled.*

TONI MORRISON, *Song of Solomon*

B. It was one of those fantastically lush May days **that** *the devious Russian spring looses suddenly upon the countryside.*

ANDREA LEE, *Russian Journal*

1. The man ____________________ (bound modifier of **man**) was very young and very thin.
2. This job also offered us access to a master key to all the rooms.
3. He has the sort of face ____________________ (bound modifier of **face**).
4. I went to a carnival in Los Angeles.
5. Residues of these chemicals linger in the soil ____________ (bound modifier of **soil**) ____________________.
6. My eyes met with those of a girl about eighteen, ____________ (free modifier of **girl**) ____________________.
7. What English he learned he picked up from truck drivers.
8. The village's only real attraction, ____________ (free modifier of **attraction**) ____________________, is the hot spring water.
9. He came from a village in a part of Extramadura.
10. There was once a French-Canadian ____________ (bound modifier of **French-Canadian**) ____________________ but ____________________ (bound modifier of **French-Canadian**).

Old Folks at Home

Combine the sentences below into a paragraph that contains several relative clauses. You can compare your paragraph with a professional or student writer's version in the Appendix.

1. Old Henry and his wife Phoebe were fond of each other.
2. They were as fond as it is possible for two old people to be.
3. The old people have nothing else in this life to be fond of.

4. He was a thin old man.
5. He was seventy when she died.
6. He was a queer person.
7. He was a crotchety person.
8. He had coarse hair and beard.
9. His hair and beard were gray-black.
10. His hair and beard were quite straggly.
11. His hair and beard were unkempt.

12. He looked at you out of dull eyes.
13. His eyes were fishy.
14. His eyes were watery.
15. His eyes had deep-brown crow's-feet at the sides.

16. His clothes were like the clothes of many farmers.
17. His clothes were aged.
18. His clothes were angular.
19. His clothes were baggy.
20. His clothes stood out at the pockets.
21. His clothes did not fit about the neck.
22. His clothes were protuberant at elbow and knee.
23. His clothes were worn at elbow and knee.

24. Phoebe Ann was thin.
25. She was shapeless.
26. She was a very umbrella of a woman.
27. She was clad in shabby black.
28. She had a black bonnet for her best wear.

29. Time had passed.
30. They had only themselves to look after.
31. Their movements had become slower and slower.
32. Their activities had become fewer and fewer.

33. The annual keep of pigs had been reduced from five to one porker.
34. The porker grunted.
35. The single horse was a sleepy animal.
36. Henry now retained the horse.
37. The horse was not over-nourished.
38. The horse was not very clean.

39. The chickens had almost disappeared.
40. Formerly there was a large flock of chickens.
41. This was owing to ferrets.
42. It was owing to foxes.
43. It was owing to the lack of proper care.
44. Lack of proper care produces disease.

45. The garden was now a memory of itself.
46. The garden was formerly healthy.
47. The memory was straggling.
48. The vines and flower-beds had now become thickets.
49. The vines and flower-beds formerly ornamented the windows and dooryard.
50. The thickets were choking.

51. A will had been made.
52. The will divided the small property among the four.*
53. The property was eaten by taxes.
54. The four remained.
55. It was really of no interest to any of them.

56. Yet these two lived together.
57. They lived in peace and sympathy.
58. Only now and then old Henry would become unduly cranky.
59. He complained almost invariably.
60. Something had been neglected.
61. Something had been mislaid.
62. Something was of no importancc at all.

Writing Suggestion 1: Using your observation, experience, and imagination, write a short story about an older couple like Henry and Phoebe. You can continue the story the exercise begins if you wish, or you can tell a different story that is all your own. As you compose your story, keep this maxim from novelist Jack Kerouac in mind: "Detail is the life of literature."

Writing Suggestion 2: As the "baby boom" generation grows older, the problem of care for the aged will grow more and more acute. Write a speculative essay in which you present the kind of care you would hope to have as a senior citizen. What kind of planning can we do today to make your dream a reality?

The Relative Clause: Sentence Acrobatics

Combine each set of sentences below into one or more "acrobatic" sentences. See if you can create at least one relative clause as you do each exercise, but feel free to try out other constructions as well. Naturally,

* the four living children of Henry and Phoebe

each problem invites more than one "correct" answer. Therefore, you must create original sentences that strike *you* as both correct and stylish.

You may enjoy comparing your combinations with the professional or student writers' versions in the Appendix. Look for both similarities and differences, but try to decide whose version is more stylish—it may well be your own.

SAMPLE EXERCISE

A species is a group.
The group can produce offspring.
The offspring are fertile.
The group crosses within itself.
The group does not cross outside itself.

STUDENT AND PROFESSIONAL WRITERS' VERSIONS

A species is a group **that** *crosses within but not outside itself and produces offspring* **that** *are fertile.*

STUDENT WRITER

A species is a group **that** *can produce fertile offspring by crosses within but not outside itself.*

CARL SAGAN, *The Dragons of Eden*

1. The battery was commanded by a captain named O'Neill.
   O'Neill's family had emigrated to France from Ireland.
   They emigrated in the seventeenth century.
2. The island is peopled.
   I live on the island.
   The people are cranks.
   The cranks are like myself.
3. He was one of those men.
   In those men the force is diffused.
   The force creates life.
   The force is not centralized.
4. The superintendent of the jail raised his head at the sound.
   He was standing apart from the rest of us.
   He was prodding the gravel.
   He prodded it with a stick.
   The prodding was moody.
5. The most famous lithotomist* of all time was not a doctor.
   He was an itinerant thug.

* *lithotomist:* a surgeon who removes mineral deposits or "stones" from the bladder

The thug was named Jacques Baulot.
Baulot's medical career began in 1680.
He was a servant to Pauloni.
Pauloni was a strolling lithotomist and curer of ruptures.

6. The man confronts a world.
The man is born into this society of ours.
The society is American.
His world differs radically in its character from that world.
His ancestors were born into that world.

7. This was one Sunday.
On this Sunday the rest of her family had gone to a barbecue.
Connie relaxed at home.
She listened to music.
She daydreamed about the times she had had.
The times were good.
The times were with the boys.

8. Liberals must insist on wage settlements.
The settlements will be at the high end of the scale.
The settlements will reduce inflation.
The settlements will encourage economic growth.
The growth will be renewed.
This is the best real hope for the poor.
This is the best real hope for the well-being of our institutions.
The institutions are political.

9. The phenomenon was huge.
The phenomenon was unprecedented.
The phenomenon was blue jeans.
The phenomenon spread from the United States to the rest of the world.
This was in the 1970s.
The phenomenon was largely a phenomenon of declassing.
This was in its early stages.

10. Many people are married to people.
The people have been married to other people.
The other people are now married to still others.
The first parties may not have been married to those others.
But somebody has likely been married to those others.

Life

Combine the sentences below into an essay that contains several relative clauses. You can compare your essay with a professional or student writer's version in the Appendix.

1. One of my favorite possessions is a copy of *Life*.
2. It is a copy of the December 21, 1942, issue.
3. I picked it up a few years ago at a flea market.

4. It cost me $1.00.
5. It cost me ten times what it would have cost my mother or my father.
6. My mother graduated from high school that year.
7. My father was soon to enlist in the Navy.

8. Recently, I have found that my issue of *Life* has gained a timely poignance.
9. My issue was once no more than a period piece.
10. My generation has begun to face the possibility of a draft registration.
11. The draft registration is in peacetime.
12. The draft registration would include both sexes.

13. It portrays a nation.
14. The nation is obsessed with war.
15. The nation is obsessed with the roles.
16. Men and women should play the roles in war.
17. It suggests a number of comparisons with our present situation.
18. The comparisons are disturbing.

19. The sacrifices pervade most of the articles.
20. The sacrifices pervade many of the advertisements.
21. The articles and advertisements are in *Life*'s 1942 Christmas issue.
22. The sacrifices are necessary to war.

23. "Please don't call long distance *this* Christmas!"
24. Bell Telephone requests this.
25. "It may be the 'holiday season'—but war needs the wires."

26. An ad portrays a young mother.
27. She explains to her son.
28. Her son is an infant.
29. His father has been lent to his country.
30. He has been lent "so that in the years to come, young mothers everywhere . . . will be able to say 'Merry Christmas' to their sons."
31. The ad is for the United States Rubber Company.

32. The magazine's cover story is a photo-essay.
33. The story is "Lonely Wife."
34. Its text offers advice to wives of servicemen.

35. Move into a smaller place.
36. Make sure "your husband is the master when he returns on furlough."

37. Take a course in camouflage.
38. The course is in the evening.

39. "Volunteer work is another good outlet."

40. The males remain at home.
41. The males are "wolves."
42. They are to be kept "at bay."

43. In one photograph Joan keeps a potential wolf's hands occupied.
44. Joan is pretty.
45. She is the Lonely Wife.
46. The keeping is enterprising.
47. She has him help wind her knitting yarn.

48. Another photo is of five women.
49. The women are playing cards.
50. It is captioned.
51. "Company of other women, of little interest when husbands are around, is now appreciated by Joan."

52. She is pictured in a church.
53. This is last.
54. She kneels.
55. She is in prayer before a war shrine.
56. Her prayer is solitary.
57. She beseeches the Lord "to take into thine own hand both him and the cause wherein his country sends him."

58. *Life*'s vision of a nation is also that of a society.
59. The nation is united in war.
60. *Life*'s vision is so different from the only American war I remember.
61. The war I remember is Vietnam.
62. During the Vietnam war my older brother's registration as a conscientious objector brought me nothing but relief.
63. The society is stratified.
64. The stratification is comfortable.
65. The stratification is secure.
66. It is stratified according to what we now popularly call role-models.

67. An ad shows a soldier.
68. He is in his berth.
69. He contemplates "a dog named Shucks, or Spot, or Barnacle Bill. The pretty girl who writes so often . . . that gray-haired man, so proud and awkward at the station . . . the mother who knit the socks he'll wear soon."
70. The ad is for the New Haven Railroad.

71. One of the articles in *Life*'s Christmas issue is a feature.
72. It is one of the few light-hearted articles.
73. The feature is on Las Vegas gamblers.
74. The article observes, "Keno is a woman's game. Like old-fashioned lotto or moviehouse bingo, it requires little intelligence."
75. The observation is straight faced.

Writing Suggestion 1: Go to the library and look up a magazine or newspaper that was published at least five years before you were born. After you've studied the issue closely, write an essay discussing how the articles and advertisements portray men and women. If you wish, consider how men's and women's roles have changed since the publication appeared.

Writing Suggestion 2: If you read a magazine regularly, whether it be *Time* or *National Lampoon,* write an essay explaining the magazine's appeal. If you do not read any magazines regularly, go to your local newsstand and survey the offerings. Buy a magazine that catches your interest, read it, and write an essay analyzing its appeal.

> ***When the struggle with somnolence has been fought out and won, when the world is all-covering darkness and close-pressing silence, when the tobacco suddenly takes on fresh vigour and fragrance and the books lie strewn about the table, then it seems as though all the rubbish and floating matter of the day's thoughts have poured away and only the bright, clear and swift current of the mind itself remains, flowing happily and without impediment.***
>
> **CHRISTOPHER MORLEY, "On Going to Bed"**

Christopher Morley's analysis of the lucid, reflective hour before bedtime is both psychologically and grammatically complex. Even before stating his main ideas, Morley takes pains to establish the exact *time* under discussion:

> The struggle with somnolence has been fought out and won.
> The world is all-covering darkness and close-pressing silence.
> The tobacco suddenly takes on fresh vigour and fragrance.
> The books lie strewn about the table.

Having set the scene in detail, Morley makes two general observations. The first offers a comparison:

> Then it seems **as though** *all the rubbish and floating matter of the day's thoughts have poured away.*

The next goes directly to the heart of the matter:

> Only the bright, clear and swift current of the mind itself remains.

This second observation, in turn, prompts a final comment:

> The current flows happily and without impediment.

While this is indeed a great deal of information to arrange in one sentence, Morley has related the ideas together coherently, thanks principally to the word **when**:

> **When** *the struggle with somnolence has been fought out and won,* **when** *the world is all-covering darkness and close-pressing silence,* **when** *the tobacco suddenly takes on fresh vigour and fragrance and the books lie strewn about the table,* then it seems as though all the rubbish and floating matter of the day's thoughts have poured away and only the bright, clear and swift current of the mind itself remains, flowing happily and without impediment.

Morley's sentence is at once *compound* in that it has two base clauses (here coordinated by **and**) and *complex* in that each of the three initial modifiers introduced by **when** is a full clause, with its own subject and verb. Furthermore, the comparison introduced by **as though** within the base is a complete clause as well:

> Then it seems **as though** *all the rubbish and floating matter*
>
> subject
>
> *of the day's thoughts have poured away*
>
> verb

In Chapter 2, you studied how writers combine words, phrases, and clauses in *equal* rank by using coordinating connectives. In Morley's sentence, however, the clauses introduced by *when* and *as though* are not in equal rank with the base clauses. Instead, they are **dependent** on the first base and unable to stand alone. The clauses introduced by *when* and *as though* are thus **modifiers** rather than independent clauses. Just what kind of modifiers are they, and what can similar modifiers add to your writing?

SUBORDINATORS AND SUBORDINATE CLAUSES

Words like *when* and *as though* are called ***subordinators.*** Placed before complete clauses, as in Morley's sentence, subordinators create ***subordinate clauses.*** The term "subordinate" comes from the Latin prefix *sub* ("under") combined with the verb *ordinare* ("to set or place"). As you will learn in Chapter 6, in terms of sentence structure, a subordinate clause is "placed under" the base clause it modifies. Subordinators make the clauses they introduce dependent on the base for the completion of their meaning. Indeed, subordinators like *when* and *as though* establish precise relationships between the base clause, which can stand on its own, and the subordinate clause, which depends on the base for completion. Thus, when you create subordinate clauses, you establish precise relationships among your ideas.

CREATING SUBORDINATE CLAUSES

For example, consider what relationships might exist between these two sentences when they are combined:

> The general atmosphere is bad.
> Language must suffer.

Much will depend on which sentence you consider to be the more important of the two, since it will become the base clause. Let us assume you aim to stress the second sentence. You might, then, subordinate the first sentence to it in any of several ways, depending on your purpose. You might express a relationship of *place:*

> **Where** *the general atmosphere is bad,* language must suffer.

On the other hand, you might show *cause and result:*

> **Because** *the general atmosphere is bad,* language must suffer.

Yet another possibility would be to express a relationship of *degree:*

> **Insofar as** *the general atmosphere is bad,* language must suffer.

Last of all, you might express the relationship that the writer George Orwell chose to establish in his essay "Politics and the English Language." Like Morley, Orwell created a relationship of *time:*

> **When** *the general atmosphere is bad,* language must suffer.

Depending on your purpose and the context of your sentence, any of these versions can be the correct one, the one that expresses exactly the relationship you seek to establish between your ideas.

SUBORDINATE CLAUSES: BOUND OR FREE MODIFIERS?

Subordinate clauses may be either **bound** modifiers, fused with the base clause, or **free** modifiers, set off by punctuation. Whether or not a subordinate clause is bound or free depends both on its position within the sentence and on the writer's meaning.

A subordinate clause may be placed in any of three positions within a sentence: **initial** position (*before* the base), **medial** position (*within* the base), or **final** position (*after* the base). For example, the sentence from Christopher Morley's "On Going to Bed" contains three subordinate clauses in initial position, each introduced by **when:**

> **When** *the struggle with somnolence has been fought out and won,* **when** *the world is all-covering darkness and close-pressing silence,* **when** *the tobacco suddenly takes on fresh vigour and fragrance and the books lie strewn about the table,* . . .

Each of these initial modifiers is punctuated as free, set off by a comma. On the other hand, the final subordinate clause introduced by **as though** is not set off by commas. Rather, it is bound directly to the base:

> . . . then it seems **as though** *all the rubbish and floating matter of the day's thoughts have poured away.* . . .

Where the initial subordinate clauses were set off as free modifiers *commenting* on the base clause, this final subordinate clause is a bound modifier *defining* exactly how "it seems." Without the modifier, the writer's meaning would be unclear.

Unfortunately, not all subordinate clauses fall into such neat categories. Positioning and pauses, however, help us determine whether a subordinate clause is bound or free. *Initial* subordinate clauses are usually set off as free modifiers, except when the subordinate clause is relatively short:

> **If** *gratitude and esteem are good foundations of affection,* Elizabeth's change of sentiment will be neither improbable nor faulty.
>
> JANE AUSTEN, *Pride and Prejudice*

> **If** *you touched him* he would sway like a boulder suspended on the precipice of a cliff.
>
> JACK KEROUAC, *On the Road*

Subordinate clauses in *medial* position within the base are even easier to manage. When a subordinate clause separates the subject and predicate, it is always set off as a free modifier, no matter what its length:

> Strange horses, **when** *there had been strange horses on that road,* had shied at the gray bulk.
>
> DONALD HALL, *String Too Short to Be Saved*

> Mr. Lee's incessant activity, **even though** *some of it is undoubtedly superfluous,* has served him well during his forty-two years on Broadway.
>
> A. J. LIEBLING, "The Boys from Syracuse"

The punctuation of *final* subordinate clauses is a matter more subtle, however, one not governed by a simple rule. Whether or not a final subordinate clause is set off depends on exactly what you choose to imply about its relationship to the base. Is the modifier a *comment,* hence set off as free, or a *definition,* hence bound to the base? As we saw, the final subordinate clause in Morley's sentence was clearly a definition, without which the base would have been incomplete.

To grasp the distinction between final subordinate clauses that comment and final subordinate clauses that define, use the subordinator **as though** to combine the paired sentences below. How should each combination be punctuated?

A. A deadened burst of mighty splashes and snorts reached us from afar.
An ichthyosaurus* had been taking a bath of glitter in the great river.

B. He looked me over.
He was examining a prize poodle.

Write your versions here:

____

____

____

____

____

____

Professional writers combined and punctuated the sentences in these ways:

A. A deadened burst of mighty splashes and snorts reached us from afar**, as though** *an ichthyosaurus had been taking a bath of glitter in the great river.*

JOSEPH CONRAD, *Heart of Darkness*

B. He looked me over **as though** *he were examining a prize poodle.*

RICHARD WRIGHT, *Uncle Tom's Children*

Each author uses **as though** to create a comparison. Nonetheless, each implies something different about the relationship of the comparison to the main idea. Joseph Conrad's rather whimsical comparison is merely a comment, a speculation. Hence, it is set off from the base clause by a comma. On the other hand, Richard Wright wishes to imply that his comparison is essential to his meaning. The subordinate clause is a definition of just how the white man looked him over. Therefore, Wright's modifier is not set off from the main clause. Fortunately, the ear and the brain work together in

**ichthyosaurus* or *ichthyosaur:* a prehistoric reptile, now extinct, that had a fishlike body, four paddle-shaped fins, and a long snout like a dolphin's

such matters. When you hear a pause between the base clause and the final subordinate clause, mark it with a comma. Although the decision is not always clear-cut, the choice is yours.

WHAT SUBORDINATE CLAUSES ADD TO YOUR WRITING

As we have seen, subordinators do not merely connect clauses; they establish precise *relationships* between clauses. These relationships may be divided into six broad categories:

1. Specifying location
2. Indicating time relationships
3. Showing manner, degree, or similarity
4. Revealing cause and result
5. Stating conditions
6. Making contrasts

Since early childhood, you have been creating subordinate clauses to establish these relationships among your ideas. Nevertheless, you may not be using subordinators as effectively as possible in your writing. To refresh your memory, then, the most common subordinators are presented below, classified by their various functions. As you will see, several categories include both simple subordinators like **as** and **if** as well as compound subordinators like **as though** and **even if.**

1. Specifying Location

We use the subordinators **where** and **wherever** almost automatically when we specify location. You can review this process by combining these two sentences into one:

> She saw charm and security.
> He saw advanced dilapidation and imprisonment.

Write your version here:

If you chose to make the second sentence the base clause, your version probably looks something like this:

> **Where** *she saw charm and security,* he saw advanced dilapidation and imprisonment.
>
> JOHN CHEEVER, "The Common Day"

Of course, it's also possible to subordinate the second sentence to the first, or, in either case, to place the subordinate clause in final rather than initial position. Try writing two more versions of the combination. If you have any doubts about how to punctuate your combinations, review pages 76–79.

Write your versions here:

____

____

____

____

____

____

2. Indicating Time Relationships

Like the first category, this function gives us little trouble. About a dozen subordinators indicate time relationships:

after	before	until
as	once	when
as long as	since	whenever
as soon as	till	while

Choose a subordinator from the list and use it to combine these two sentences into one:

A headache and he went to bed together.
They were a noisy pair.

Write your version here:

____

____

____

Naturally, several words from the list can make the connection: **after**, **as soon as**, **once**, **when**, and **whenever.** In his story "Father Is Firm with His Ailments," Clarence Day made the following combination:

When *a headache and he went to bed together,* they were a noisy pair.

Again, try writing out two more versions, punctuating each one appropriately.

Write your versions here:

____

____

____

____

____

____

As you will recall from Chapter 3, **where** and **when** can also function as *relatives* that replace repeated nouns and mean "at which" or "on which." To grasp this, compare the sentences above with these:

> Abe North was still at the Ritz bar, **where** *he had been since nine in the morning.*
>
> F. SCOTT FITZGERALD, *Tender Is the Night*

> The next day was one of those crisp late fall days **when** *one feels so good that he wants to stay right in bed under the blankets all morning.*
>
> ROBERT BENCHLEY, "The Helping Hand"

In these sentences **where** and **when** introduce relative clauses. We can substitute "at which" and "on which" for **where** and **when**, respectively. This is not the case, however, in the sentences by Cheever and Day, in which **where** and **when** are subordinators. There, the words cannot be replaced by "at which" or "on which," since in these cases **where** and **when** are subordinators of place and time, not relatives that replace repeated nouns.

3. Showing Manner, Degree, or Similarity

Notice that several of the subordinators that indicate these relationships consist of two words, either together or separated by other words in the sentences they combine:

as	insofar as	more . . . than
as . . . as	less than	not so . . . as
as if	less . . . than	so . . . (that)
as though	like	than
inasmuch as	more than	to the extent that

Try combining the paired sentences below so as to establish relationships of degree—"how much" relationships:

A. I was glad to have the equipment.
I didn't stop to think where it had come from.

B. You could also fly out of places that were grim.
They turned to black and white in your head five minutes after you'd gone.

Write your versions here:

____

____

____

____

____

____

In his book *Dispatches,* Michael Herr made the two connections in similar ways. Compare your versions with his:

A. I was **so** glad to have the equipment **that** *I didn't stop to think where it had come from.*

B. You could also fly out of places that were **so** grim *they turned to black and white in your head five minutes after you'd gone.*

Herr's combinations show how the subordinator **that** can sometimes be omitted from the **so . . . that** construction. As you can tell if you read the sentences aloud, the omission creates an impression of informality, an impression that will not suit every subject or audience. You must choose the right subordinator not only by function, but by effect as well.

4. Revealing Cause and Result

The cause-and-result relationship is one of the most important relationships in *expository* writing, writing that seeks to *explain* rather than simply present data. Some ten subordinators reveal cause-and-result relationships:

as	in order that	so . . . that
because	now that	so (that)
considering that	once	
in that	since	

The subordinators **as** and **since,** like several others we have examined, can perform more than one function and are therefore listed in more than one category. In addition to revealing cause and result, **as** can also indicate time, manner, or degree. Similarly, **since** can indicate cause and result as well as time. Try using these two subordinators to reveal cause and result when you combine these paired sentences:

A. The clients were both male.
   The chief clerk allowed himself a laugh.

B. Grammar is a piano I play by ear.
   I seem to have been out of school the year the rules were mentioned.

Write your versions here:

____

____

____

____

____

____

As usual, more than one correct combination is possible, depending on which subordinator you use and where you place the resulting subordinate clause. You can compare your versions with these:

A. **As** *the clients were both male,* the chief clerk allowed himself a laugh.

   JAMES JOYCE, "Counterparts"

B. Grammar is a piano I play by ear, **since** *I seem to have been out of school the year the rules were mentioned.*

   JOAN DIDION, "Why I Write"

5. Stating Conditions

When we state conditions, we state logical requirements. In a conditional relationship, the truth of one statement depends on the truth of another:

If *it rains, we will stay home.* Several subordinators establish various conditional relationships between clauses:

assuming that	provided (that)
if	unless
lest	whether or not
provided that	

Read the following pairs of sentences to determine exactly what conditions obtain between each pair. Then combine the pairs by selecting subordinators from the list above:

A. The student doubts that style is something of a mystery.
Let him try rewriting a familiar sentence.

B. Even the smallest boys brought little pieces of wood and threw them in.
If fruit claimed them, they did not bring wood.

C. She may or may not have meant to.
She had made his day.

Write your versions here:

____

____

____

____

____

____

____

____

____

You can compare your versions with these:

A. **If** *the student doubts that style is something of a mystery,* let him try rewriting a familiar sentence.

E. B. WHITE, *The Elements of Style*

B. Even the smallest boys, **unless** *fruit claimed them,* brought little pieces of wood and threw them in.

WILLIAM GOLDING, *Lord of the Flies*

C. **Whether or not** *she meant to,* she had made his day.

STUDENT WRITER

As these combinations suggest, different subordinators establish different sets of conditions. For instance, **if** states a positive condition, while **unless** states a negative one. On the other hand, **whether or not** states a pair of alternative conditions, either of which may apply indifferently.

6. Making Contrasts

Finally, writers use subordinators to make contrasts between statements. Just as different conditional subordinators establish different kinds of conditional relationships, so different subordinators in this category establish varying degrees of contrast:

albeit	however	whatever
although	no matter how	whereas
even though	no matter what	while
even if	though	

You will recall that **however** can also serve as a conjunctive adverb linking independent clauses. When **however** functions as a subordinator, it means *no matter how:* **However** *we tried, we rarely succeeded.* Likewise, as a subordinator **whatever** means *no matter what:*

Whatever *their private opinions of Painesville had been,* they had been much too guarded to express them.

CLARENCE DAY, "Father's Methods of Courtship"

To practice using the subordinators in the list above, try combining the paired sentences below. Determine exactly what degree of contrast each pair implies, and then choose the right subordinator for the job:

A. He wasn't engaged yet.
He already wore a silver watch in his vest pocket.

B. She was deserted forever.
She would not want to marry again.

Write your versions here:

____

____

____

____

____

____

In his stories "Two" and "Yochna and Shmelke," respectively, Isaac Bashevis Singer combined the sentences in these ways:

A. **Although** *he wasn't engaged yet,* he already wore a silver watch in his vest pocket.

B. She was deserted forever, **albeit** *she would not want to marry again.*

In the second combination, Singer used the comparatively rare subordinator **albeit,** which means much the same thing as **although.** What other subordinators from the list might have expressed different degrees of contrast between the paired sentences?

CHOOSING WHETHER TO COORDINATE OR SUBORDINATE

To young children first beginning to speak, all things seem equal. If you ask a three-year-old to repeat the sentence *The boy* **who** *got wet ran home,* she will very likely say, "The boy got wet **and** he ran home." That is, the child will coordinate the ideas rather than subordinate one to the other logically. Instead of repeating the *complex* sentence, the child will produce a *compound* sentence. No doubt, a child could go on in this vein almost endlessly: ". . . **and** he caught cold **and** he missed school **and**. . . ." Perhaps your teachers have cautioned you against this childish kind of writing, urging you instead to subordinate ideas one to another in the ways we have just examined. It's true that as we grow up, we rely more on subordination and less on coordination to express our ideas. Nevertheless, as the many examples in Chapter 2 revealed, professional writers regularly use coordinating connectives to link related ideas. The choice between coordination and subordination is not an absolute one, but rather a matter of style and meaning.

For this reason, let us pursue the relationship between subordination and coordination a little further. To begin, consider how you might best combine each of these two groups of sentences:

A. Nature has introduced great variety into the landscape.
Man has displayed a passion for simplifying it.
He undoes the built-in checks and balances.
By these checks and balances nature holds the species within bounds.

B. We allow the chemical death rain to fall.
We imagine there is no alternative.
In fact there are many.
Our ingenuity could soon discover many more.
It would have to be given opportunity.

Write your versions here:

____

____

____

____

____

____

____

____

As it happens, the two sequences come from the same chapter of one book by a single author. Here's how Rachel Carson combined the ideas in the first chapter of *Silent Spring,* her sobering study of the impact of pesticides on our environment:

A. Nature has introduced great variety into the landscape, **but** man has displayed a passion for simplifying it. **Thus,** he undoes the built-in checks and balances by *which* nature holds the species within bounds.

B. We allow the chemical death rain to fall *as though* there were no alternative, *whereas* in fact there are many, **and** our ingenuity could soon discover many more *if* given opportunity.

First off, note that Carson used *both* coordination and subordination in each passage (passage A includes a relative clause introduced by *which*). Nevertheless, because one kind of connective predominates in each passage, each has a distinctive effect.

Carson relied more heavily on coordinating connectives in creating passage A. There, **but** indicates a contrast between equal forces, man and nature. Furthermore, she chose to combine the four group A sentences into not one but two sentences—a balanced pair. She then added the conjunctive adverb **thus** at the beginning of the second sentence to lead us to a conclusion as we pass from the *cause* of the problem, stated in the first sentence, to the *result,* stated in the second. Overall, these coordinating connectives create an effect of evenhanded deliberation. Developed step by sure step, Carson's case seems irrefutable, almost self-evident.

On the other hand, while Carson's sentence B includes the coordinating conjunction **and,** its overall effect is quite different from that of passage A. Here, three out of four connectives are subordinators, which serve to indicate *unequal* relationships. Such connectives are indeed appropriate, since in this sentence Carson steadfastly distinguishes between appearance (*as though*) and reality (*whereas*). Having made such a distinction between things unequal, she goes on to propose a condition (*if*) for a radical change in our behavior. All in all, these subordinators create an effect of penetrating, close-knit argumentation. But far from seeming self-evident, the case here seems hard won.

Students sometimes struggle on the horns of a false dilemma by asking which of the two strategies, subordination or coordination, is the better. As the paired passages from *Silent Spring* should indicate, the answer is either—or both. The real difference between subordination and coordination is not functional but structural. Subordinators create *dependent* clauses, clauses that cannot stand alone. Coordinating connectives, on the other hand, can link up *independent* clauses—complete sentences—as well as words or phrases that seem of equal importance to the writer. Thus, whether you subordinate or coordinate ideas depends on your material, your audience, and your purpose.

PULLING IT ALL TOGETHER

Finally, to conclude our study of subordination, let us turn to that most argumentative of all realms, political philosophy. There, because the relationships among ideas are at once logical and complex, subordination abounds. Imagine, for instance, that you want to make a point about the President's legislative powers. You begin by noting a speculation:

> The President can legislate better than Congress.

Then follows a sentence of examples:

> Roosevelt and Wilson could.

Finally, you note what is really your general point:

> The people will support the President.

The ideas are provocative, but they prompt a contrast:

> Many lawyers will shout that the rights of Congress are being violated.

Here, then, are the sentences for you to combine into one assertion:

> The President can legislate better than Congress.
> Roosevelt and Wilson could.
> The people will support the President.
> Many lawyers will shout that the rights of Congress are being violated.

Naturally, several combinations are possible. The first sentence states what is likely a condition: **if.** The second offers what is really a comparison: **as.** The third is, of course, the base clause on which the others will depend. Finally, the fourth sentence makes a contrast: **no matter how.** Using these subordinators, in his early book *Drift and Mastery,* the political philosopher Walter Lippmann combined the ideas this way:

> **If** *the President can legislate better than Congress,* **as** *Roosevelt and Wilson could,* the people will support the President, **no matter how** *many lawyers shout that the rights of Congress are being usurped.*

Although Lippmann's sentence is both logically and grammatically complex, we can read it with ease because the subordinators within it establish relationships among the ideas. Indeed, that's the real value of the subordinate clause: to establish *exact* relationships among ideas.

The Subordinate Clause: Combinations

Combine each set of sentences below into one sentence that contains at least one subordinate clause. You can compare your combinations with professional or student writers' sentences in the Appendix.

SAMPLE EXERCISE

New kinds of thinking are about to be accomplished.
New varieties of music are about to be accomplished.
There has to be an argument beforehand.

PROFESSIONAL WRITER'S VERSION

Whenever *new kinds of thinking are about to be accomplished, or new varieties of music,* there has to be an argument beforehand.

LEWIS THOMAS, "To Err Is Human"

1. People often write obscurely.
   They have never taken the trouble to learn to write clearly.
2. The twentieth century approaches its end.
   The conviction grows that many other things are ending too.

3. A. Hopkins Parker was living in a fool's paradise.
   It did not matter where he was.
4. We are aware of these contradictions.
   This disorder among our statements is itself a source of tension.
5. A married woman doesn't dare reveal her bare head.
   It might rouse the lust of strange men.
6. The Japanese believed fireflies to be transformed from decaying grasses.
   Glowworms were said to arise from bamboo roots.
7. Ellen felt her eyes brighten.
   She leaned over the cooking pots to gather them together.
8. On one of these Saturdays Father put on his derby.
   It was sunny.
9. The spring rains and mounting sun begin to tint the meadow grass.
   The alewives run up the streams.
   The blackbirds and the spring frogs sing their full chorus.
   Then the snipe arrives at night on the south wind.
10. Pilings passed alongside.
    The old man guided us out with ease.
11. The people behave.
    I respect them most.
    They were immortal.
    Society was eternal.
12. I walked up to the end of one trench.
    Its proprietor looked at me.
    Its proprietor was a tan man.
    The other soldier continued to regard the sky.
13. There is some exceptionally strong biological necessity for sleep.
    Natural selection would have evolved beasts that sleep not.
14. Thoreau had merely left us an account of a man's life in the woods.
    Or he had simply retreated to the woods and there recorded his complaints about society.
    Or he had contrived to include both records in one essay.
    Walden would probably not have lived a hundred years.
15. The people's representatives have sought to govern.
    They had inherited the royal prerogatives.
    They soon produced the same evils.
    Men had complained about the evils under royal government.

Jody

Combine the sentences below into a paragraph that contains at least one subordinate clause. You can compare your paragraph with a professional or student writer's version in the Appendix.

1. The little boy walked along the road toward his home ranch.
2. The little boy was Jody.
3. He walked in a mid-afternoon of spring.
4. His walk was martial.
5. The road was lined with brush.

6. He banged his knee against the golden lard bucket.
7. He used the bucket for school lunch.
8. He contrived a good bass drum.
9. His tongue fluttered sharply against his teeth.
10. Its purpose was to fill in snare drums and trumpets.
11. The trumpets were occasional.

12. Some time back the other members of the squad had turned.
13. The squad walked so smartly from the school.
14. They had turned into the various little canyons.
15. They had taken the wagon roads.
16. The roads led to their own home ranches.

17. Now Jody marched seemingly alone.
18. His knees were lifted high.
19. His feet pounded.

20. Behind him there was a phantom army.
21. The army had great flags and swords.
22. The army was silent.
23. The army was deadly.

Writing Suggestion 1: Only an adult would call Jody's army a phantom. To a child, imaginary companions are often more real than flesh-and-blood friends. Write a paragraph describing one of the phantom friends you had when you were Jody's age.

Writing Suggestion 2: War games from "cowboys and Indians" to "G.I. Joe" strongly appeal to young boys. Write an essay in which you discuss why this is so.

The World's Biggest Membrane

Combine the sentences below into a paragraph that contains at least one subordinate clause. You can compare your paragraph with a professional or student writer's version in the Appendix.

1. The earth is viewed from the distance of the moon.
2. The astonishing thing about the earth is that it is alive.
3. The astonishing thing catches the breath.

4. The photographs show the surface of the moon in the foreground.
5. The surface is dry.
6. The surface is pounded.
7. The moon is dead as an old bone.

8. The earth is aloft.
9. It floats free beneath the membrane of the sky.
10. The membrane is moist.
11. The membrane gleams.
12. The sky is bright blue.
13. The earth is rising.
14. The earth is the only exuberant thing in this part of the cosmos.

15. Suppose you could look long enough.
16. You could see the swirling of the great drifts of white cloud.
17. The drifts cover and uncover the masses of land.
18. The masses of land are half-hidden.

19. Suppose you had been looking for a very long time.
20. The time is geologic.
21. You could have seen the continents themselves.
22. The continents are in motion.
23. They drift apart on their crustal plates.
24. They are held afloat by the fire beneath.

25. It has the look of a live creature.
26. The look is organized.
27. The look is self-contained.
28. The creature is full of information.
29. The creature is skilled in handling the sun.
30. Its skill is marvelous.

Writing Suggestion 1: In this passage, the author describes the earth as though the entire planet were alive. Write a paragraph describing something we usually consider nonliving—a machine, a building, a work of art, for example—as though it were alive.

Writing Suggestion 2: When American astronauts landed on the moon in 1969, mankind's ancient dream of space travel became a reality. Write an essay arguing for or against a vigorous program of space exploration. Is America's investment in outer space well spent?

The Subordinate Clause: Creations

Create at least one subordinate clause in each sentence below. While most of the exercises ask you to create specific kinds of subordinate clauses, some leave you free to create any kind of subordinate clause that seems appropriate. You can compare your creations with professional or student writers' sentences in the Appendix.

SAMPLE EXERCISES

A. Her body swayed ______________________________,
(time)

______________________________ . [signaled format]
(comparison)

B. The main issue was the First Amendment. [open format]

PROFESSIONAL WRITERS' VERSIONS

A. Her body swayed **while** *she danced,* **as** *a plant sways in the water.*
OSCAR WILDE, *The Picture of Dorian Gray*

B. **Although** *there were some other issues in the case,* the main issue was the First Amendment.
CHARLES REMBAR, "For Sale: Freedom of Speech"

1. ______________________________,
(time)
hundreds of thoughts ran through my head.

2. Childbirth is painful ______________________________
(cause)
______________________________ .

3. I have noticed that most men drop into a chair and pick up a magazine.

4. ______________________________,
(place)
public officials intervene.

5. He had such a long and dull evening.

6. ______________________________,
(contrast)
there is still the radio or television to fill the void.

7. I would have been tempted to jump from it.

8. Even the smallest boys, ______________________________
(negative condition)
______________, brought little pieces of wood and threw them in.

9. Our trigger finger tenses.

10. ____
(time)

an Indian may occasionally emerge for air, ________________
(negative condition and

____
degree)

____.

Something Happened

Combine the sentences below into one or two paragraphs that contain several subordinate clauses. You can compare your paragraphs with a professional or student writer's version in the Appendix.

1. The brakes gave way.
2. The loaded Coca-Cola truck began its descent of the final hill.
3. The hill led into the village.

4. The truck careened wildly.
5. The driver fought for control.

6. He was near the bottom of the hill.
7. He lost the battle.

8. The truck snapped into a field.
9. It jumped a stone wall.
10. It flung bottles in every direction.
11. It was as if the truck were trying to lighten the load.
12. It was as if the truck were trying to lessen the impact.
13. The impact was coming.

14. In a few seconds, it rested on its side.
15. Its resting was quiet.
16. It was among the daisies.
17. It was near a chapel.
18. The chapel was small.
19. The chapel was white.
20. The chapel was in the center of my home town.
21. Nothing ever happens in my home town.

22. The dust settled.
23. People began emerging from their homes.
24. Their homes were nearby.

25. They were like bees.
26. The bees were drawn to honey.
27. They gathered.
28. They were children.

29. They were grandparents.
30. They were employees.
31. And they were housewives.
32. They were nearly the entire village population.

33. They hovered near the accident.
34. They formed into colonies.
35. A few darted back and forth from group to group.
36. They buzzed with excitement.
37. They compared notes.

Writing Suggestion 1: Even in the sleepiest village, now and again something happens that stirs up the hive and gets people buzzing. The exercise above gets a story started with a crash. If you use your imagination, you should be able to write a few original paragraphs that carry the tale to its logical (and psychological) conclusion. What happened to all that "free" Coke?

Writing Suggestion 2: Disaster is always a test of character. When an accident occurs, some people rise to the occasion, while others become their worst selves. Write an essay in which you discuss people's reactions to a disaster, private or public, to which you were a witness.

The Subordinate Clause: Sentence Acrobatics

Combine each set of sentences below into one or more "acrobatic" sentences. See if you can create at least one subordinate clause as you do each exercise, but feel free to try out other constructions as well. Naturally, each problem invites more than one "correct" answer. Therefore, you must create original sentences that strike *you* as both correct and stylish.

You may enjoy comparing your combinations with the professional or student writers' versions in the Appendix. Look for both similarities and differences, but try to decide whose version is the more stylish—it may well be your own.

SAMPLE EXERCISE

You write a book.
The book is boring enough.
Even you cannot bear to read it over.
Then you become a professor.

STUDENT AND PROFESSIONAL WRITERS' VERSIONS

If *you write a boring enough book*—a book that even you cannot bear to read over—then you become a professor.

STUDENT WRITER

Before *you become a professor,* you have to write a book which is boring enough **so that** *even you cannot bear to read it over.*

MARK HELPRIN, "A Vermont Tale"

1. There is a brilliant statement of Freud's.
   Freud states that in the Middle Ages people withdrew to a monastery.
   In modern times they become nervous.

2. Every competition is just an echo of the spermatozoids' race for their place under the sun.
   This is as the behaviorists insist.
   The Olympic Games could be regarded as a somewhat gigantic insemination.

3. This was prior to 1919.
   In 1919 the legislators made the practice of the bookmaking trade a misdemeanor.
   The legislators did this at the urging of Charles Evans Hughes.
   Hughes was then governor.
   The bookies of New York formed an honorable and highly respected guild.

4. The scuba diver's first rule is this.
   Never dive alone.
   Your equipment gives out.
   You become panicky.
   Your buddy can share his gear with you.
   Your buddy can calm you down.

5. You are lucky enough.
   You have lived in Paris.
   You were a young man.
   It does not matter where you go for the rest of your life.
   It stays with you.
   Paris is a feast.
   The feast is moveable.

6. The paradox of Japan is that its emergence as a superpower has so overwhelmed it.
   Its emergence has been swift.
   The superpower is economic.
   This is thirty-five years after Japan was left shattered and desolate.
   The Second World War left it shattered and desolate.
   It is overwhelmed with plenty.
   It is not unlike some heir to sudden huge wealth.
   The heir is embarrassed, bewildered, and somewhat lonely.
   He does not feel elated.
   He tries to adjust to the shock of affluence.

7. It was late one evening.
   I was lying on my bed.

I was fully dressed.
I was brooding about my laziness.
I was brooding about my neglected work.
I was brooding about my lack of will power.
I got the signal.
I was wanted on the pay telephone downstairs.

8. The absolute consistency of styles now seems a bit baffling.
The consistency was in any given year in the past.
It is not because fashion was once a conspiracy.
A good many people think fashion was once a conspiracy.
They think designers, editors, and department-store buyers were all closeted in a back room at Maxim's.
The designers, editors, and department-store buyers were deciding how women should dress.

9. Technological advances have been prodigious.
The advances have been since 1925.
Science news magazines are springing up.
They are like toadstools.
The American public appears to be badly informed.
It is badly informed about the real nature of science.
It is as badly informed as it ever was.

10. This was in Brazil.
Prisoners are hooded.
They cannot see their captors.
An American minister nevertheless had an encounter.
The encounter was with Luis Miranda Filho.
The encounter was face-to-face.
Filho was the most vicious of the minister's torturers.
He ceased administering electric shock for a minute.
He knelt before his victim.
He threatened to kill him.
He would kill him if he did not cooperate.

The End of Modernism

Combine the sentences below into a paragraph that contains several subordinate clauses. You can compare your paragraph with a professional or student writer's version in the Appendix.

1. Vanguard art seems to have lost its role.
2. The role is "political."
3. This is in the past thirty years.

4. We still have lots of art.
5. We have a stream of it.
6. The stream feeds a market.

7. The market is apparently insatiable.
8. The stream provides opportunities for argument, exegesis, and comparison.
9. The opportunities are endless.
10. At the same time, painting and sculpture have ceased to act with the urgency.
11. The urgency was once part of the contract.
12. The contract was modernist.

13. Painting and sculpture change.
14. But their changing no longer seems as important.
15. It seemed important in 1900, or 1930, or even 1960.

16. One speaks of the end of modernism.
17. One does not invoke a terminus.
18. The terminus is sudden.
19. The terminus is historical.

20. Histories do not break off clean.
21. They are not like a glass rod.

22. They fray.
23. They stretch.
24. They come undone.
25. They are like rope.

26. There was no specific year.
27. The Renaissance ended in that year.

28. It did end.
29. Culture is still permeated.
30. The remnants of Renaissance thought permeate it.
31. The remnants are active.

Writing Suggestion 1: Visit a local museum or gallery that displays contemporary art. After you have studied the collection, pick out one or more pieces that strike you as particularly interesting. Write an essay in which you describe the works you chose and explain their appeal.

Writing Suggestion 2: Do you agree that the period of what we have come to know as "modern" art is drawing to a close? If so, where is art heading? Write a short essay discussing this issue in any of the arts—from painting and sculpture to music and dance.

The review exercises in this chapter will help you practice using **coordinating connectives, relative clauses,** and **subordinate clauses** along with other combinations.

Fenway Park

Combine the sentences below into a paragraph that contains both bound and free modifiers. You can compare your paragraph with a professional or student writer's version in the Appendix.

1. Fenway Park is in Boston.
2. Fenway Park is a ballpark.
3. Fenway Park is a lyric little bandbox.

4. Everything is painted green.
5. Everything seems in sharp focus.
6. The sharpness is curious.
7. Everything seems like the inside of an Easter egg.
8. The Easter egg is old-fashioned.
9. The Easter egg is the peeping type.

10. It was built in 1912.
11. It was rebuilt in 1934.
12. It offers a compromise.
13. The compromise is between Man's determinations and Nature's irregularities.

14. Man's determinations are Euclidean.
15. Nature's irregularities are beguiling.
16. Most Boston artifacts offer this compromise.

17. Its right field is one of the deepest in the American League.
18. Its left field is the shortest in the American League.

19. The left-field wall virtually thrusts its surface at hitters.
20. The hitters are right-handed.
21. The wall is high.
22. The wall is three hundred and fifteen feet from home plate along the foul line.

Writing Suggestion 1: Do you know of a place that, like Fenway Park, offers a compromise between Man's geometric determinations and Nature's softer edges? If so, write a paragraph describing the place in detail, stressing both sides of the architectural compromise it represents.

Writing Suggestion 2: From Boston to Los Angeles and beyond, America is a nation obsessed with spectator sports. Write an essay in which you analyze our national passion for baseball, football, or any other sport. What is it that keeps people glued to the tube on Superbowl Sunday?

Monkey Business

Combine the sentences below into a paragraph that contains both bound and free modifiers. You can compare your paragraph with a professional or student writer's version in the Appendix.

1. Squirrel monkeys have a kind of ritual or display.
2. The squirrel monkeys have "gothic" facial markings.
3. They perform the ritual or display.
4. They greet one another.

5. The males bare their teeth.
6. They rattle the bars of their cage.
7. They utter a squeak.
8. The squeak is high-pitched.
9. The squeak is possibly terrifying to squirrel monkeys.
10. They lift their legs.
11. They exhibit an erect penis.

12. Such behavior would border on impoliteness in many gatherings.
13. The gatherings are contemporary.
14. The gatherings are social.
15. It is a fairly elaborate act.
16. It serves to maintain dominance hierarchies in squirrel-monkey communities.

Writing Suggestion 1: Although the squirrel-monkey ritual described above seems gross and crude, it suggests a truth about human as well as animal behavior. Like the squirrel monkeys, we humans have developed social rituals that tell us who's who in terms of status and power. Describe one kind of ritual display by which humans, male or female, establish social hierarchies.

Writing Suggestion 2: If you have owned a pet or visited a large zoo, you have observed the social behavior of animals. Using your observations, write a short essay on one aspect of animal society. You might focus on the dominance rituals or "pecking orders" as in the exercise above. On the other hand, there are many other topics worth exploring: territorial rights, familial patterns, and relationships with humans, to name only a few.

Review of Chapters 2, 3, 4: Sentence Acrobatics

Combine each set of sentences below into one or more "acrobatic" sentences. See if you can use coordinating connectives, relative clauses, and subordinate clauses as you do the exercises, but feel free to try out other constructions as well. Naturally, each problem invites more than one "correct" answer. Therefore, you must create original sentences that strike *you* as both correct and stylish.

You may enjoy comparing your combinations with the professional or student writers' versions in the Appendix. Look for both similarities and differences, but try to decide whose version is the more stylish—it may well be your own.

SAMPLE EXERCISE

They drank the bottle of wine.
A faint wind rocked the pine needles.
The sensuous heat of early afternoon made freckles on the luncheon cloth.
The freckles were blinding.
The luncheon cloth was checkered.

STUDENT AND PROFESSIONAL WRITERS' VERSIONS

After *they drank the bottle of wine,* a faint wind rocked the pine needles **as** *the sensuous heat of early afternoon made blinding freckles on the luncheon cloth,* **which** *was checkered.*

STUDENT WRITER

They drank the bottle of wine **while** *a faint wind rocked the pine needles* **and** *the sensuous heat of early afternoon made blinding freckles on the checkered luncheon cloth.*

F. SCOTT FITZGERALD, *Tender Is the Night*

1. A provincial city is not like a boom town.
   The provincial city becomes overnight the capital of a great nation.
   The provincial city has no ebullience.

2. It was one of those motels.
   Those motels give you a two-by-four towel.
   You want to dry a three-by-five body.

3. He was born in Tupelo, Mississippi.
   He was an only child.
   His parents scraped along on odd jobs.
   The family moved to Memphis.
   Elvis was thirteen.

4. The appellations sound extreme.
   The appellations are "socialist" and "communist."
   The appellations are much used.
   They are like the cry of "wolf."
   They have been overdone.

5. She wore a knit sweater-suit of hard, bright blue.
   The suit did not sag.
   The suit did not pull.
   The suit gave her figure the perfection of a model.
   Her figure was admirable.
   The perfection was wooden.
   The model was in a store window.

6. A cardinal rule is that all systems must be installed in duplicate.
   This is at least.
   The rule is for the designers of commercial nuclear power plants.
   The systems are essential to safety.
   Some of the apparatus fails.
   There will always be enough extra equipment.
   The extra equipment will keep the plant under control.

7. One night there was to be a grand display of fireworks in the Bois.
   Mother insisted on going.
   After dinner they drove out there in their evening clothes.
   Both of them enjoyed it immensely.
   It came time to go back.
   They found that they could not get a carriage.

8. In fact fireflies are not flies.
   They are not bugs.
   They are not worms.
   They are beetles.
   The beetles have soft bodies.
   The beetles are called Lampyridae.
   The name is based on an old Greek word.
   The word also evolved into our word "lamp."

9. The boy was stocky.
   The boy was sharp-eyed.
   The boy was talkative.
   The boy was a towhead of about twelve.
   The boy was exuberantly grateful.
   The old man feebly crawled into the back seat.
   The old man slumped there silently.
   The old man's face was seamed.
   The old man's face was yellow.

10. The day comes for the first grass-cutting.
    The mower starts.
    The mower stops.
    The mower starts.
    The mower sends out a cloud of smoke.
    The mower has to go into the shop.
    In the shop it is diagnosed.
    It needs professional attention.
    It is tagged.
    It takes its place in a line of machines.
    The line is endless.
    We get in touch with a neighbor.
    The neighbor is in command of a sickle.

Monument Valley

Combine the sentences below into a paragraph that contains both bound and free modifiers. You can compare your paragraph with a professional or student writer's version in the Appendix.

1. All Navajo dwellings face east.
2. Our camp faced east.
3. It faced toward the rising sun and the rising moon.
4. It faced across a limitless expanse of tawny desert.
5. The desert is that ancient sea.
6. The sea is framed by the towering nearby twin pinnacles.
7. The pinnacles are called The Mittens.

8. We began to feel the magic.
9. We felt it even before the sun was fully down.

10. It occurred when a diminutive wraith drifted silently by.
11. The wraith was of a Navajo girl.
12. She was wearing a long, dark, velvet dress.
13. The dress gleamed with silver ornaments.
14. She was herding a flock of sheep to a waterhole somewhere.
15. The sheep were ghostly.

16. A bell on one of the rams tinkled faintly.
17. Its music was lost in the soft rustle of the night wind.
18. It left us with an impression.
19. Perhaps we had really seen nothing at all.

Writing Suggestion 1: Every tribe and culture has its own folkways, mores, and style of living. While you may not be able to visit and observe a Navajo village, you can easily study a local subculture. Pick a distinctive group of people in your neighborhood—perhaps an ethnic group, perhaps a religious sect—for informal observation. Write a report on the folkways and values of the group you study.

Writing Suggestion 2: Write a paragraph describing the sounds and silences of a place you know well. While the loud noises are fun to describe, you should also try to capture the soft sounds and silences as well.

America the Comfortable

Combine the sentences below into a paragraph that contains both bound and free modifiers. You can compare your paragraph with a professional or student writer's version in the Appendix.

1. Fashion began in the seventies to appropriate plain clothes.
2. Plain clothes are the dutiful, sensibly planned sportswear.
3. The sportswear has historically been the American garment industry's mainstay.
4. American style finally came of age.

5. This is the way of dressing we know best.
6. It may or may not look especially attractive.
7. It's comfortable.
8. We're comfortable with the idea of it.

9. The idea is essentially a moral one.
10. It is a matter of ethics.
11. Aesthetics are aside.

12. The religion may have been lost along the way.
13. The Puritan sensibility holds our material desires in check.
14. The Puritan sensibility is instilled in many Americans.
15. It is instilled to this day.
16. It is instilled from birth.

17. Objects are defined.
18. A chair, a spoon, a shoe are objects.
19. The function defines them.
20. They perform the function.

21. Any detail is frivolous.
22. The detail doesn't serve that function.
23. The detail is mere trimming.

24. A Shaker chair is beautiful.
25. The beauty is in its integrity.

26. Good prose must be pared down.
27. It must be stripped of decoration.
28. It's to follow the example.
29. The example is plainspoken.
30. *The Elements of Style* set the example.

31. Elegance is a little austere.
32. This is to the American way of thinking.

Writing Suggestion 1: Once you have completed the exercise above, write a paragraph analyzing your own taste in fashions. Cite details and examples from your own and others' wardrobes, but don't simply list what you like. Interpret your data in the light of the analysis proposed in the exercise. Do you agree that elegance should be a little austere?

Writing Suggestion 2: In her book *The Language of Clothes,* Alison Lurie argues that what we wear reveals much about who we are, who we hope to be, and whom we seek to impress. Using observations of the fashions around you, write an essay on the "language of clothes." What are the clothes saying?

Shreve was coming up the walk, shambling, fatly earnest, his glasses glinting beneath the running leaves like little pools.

WILLIAM FAULKNER, *The Sound and the Fury*

As you will recall from Chapter 1, our study of sentence combining began with the sentence above. Faulkner's sentence, we discovered, is grammatically simple. That is, it contains only one independent clause: *Shreve was coming up the walk.* After this independent or **base clause** come several **modifiers:** *shambling, fatly earnest, his glasses glinting beneath the running leaves like little pools.* Because the sentence develops by addition or accumulation, it is called a **cumulative sentence.** A cumulative sentence is constructed in such a way that the main idea comes first, in the base, and is then developed in the modifiers that follow the base.

In Chapters 2, 3, and 4, you learned how to create compound and complex sentences by using coordinators, relatives, and subordinators. Note that all these strategies involve linking up complete clauses. For most of the remainder of this book, however, we shall be concerned with cumulative sentences. Cumulative sentences usually contain only one complete clause, the base, which is followed by one or more modifying phrases:

CUMULATIVE SENTENCE

Base clause	***Modifying phrases***
Shreve was coming up the walk,	shambling, fatly earnest, his glasses glinting beneath the running leaves like little pools.

Naturally, in order to write effectively, you need to be able to create simple, compound, and complex sentences. Indeed, variety is one of the hallmarks of an effective style. Nevertheless, the modern rhetorician Francis Christensen argued persuasively that among professional writers it is the cumulative sentence that is "the typical sentence of modern English."* Christensen based this conclusion on a long study of modern writers like William Faulkner, Ernest Hemingway, and E. B. White—all master stylists. Of course, none of these writers creates cumulative sentences only. To do so would be artificial and tedious. But as Christensen believed, mature writers do use cumulative sentences regularly, while less mature writers use them but seldom. Therefore, having studied compound and complex sentences, we shall now consider cumulative sentences, sentences in which a base clause is followed by one or more modifiers. As you will find with practice, the cumulative sentence does indeed strike the modern mind as a natural medium for expressing and developing ideas.

WHAT CUMULATIVE SENTENCES ADD TO YOUR WRITING

As the sentence by William Faulkner reveals, a cumulative sentence hangs loose, almost effortlessly, shaped by the contour of the writer's mind in action. Christensen himself at once gracefully explained and exemplified this kind of sentence in the following passage from his essay "A Generative Rhetoric of the Sentence":

> The main clause, which may or may not have a sentence modifier before it, advances the discussion; but the additions move backward, as in this clause, to modify the statement of the main clause or more often to explicate or exemplify it, so that the sentence has a flowing and ebbing movement, advancing to a new position and then pausing to consolidate it, leaping and lingering as the popular ballad does.

* The following discussion—and, indeed, much of *Combining and Creating* at large—grows out of Christensen's essays "A Generative Rhetoric of the Sentence" and "A Lesson from Hemingway," both of which are reprinted in *Notes Toward a New Rhetoric: Nine Essays for Teachers* (New York: Harper & Row, 1978).

Christensen called the cumulative sentence "generative" because he believed that its very form encourages the writer to *generate* ideas: "It serves the needs of both the writer and the reader, the writer by compelling him to examine his thought, the reader by letting him into the writer's thought."

THE FOUR ELEMENTS OF STYLE

Christensen's theory is compelling, but how can you translate it into practice in your own writing? Sentence-combining exercises alone might help you learn to add modifiers to base clauses, but without some guiding principles your progress would be hit-or-miss at best. Fortunately, in his study of modern writing Christensen discovered four simple principles that can guide you in your sentence-combining practice and in your original writing as well. These principles are **addition, direction of movement, levels of structure,** and **texture.** Together, these constitute the four elements of style.

1. Addition

As you have probably realized, writing well is a process of **addition.** Christensen found this to be the case in the work of the professional writers he studied, but it was confirmed for him by a comment the teacher-novelist John Erskine made in "A Note on the Writer's Craft":

> Let me suggest here one principle of the writer's craft, which though known to practitioners we have never seen discussed in print. The principle is this: When you write, you make a point, not by subtracting as though you sharpened a pencil, but by adding.

This principle applies not just to the sentence, of course, but to all of writing: to words, phrases, sentences, paragraphs, and essays. Indeed, a sentence-combining exercise is really a verbal addition problem. For instance, try to add up these six sentences into one:

The men were sitting.
They were old.
They were in prayer shawls.
The prayer shawls were torn.
Their robes were riddled.
Holes riddled the robes.

Write your version here:

____

____

____

In the broadest sense, the **topic** of this exercise is fully stated in the very first sentence, "The men were sitting." All the new information contained in the other sentences is really a **comment** on this topic: What sort of *men? Sitting* in what way? But until we've practiced the craft of writing for some time, Erskine argued, we imagine that the base clause—the topic—is more significant than the comments made on it:

> In the use of language, however, the truth is precisely the reverse. What you wish to say is found not in the noun but in what you add to qualify the noun. The noun is only a grappling iron to hitch your mind to the reader's. The noun by itself adds nothing to the reader's information; it is the name of something he knows already, and if he does not know it, you cannot do business with him. The noun, the verb, and the main clause serve merely as a base on which the meaning will rise.

"The modifier is the essential part of any sentence," Erskine concluded. The way to do our sentence-combining exercise, then, is to convert the *comment* sentences into modifiers of the *topic,* which can be expressed in a base clause:

> The old men were sitting in torn prayer shawls, their robes riddled with holes.

This is how Isaac Bashevis Singer added up the sentences in his "Stories from Behind the Stove."

Bound and Free Modifiers Again

Note that when Isaac Bashevis Singer "added up" the six sentences, he created modifiers of two sorts: bound and free. First, there are several **bound modifiers** embedded within the sentence. Bound modifiers are *not* set off by punctuation. They comment on single words and are usually locked in place next to the words they modify. The bound modifiers in Singer's sentence include "the **old** men," "sitting **in torn prayer shawls**," and "riddled **with holes**." Here are some more sentences that contain bound modifiers:

> The water was a **rising cold** shock.
>
> ERNEST HEMINGWAY, "Big Two-Hearted River" (Part II)

> We are a family **that has always been very close in spirit.**
>
> JOHN CHEEVER, "Goodbye, My Brother"

> He looked **like a bowling ball fueled with liquid oxygen.**
>
> TOM WOLFE, "The New Journalism"

The second kind of modifier in Singer's sentence is a **free modifier.** Indeed, it is the addition of this free modifier after the base clause that makes Singer's sentence cumulative:

The old men were sitting in torn prayer shawls, **their robes riddled with holes.**

Like bound modifiers, free modifiers can comment on single words. Thus, in Singer's sentence, the free modifier "their robes riddled with holes" comments on a noun, "men."

But a free modifier can also modify not just a single noun or verb but an entire clause:

On most important matters, each state makes its own laws and settles its own arguments.

MICHAEL KINSLEY, "The Withering Away of the States"

The free modifier in Kinsley's sentence comments on the base clause at large. Whether they comment on single words or on complete clauses, free modifiers are always set off by a pause when we speak and by punctuation when we write. Furthermore, because they are set off from what they modify, free modifiers can often be moved to any of several positions before, within, or after the base. Here are some further examples of free modifiers:

A college student with limited funds, I searched for fairly inexpensive restaurants.

STUDENT WRITER

Her hand, **which dangles over the side,** sparkles cold with jewels.

F. SCOTT FITZGERALD, *The Great Gatsby*

Maybe altruism is our most primitive trait, **out of reach, beyond control.**

LEWIS THOMAS, "The Tucson Zoo"

Bound and free modifiers are thus the building blocks of good writing. Added to a base clause, modifiers are indeed what bring the writer's point into focus, as John Erskine suggested. In the next several chapters, we shall study a wide range of modifying phrases, most of which may be either bound or free, depending on their relationship to the words they modify.

2. Direction of Movement

Good writing is dynamic. That is, it follows the movements of the writer's mind. Furthermore, by arranging modifiers in various positions before, after, or within the base clause, we can direct the reader's mind forward or backward—or make it pause and ponder a key point.

Whether bound or free, initial modifiers—modifiers placed *before* the word or clause they modify—give the sentence a forward thrust:

INITIAL MODIFIERS

The **tall dark** → [girl] did not pay any attention. [bound modifiers]

SHERWOOD ANDERSON, *Winesburg, Ohio*

Without adequate irrigation and fertilizers, crop yield could not be raised nor poor soils be made productive. [free modifier]

BARBARA W. TUCHMAN, *A Distant Mirror: The Calamitous 14th Century*

Medial modifiers, on the other hand, inserted between the subject and the predicate of the base, slow down or interrupt the forward movement of the sentence. Medial free modifiers—like the phrase you are now reading—create a pause in mid-sentence. They thus force the reader to ponder the subject before moving ahead to the predicate:

MEDIAL MODIFERS

The mixture **of duty, ego, and seduction which motivates politicians** is difficult to sort out. [bound modifiers]

ELIZABETH DREW, "A Reporter at Large"

Miss Buell's face , **which was old and grayish and kindly, with gray stiff curls beside the cheeks, and eyes that swam very brightly, like little minnows, behind thick glasses,** wrinkled into a complication of amusements. [free modifiers]

CONRAD AIKEN, "Silent Snow, Secret Snow"

Final modifiers of a word or clause create a gradual forward movement by simultaneously advancing the discussion and recalling our attention to the original topic, rather like two steps forward and one step back. Final free modifiers are, of course, what make cumulative sentences cumulative. They add new information to the base clause, thereby bringing the idea gradually into focus:

FINAL MODIFIERS

He was shaking **like the lead singer in a rhumba band**. [bound modifiers]

WOODY ALLEN, "The Whore of Mensa"

There are two sides to a raccoon— **the arboreal and the terrestrial.** [free modifier]

E. B. WHITE, "Coon Tree"

Jasper went plodding over the fields, **laboring without end, a great man, tall in a doorway, bent a little forward when he walked.** [free modifiers]

ELIZABETH MADOX ROBERTS, *The Time of Man*

Because the typical sentence of modern English is cumulative in its structure, professional writers tend to add their free modifiers after the base clause, in final position. Nevertheless, combinations of initial, medial, and final free modifiers in a single sentence are not at all unusual:

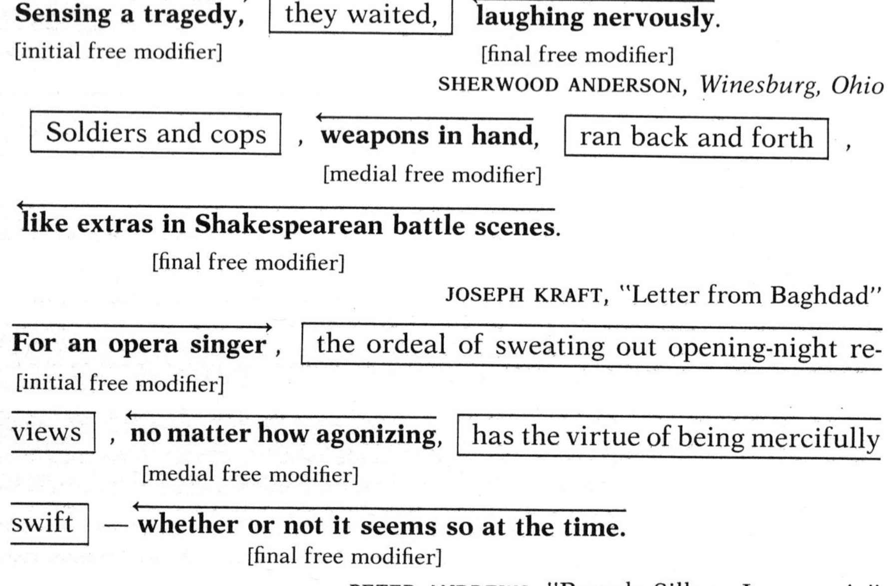

Direction of movement is what makes writing dynamic. By varying the position of the modifiers in your sentences, you can create prose that moves on paper—and in the reader's mind.

3. Levels of Structure

Good writing, then, moves horizontally, forward and back, with the ebb and flow of the mind in action. But writing has a second dimension of movement as well: its vertical movement into depth. Typically, the base clause of a cumulative sentence is a broad, shallow statement. It may be **general:**

> **Everything about the experience frightened and repelled me. . . .**

It may be **abstract:**

> **There is a frenzy of multiplicity. . . .**

Or it may be **plural:**

> **They were watching the midnight news. . . .**

Paradoxically, by telling us "everything," the base clause usually tells us very little. As Erskine stressed, "The modifier is the essential part of any sentence." It is the modifiers added to the base clause that give writing depth. In effect, by adding modifiers to the base, we downshift the sentence to a lower level of structure. The shift may be from the **general** to the **specific:**

Everything about the experience frightened and repelled me: [general base clause]
↓ the taste of salt in my mouth, [specific free modifier]
the foul chill of the wooden bathhouse, [specific free modifier]
the littered sand, [specific free modifier]
the stench of the tide flats. [specific free modifier]

E. B. WHITE, "The Sea and the Wind That Blows"

The shift may be from the **abstract** to the **concrete:**

There is a frenzy of multiplicity: [abstract base clause]
↓ planes behind planes, [concrete free modifier]
shapes within shapes, [concrete free modifier]
colors over colors, [concrete free modifier]
all shifting, [concrete free modifier]
changing. [concrete free modifier]

JAMES STEVENSON, "Painting: A Journal"

Or the shift may be from the **plural** to the **singular:**

They were watching the midnight news, [plural base clause]
↓ Bird in bed on his stomach, [singular free modifier]
Himiko hugging her knees on the floor. [singular free modifier]

KENZABURO OË, *A Personal Matter*

Levels of structure is thus the third element of style. The base clause of a cumulative sentence sketches the broad surface of an idea, but the added modifiers expose the depths of the writer's perception.

Analyzing Levels of Structure

By analyzing the levels of structure within a sentence, we can graphically outline the relationships among ideas within the sentence. For example, consider this sentence-combining exercise:

He broke off.
He was frowning.
He was thinking the thing out.
He was tugging at the stub of a nail.
He tugged with his teeth.
The tugging was unconscious.

Write your version here:

____

____

____

The challenge here is to select the most general or abstract sentence as the base clause and then to convert the remaining sentences into free and bound modifiers. Naturally, several combinations are possible. For instance, here is the professional writer's version from which the exercise was created:

> He broke off, frowning, thinking the thing out, unconsciously tugging at the stub of a nail with his teeth.
>
> WILLIAM GOLDING, *Lord of the Flies*

Golding selected the first sentence, "He broke off," as the base. Then, by consolidating several of the remaining sentences, he created three final free modifiers. A structural analysis of the result looks like this:

1 He broke off,
    2 **frowning,**
    2 **thinking** the thing out,
    2 unconsciously **tugging** at the stub of a nail with his teeth.

Since the base clause represents the highest level of generality or abstraction in the sentence, we number it level 1. Then, because each of the three final free modifiers refers to the base, we indent them and number them level 2. The result is what we shall call a **coordinate sequence** of modifiers, a sequence in which all the modifiers are at the same level of structure. Notice that the very form of the modifiers—each one containing an **-ing** word—suggests a parallel structure.

By experimenting with various sentence combinations and then contrasting their levels of structure, you can heighten your appreciation of professional writing and sharpen your own style as well. How might you combine the following sentences?

> Leeches have been heard to tap on leaves.
> The tapping is rhythmic.
> They engage the attention of other leeches.
> The other leeches tap back.
> The tapping is in synchrony.

Write your version here:

____

____

____

A famous "biology watcher" organized the data in this way:

> Leeches have been heard to tap rhythmically on leaves, engaging the attention of other leeches, which tap back, in synchrony.
>
> LEWIS THOMAS, "The Music of *This* Sphere"

Like Golding, Thomas begins this sentence with the base clause. He, too, creates three final free modifiers. But a structural analysis reveals that the sequence of modifiers here is quite different from the sequence in Golding's sentence:

1 Leeches have been heard to tap rhythmically on leaves,
  2 **engaging** the attention of other leeches,
    3 **which** tap back,
      4 **in** synchrony.

Once again, we number the most general statement, the base clause, level 1. Since the next phrase modifies the base, we indent it and label it level 2. But the third phrase does not refer back to the base but rather to the "other leeches" mentioned at level 2. For this reason, we indent again and number the third item level 3. Likewise, the last phrase, "in synchrony," modifies the verb "tap" at level 3. Therefore, we indent still another notch and label the final modifier level 4.

We shall call this kind of structure a **subordinate sequence** of modifiers. Such a sequence creates an impression of depth, since each modifier is a comment on the last. The **level of structure** always determines how you indent and number a free modifier. Nevertheless, you can often detect a subordinate sequence from the very form of the modifiers in a sentence. Note that each modifier in Thomas's sentence begins with a different kind of word.

Of course, not every cumulative sentence includes a rigidly coordinate or subordinate sequence of final free modifiers. A **mixed sequence** of modifiers in various positions is common in professional writing. Consider the following sentence:

> After the lions had returned to their cages, creeping angrily through the chutes, a little bunch of us drifted away and into an open doorway nearby, where we stood for a while in semidarkness, watching a big brown circus horse go harumphing around the practice ring.
>
> E. B. WHITE, "The Ring of Time"

In analyzing any sentence, the first thing to do is to locate the base clause. In White's acrobatic sentence, two free modifiers precede the base and two follow it. Once we determine each modifier's relationship to the base and to the other modifiers, the following analysis takes shape:

  2 After the lions had returned to their cages,
    3 creeping angrily through the chutes,
1 a little bunch of us drifted away and into an open doorway nearby,
  2 where we stood for a while in semidarkness,
    3 watching a big brown circus horse go harumphing around the practice ring.

As is often the case, the analysis reveals a hidden symmetry within a writer's work. As you practice combining and creating sentences of your own, you will gradually become more and more aware of such artful patterns in your writing.

So much for sentences with initial and final free modifiers. But what about a sentence like this one?

> The future, like the recorded past, is a specifically human dimension.
>
> S. I. HAYAKAWA, *Language in Thought and Action*

Hayakawa's sentence has a medial modifier set off by commas between the subject and the predicate of the base. By using a slash mark (/), we can mark the position of such a modifier and then indicate its level of structure:

1 The future, / , is a specifically human dimension.
  2/ like the recorded past

The slash mark is inserted between the commas that enclosed the medial modifier in Hayakawa's sentence. The slash acts as a placeholder in the analysis, and it is repeated after the number 2 that indicates the modifier's level of structure. Because the commas that enclosed the modifier remain in the base clause, we do not put any punctuation before or after the medial modifier at level 2.

Given this notation system, we can express the levels of structure in any sentence that has one base clause and one or more free modifiers. Indeed, the number of possible levels within a single sentence is limited only by the writer's imagination. But for the notation system to be complete, it should be able to accommodate sentences like this one as well:

> A tragic writer does not have to believe in God, **but** he must believe in man.
>
> JOSEPH WOOD KRUTCH, *The Modern Temper*

Krutch's sentence is, of course, a **compound sentence,** made up of two simple sentences linked by a coordinating connective. In effect, the sentence has two base clauses and no free modifiers. Therefore, we can express its levels of structure in the following way:

1 A tragic writer does not have to believe in God,
but
1 he must believe in man.

Note that since the coordinating connective **but** is a link *between* the two bases, it is set apart from them on its own line.

Our third element of style, **levels of structure,** thus proves to be an immensely useful principle. For one thing, by numbering levels of structure, we can visualize the relationships among ideas in a given sentence. But more important, the principle of levels of structure suggests that *any* sentence can be developed, expanded into greater depth. Naturally, how we indent and number the levels of structure in a particular sentence is sometimes a matter of interpretation, open to discussion. This is as it should be, since what matters is not the static diagram of a sentence, but the dynamic relationships among its parts. And those relationships ultimately exist not only on the page, but in the mind, where good writing begins and ends.

4. Texture

Addition, direction, and levels help define the structure of good writing, how it works. But what about its texture, the way it *feels?* As we have seen, good writing has breadth of movement and depth of structure. In combination, these elements give good writing a final dimension of value: its rich, dense **texture.** Texture is thus the cumulative effect of a writer's style.

This chapter opened with a richly textured sentence from William Faulkner's novel *The Sound and the Fury:*

> Shreve was coming up the walk, shambling, fatly earnest, his glasses glinting beneath the running leaves like little pools.

We can outline the structure of this sentence as a coordinate sequence of final free modifiers:

1 Shreve was coming up the walk,
  2 shambling,
  2 fatly earnest,
  2 his glasses glinting beneath the running leaves like little pools.

This is the structure of the sentence, but what about its texture? What is it about the modifiers that adds up to so compelling a picture? To answer this question, we must examine the purpose and effect of each of the additions Faulkner made to the base.

Detail, Quality, and Comparison

The first addition, "shambling," provides a **detail,** a key part of the whole picture broadly sketched in the base. The second addition, "fatly earnest," provides a different kind of information. "Fatly earnest" is a **quality** or attribute of Shreve. Where the detail "shambling" was an objective description, the quality "fatly earnest" is a subjective response, the writer's opinion. Finally, while the last addition provides a detail about Shreve's glasses, it also includes a **comparison,** "glinting beneath the running leaves like little pools."

In a provocative essay entitled "A Lesson from Hemingway," Francis Christensen argued that **detail, quality,** and **comparison** are the three fundamental methods of bringing an image or idea into focus. By adding details, qualities, and comparisons to a base clause, a writer creates a dense verbal texture, a fabric that "feels" as rich and varied as life itself. Here, in a passage from the great bullfighting story "The Undefeated," Hemingway, like Faulkner, uses all three methods in a single sentence:

> 1 The gypsy was walking out toward the bull again,
> 2 walking heel-and-toe,
> 3 insultingly, [quality]
> 3 like a ball-room dancer, [comparison]
> 3 the red shafts of the banderillos twitching with his walk. [detail]

Naturally, not every sentence need be as textured as this one. Even a single addition to a broad base clause can significantly increase the texture of a sentence:

> 1 The human brain seems to be in a state of uneasy truce,
> 2 with occasional skirmishes and rare battles. [detail]
>
> CARL SAGAN, *The Dragons of Eden*

> 1 Americans, / , have always been obstinate about being peasantry.
> 2/ while occasionally willing to be serfs [quality]
>
> F. SCOTT FITZGERALD, *The Great Gatsby*

> 2 Like most branches of mathematics, [comparison]
> 1 game theory has its roots in certain problems abstracted from life situations.
>
> ANATOL RAPOPORT, *Two-Person Game Theory*

To write with texture, then, is to combine style with substance. Textured writing has movement, depth, and density in proportion to the details, qualities, and comparisons that writers create to clarify their thoughts.

PULLING IT ALL TOGETHER

Addition, direction of movement, levels of structure, and texture are, then, the four elements of style, the fundamental principles of good writing. One of the best ways to appreciate this is to "de-write" a piece of excellent writing and then re-create it. To "de-write" a passage, we simply remove all the free and bound modifiers that give it its rich texture. Here, then, is the opening paragraph of a well-known story, stripped down to its barest bones:

> It was December. There was a Negro woman. Her name was Phoenix Jackson. She was old and small and she walked. She carried a cane, and she kept tapping the earth. This made a noise.

These simple and compound sentences may well remind you of the primer-prose stories you studied years ago. Yet upon these bare bones a master writer created a flesh-and-blood character. Clearly, the difference between the two kinds of writing is a matter of addition. Therefore, let us first add the **bound modifers** the professional writer created:

> It was December. *Far out in the country* there was an *old* Negro woman *with her head tied in a red rag.* Her name was Phoenix Jackson. She was *very* old and small and she walked *slowly in the dark pine shadows.* She carried a *thin, small* cane *made from an umbrella,* and *with this* she kept tapping the *frozen* earth *in front of her.* This made a *grave and persistent* noise *in the still air.*

Gradually, Phoenix Jackson is coming into focus. The bound modifiers add essential details and qualities to the picture. What is of more importance, however, is that they begin to create an atmosphere, a texture that feels authentic.

But while this version is promising, it remains deficient in two basic elements of style: movement and depth. It is essentially two-dimensional, a sketch. When we restore the **free modifiers,** however, the scene comes to life, and the old woman begins to move:

> It was December—*a bright frozen day in the early morning.* Far out in the country there was an old Negro woman with her head tied in a red rag, *coming along a path through the pinewoods.* Her name was Phoenix Jackson. She was very old and small and she walked slowly in the dark pine shadows, *moving a little from side to side in her steps, with the balanced heaviness and lightness of a pendulum in a grandfather clock.* She carried a thin, small cane made from an umbrella, and with this she kept tapping the frozen earth in front of her. This made a grave and persistent noise in the still air, *that seemed meditative like the chirping of a solitary little bird.*

This final version, rich in its texture and dynamic in its movement, is the opening paragraph of Eudora Welty's haunting tale "A Worn Path." Thanks to Welty's command of the four elements of style, old Phoenix Jackson wends her way through a forest of vivid details, qualities, and comparisons.

The Four Elements of Style: Combinations

Combine each set of sentences below into one sentence that includes both bound and free modifiers. Keep in mind the four basic elements of style: addition, direction of movement, levels of structure, and texture. You can compare your combinations with professional or student writers' versions in the Appendix.

SAMPLE EXERCISE

I walked far down the beach.
I was soothed by the rhythm of the waves.
The sun was on my bare back and legs.
The wind and mist from the spray were on my hair.

PROFESSIONAL WRITER'S VERSION

I walked far down the beach, soothed by the rhythm of the waves, the sun on my bare back and legs, the wind and mist from the spray on my hair.

ANNE MORROW LINDBERGH, *Gift from the Sea*

1. The sun was coming over the ridge now.
   It was glaring on the whitewash of the houses and barns.
   It was making the wet grass blaze softly.
2. The early Hebrew world must have been polydemonistic.
   It must have been fearful of every phenomenon.
3. The bull was hooking wildly.
   It was jumping like a trout.
   All four feet were off the ground.
4. Most olfactory processing is in the limbic system.
   Some occurs in the neocortex.
5. I stood on the balcony that summer afternoon.
   I was in my long gaberdine.
   A velvet cap was over my red hair.
   I had two disheveled sidelocks.
   I was waiting for something more to happen.
6. That constitutional advance has been accepted.
   The advance is the end of literary censorship.
7. Young artists are primed by art schools' vision of the modernist past.
   The vision is often starry-eyed.
   Young artists are faced with a market.
   The market is voracious for new styles.
   The market is voracious for new looks.
8. My wife was inviting me to sample her very first soufflé.
   She accidentally dropped a spoonful of it on my foot.
   This fractured several small bones.
9. He sat and stared at the sea.
   The sea appeared all surface and twinkle.
   It appeared far shallower than the spirit of man.

10. The public listens to these forecasts.
The listening is respectful.
The public does not believe them.
This is in accordance with a convention.
The convention is well-established.

11. I worked during my last two years of high school.
I worked as a maintenance man.
I was one of two.
I worked at a motel in Portland, Maine.
Portland, Maine, is my home town.

12. The Marine Biological Laboratory in Woods Hole is a paradigm.
The Laboratory is a human institution.
The institution is possessed of a life of its own.
The institution is self-regenerating.
The institution is touched all around by human meddle.
But it is constantly improved by human meddle.
It is constantly embellished by human meddle.

13. Wash was there to meet him.
Wash was unchanged.
Wash was still gaunt.
Wash was still ageless.
Wash had his gaze.
The gaze was pale.
The gaze was questioning.
Wash's air was diffident.
He was a little servile.
He was a little familiar.

14. This was during the three centuries following the fourteenth.
History was virtually a genealogy of nobility.
It was devoted to tracing dynastic lines.
It was devoted to tracing family connections.
It was infused by the idea of the noble as a superior person.

15. The mornings are the pleasantest times in the apartment.
Exhaustion has set in.
The mosquitoes are at rest on ceiling and walls.
The mosquitoes are sated.
The mosquitoes are sleeping it off.
The room is a swirl of bedclothes and garments.
The bedclothes are tortured.
The garments are abandoned.
The vines are in their full leafiness.
The vines are filtering the hard light of day.
The air conditioner is silent at last.
The air conditioner is like the mosquitoes.

A Parable

Combine the sentences below into a short essay that contains both bound and free modifiers. You can compare your essay with a professional or student writer's version in the Appendix.

1. Buddha told a parable.
2. He told it in a sutra.*

3. A man encountered a tiger.
4. The man was traveling across a field.

5. He fled.
6. The tiger was after him.

7. He came to a precipice.
8. He caught hold of the root of a wild vine.
9. He swung himself down over the edge.

10. The tiger sniffed at him from above.

11. The man trembled.
12. The man looked down.
13. He looked to somewhere far below.
14. Another tiger was waiting.
15. The tiger wanted to eat him.

16. Only the vine sustained him.

17. Two mice started to gnaw away the vine.
18. One mouse was white.
19. One mouse was black.
20. They started little by little.

21. The man saw a strawberry near him.
22. The strawberry was luscious.

23. He grasped the vine.
24. He grasped it with one hand.
25. He plucked the strawberry.
26. He plucked it with the other.

27. How sweet it tasted!

Writing Suggestion 1: A parable is a short, simple story that illustrates a lesson, usually moral or religious. As in the case of Buddha's parable in the exercise above, the lesson is often suggested rather than explained. Write a paragraph in which you fully explicate (from the Latin *explicare,* "to unfold") the meaning of Buddha's parable.

* *sutra:* a Buddhist sermon or religious dialogue

Writing Suggestion 2: Using Buddha's parable as a model, write a parable illustrating one of your own ideas. For an example of a parable from the New Testament, see Luke 13:6–9, Christ's parable of the fig tree.

Midsummer

Combine the sentences below into a paragraph that contains both bound and free modifiers. You can compare your paragraph with a professional or student writer's version in the Appendix.

1. They would ride through the woods that August.
2. The woods were hot.
3. The woods were dim.
4. That August was sultry.
5. That August was ominous.

6. Their horses would carry them in a minute to the hollows.
7. The horses carried them from the hard ground.
8. The ground was littered with spots of sifted sun.
9. The horses carried them on the hills.

10. There was something terrible about the hollows.
11. The hollows were deep-bottomed with decaying leaves.
12. The hollows smelled of dead water.
13. The hollows smelled of dark leafage.
14. The hollows smelled of insufferable heat.

15. The sound of the horses' feet was like a heartbeat.
16. The heartbeat was confused.
17. The heartbeat was on the swampy ground.

18. They both felt it.

19. They used to get off their horses.
20. They had not said a word.
21. They used to submerge themselves in each other's arms.
22. The submerging was helpless.
23. The sweat ran down their backs.
24. Their backs were under their shirts.

25. They never talked there.

26. They stood together.
27. They were swaying.
28. Their feet were deep in the mulch.
29. Their feet were booted.
30. They held each other.
31. They were hot.
32. They were mystified.
33. They were in this green gloom.

34. They could always hear the cicada.
35. They heard it from far away.
36. It was in the upper meadows.
37. The cicada reached a crescendo.
38. The crescendo was unbearable.
39. The crescendo was sharpened.

Writing Suggestion 1: Once you have written a version of *Midsummer*, use your paragraph as the basis for an exercise in imitation. The two lovers in *Midsummer* ride their horses deep into the woods in order to escape detection. In your imitation, change the characters, situation, and setting, but follow the phrasing of your *Midsummer* paragraph. Thus, if your first sentence in *Midsummer* was "That sultry, ominous August they would ride through the hot, dim woods," your imitation might be "That frozen, tranquil December they would ski down the cold, bright slopes."

Writing Suggestion 2: In *Midsummer*, the two lovers flee from society in order to be alone together. Write a short essay discussing young people's need for privacy. How much privacy should a teenager be allowed? What restrictions, if any, should be placed on a teenager's privacy?

The Four Elements of Style: Creations

By adding bound and free modifiers to your sentences, you add texture to your writing. Create details, qualities, and comparisons that enrich the texture of the sentences below. While most of the exercises call for specific kinds of additions, some leave you free to add any modifiers that seem appropriate. You can compare your creations with professional or student writers' sentences in the Appendix.

SAMPLE EXERCISES

A. With ______________ (detail), the ______________ (quality) woman waited, ______________ (detail), ______________ (detail), and ______________ (detail), as if ______________ (comparison). [signaled format]

B. There is no evidence. [open format]

PROFESSIONAL WRITERS' VERSIONS

A. With **her hands on her knees,** the **old** woman waited, **silent, erect,** and **motionless,** as if **she were in armor.**

EUDORA WELTY, "A Worn Path"

B. **Despite all the talk of unidentified flying objects and ancient astronauts,** there is no **serious** evidence **that we have been or are being visited.**

CARL SAGAN, *The Dragons of Eden*

1. The men of the sardine fleet, ______________________ (detail), were in and out all afternoon.

2. However ______________________ (quality), one can exist alone.

3. The whole school seemed united behind the team.

4. The kitchen was ______________________ (quality) and ______________ (quality), with ______________________ (detail).

5. Working a typewriter by touch, like ______________________ (comparison) or ______________________ (comparison), is best done by not giving it a glancing thought.

6. He looked down at me.

7. In ______________ (detail), an additional element is needed to account for the working of the system: ______________________ (detail).

8. Like ______________________ (comparison), she changes the subject.

9. The newcomer is a lady of about thirty.

10. They listen, ______________ (quality), ______________________ (detail), ______________________ (detail).

Bat-Chat

Combine the sentences below into a paragraph that contains both bound and free modifiers. You can compare your paragraph with a professional or student writer's version in the Appendix.

1. Bats are obliged to make sounds.
2. They make them almost ceaselessly.
3. They make them to sense all the objects in their surroundings.
4. They sense the objects by sonar.

5. They can spot small insects.
6. They can spot them with accuracy.
7. They can spot them on the wing.

8. They will home onto things they like.
9. They home with infallibility.
10. They home with speed.

11. Such a system is for the equivalent of glancing around.
12. They must live in a world of bat-sound.
13. The sound is ultrasonic.
14. Most of it has an industrial sound.
15. Most of it has a machinery sound.

16. Still, they communicate with each other as well.
17. They communicate by clicks.
18. They communicate by greetings.
19. The greetings are high-pitched.

20. They have been heard to produce notes.
21. The notes are strange, solitary, and lovely.
22. The notes are like bells.
23. The bats produce them while hanging at rest upside-down in the depths of woods.

Writing Suggestion 1: Although you may never have eavesdropped on a bat-chat, you have probably witnessed instances of what appeared to be animal communication. Write a paragraph explaining such an instance—between animal and animal or between animal and human. How did the communication occur? How effective was it for each party?

Writing Suggestion 2: Not all of human communication is verbal. People communicate by gestures, expressions, and postures as well as by speech and writing. Gather examples of human nonverbal communication and then write an essay in which you analyze your findings.

The Four Elements of Style: Analyzing Levels of Structure

Following the guidelines set forth on pages 113–117, analyze the sentences below in terms of levels of structure, indicating the various levels by number and indentation. You can compare your analyses with the sample analyses in the Appendix.

SAMPLE SENTENCE

The pool itself, gently steaming in the cold of the building, was a gloomy tank, trapezoidal in shape, and I learned later that it was twenty-five yards long on one side and exactly twenty-two and one-half yards long on the other—which made for some tricky finishes in a race.

ALLAN SEAGER, "The Joys of Sport at Oxford"

SAMPLE ANALYSIS

1 The pool itself, / , was a gloomy tank,
    2/ gently steaming in the cold of the building
    2 trapezoidal in shape,

and

1 I learned later that it was twenty-five yards long on one side and exactly twenty-two and one-half yards long on the other—
    2 which made for some tricky finishes in a race.

Explanation: This compound sentence contains two base clauses and three free modifiers. Note that the medial free modifier in the first base is replaced by a slash (/), which is repeated when the modifier is placed at level 2 (2/). The coordinator **and** links the two bases, so it is set off on its own line between them.

1. He would stand there, hatless and tanned, chin down almost to his chest, his hands dug deep in the pockets of his handsome tweed topcoat.

   JOHN O'HARA, "Are We Leaving Tomorrow?"

2. Whether or not the clothes make the person, they do make the movement. People walk down the street, sit in a chair, or illustrate conversation with gestures in ways that change from one era to the next.

   HOLLY BRUBACH, "Designer Dancing"

3. A force that would not be important in the Libyan theater, where the armies were relatively large, might be strong enough to upset the whole balance of strength in Tunisia, where battalions were still considered important units.

   A. J. LIEBLING, "Giraud Is Just a General"

4. By this time they were on the bridge, crossing the shining water far below—that day an interesting slate blue, a color that wet stones sometimes are.

   ALICE ADAMS, "Berkeley House"

5. Mr. Whipple squeezed the Charmin like a man possessed, cackling softly, eyes closed, alone in the supermarket.

   STUDENT WRITER

6. He sat at the round wicker table and fondled his discovery: a half-woman, half-lion figurine made of terra-cotta, displaying thick lips and a flat nose and large breasts, with a slightly broken tail.
   ALAN LELCHUK, "The Doctor's Holiday"

7. Nancy held the cup in both hands, looking at us, making the sound, like there were two of them, one looking at us and the other making the sound.
   WILLIAM FAULKNER, "That Evening Sun"

8. By the time the murals were installed, the following year, in the Orangerie in Paris, Monet's reputation among critics and the public had suffered a reversal.
   JEROME KLEIN, "The Strange Posthumous Career of Claude Monet"

9. The hostess, a fat woman in a green gown, with thick strings of jewels on her exposed chest, walked toward them, arms outstretched.
   JERZY KOSINSKI, *Being There*

10. The reformers exalted the rights of the state, the conservatives the rights of the individual; the one doctrine became collectivism, which ends in militarized despotism, and the other doctrine became *laissez faire,* which meant at last that no one must do anything.
    WALTER LIPPMANN, *The Good Society*

11. On his feet were single-thong flip-flops, which, when he kicked them off—as he did in the car, to sit cross-legged on the bucket seat—showed his toes to be growing in separate directions.
    PAUL THEROUX, "Yard Sale"

12. In Tanzania, south of the railway the Chinese have built from Dar-es-Salaam to the Zambian frontier, north of the Mbungu country, there lies the Selous Game Reserve, named for the great hunter Frederick Selous, established by the British during their mandatory rule of Tanganyika, and now the biggest, wildest, and least-known animal sanctuary of all Africa.
    JAN MORRIS, "Visions of Wilderness"

13. All of the other guests had gone upstairs to bed, and the ladies, having a last drink together, had turned their backs on Mr. Payson, who, unaware of the affront, was resting stuporously with his chin fallen forward on the bulge of his shirt front, his eyes closed.
    MARK SCHORER, "Portrait of Ladies"

14. Having no hope of improving their lives in any of the ways that matter, people have convinced themselves that what matters is psychic improvement: getting in touch with their feelings, eating health food, taking lessons in ballet or belly-dancing, immersing

themselves in the wisdom of the East, jogging, learning how to "relate," overcoming the "fear of pleasure."

CHRISTOPHER LASCH, *The Culture of Narcissism*

15. Dr. Harrington, tall and thin in his white flannels, stood beside the gramophone, singing with wide open mouth, his eyes comically upturned towards the low cabin ceiling; his white flannel arm was round Miss Paine's waist.

CONRAD AIKEN, "Bring! Bring!"

Sky-Change

Combine the sentences below into a paragraph that contains both bound and free modifiers. You can compare your paragraph with a professional or student writer's version in the Appendix.

1. The sky was really changing now.
2. It was changing fast.

3. It was coming on to storm.
4. Or I didn't know signs.

5. Before it had been mostly sunlight.
6. Only a few cloud shadows moved across fast in a wind.
7. The wind didn't get to the ground.
8. And the cloud shadows looked like burnt patches on the eastern hills.
9. In the eastern hills there was little snow.

10. Now it was mostly shadow.
11. Just gleams of sunlight were breaking through.
12. The gleams shone for a moment on all the men and horses in the street.
13. They made the guns and metal parts of the harness wink.
14. They lighted up the big sign on Davies' store.
15. They lighted up the white veranda of the inn.
16. The veranda sagged.

17. And the wind was down to earth.
18. It was continual.
19. It flapped the men's garments.
20. It blew out the horses' tails.
21. The tails were like plumes.

22. The smoke from houses was lining straight out to the east.
23. In the houses supper had been started.
24. And the smoke was flawing down, not up.

25. It was a heavy wind.
26. It had a damp, chill feel to it.
27. It was a wind like comes before snow.

28. And it was strong enough so it wuthered under the arcade and sometimes whistled.
29. It was the kind of wind that even now makes me think of Nevada quicker than anything else I know.

30. The look of the mountains had changed too.
31. It had changed out at the end of the street.
32. At the end the street merged into the road to the pass.

33. Before the mountains had been big and shining.
34. You didn't notice the clouds much.

35. Now the mountains were dark.
36. They were crouched down.
37. They looked heavier.
38. But they did not look nearly so high.
39. And it was the clouds that did matter.
40. The clouds came up so thick and high.
41. You had to look at them instead of the mountains.

42. And they weren't firm, spring clouds.
43. Spring clouds have shapes.
44. They weren't the deep, blue-black kind.
45. The blue-black kind mean a quick, hard rain.
46. But they were thick.
47. They were shapeless and gray-white.
48. They were like dense steam.
49. They shifted so rapidly.
50. They had so little outline.
51. You more felt than saw them changing.

Writing Suggestion 1: As you probably guessed from the dialect in the exercise above, the speaker is a westerner. The Southwest is famous for its big sky, which can change its mood dramatically from moment to moment. Whether or not you live in the West, however, you can enjoy sky-watching. The next time you notice the sky above you changing its mood—from sun to shadow or from night to dawn—compose a paragraph describing the sky-change in close detail, from moment to moment.

Writing Suggestion 2: People's language—their grammar, word choice, and pronunciation—tells us much about where they come from and who they are. After listening closely to the language around you for a few days, write an essay analyzing the language of your friends, family, co-workers, or peers. You might consider such matters as regional dialects, nonstandard forms, slang, shoptalk, and professional jargon. What does the style of one's language reveal about the style of one's life?

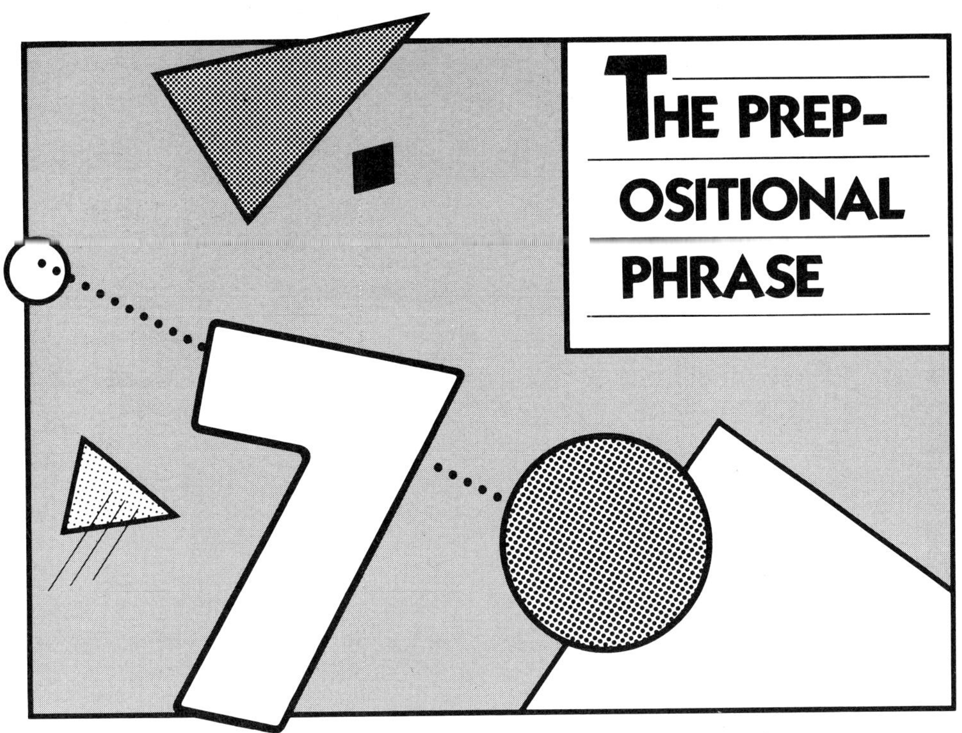

My experiences with underwater exploration began on television after dinner, with Jacques Cousteau and his intrepid divers, who floated like fish through the flickering blue-green ocean on my screen.

STUDENT WRITER, "Rapture of the Deep"

"Detail is the life of literature," observed the novelist Jack Kerouac. Kerouac's observation holds true not only for stories and poems, but for essays as well. It is the wealth of specifics—details, qualities, and comparisons—that makes the student writer's sentence above so vivid and compelling. Perhaps even more important, the student has artfully combined the details into orderly relationships that set her experiences in perspective.

The base clause of the sentence establishes the place, the time, and the kind of experiences under discussion:

My experiences began on television.
My experiences began after dinner.
My experiences were with underwater exploration.

Having told when and where the experiences began, the student next tells with whom they began:

They began with Jacques Cousteau and his divers.
The divers were intrepid.

But the picture is not yet in sharp enough focus. Therefore, the writer continues adding information, first a comparison, then the direction and location of the action:

> They floated like fish.
> They floated through the flickering blue-green ocean.
> The ocean was on my screen.

Despite this wealth of information, the student's combination is simple and direct, thanks to the precise relationships she establishes among her ideas:

1 My experiences with underwater exploration began on television after dinner,
  2 with Jacques Cousteau and his intrepid divers,
    3 who floated like fish through the flickering blue-green ocean on my screen.

By creating both bound and free modifiers, the writer pulled all her information into a single sentence that steadily downshifts to lower and lower levels of generality. Moreover, the author organized the facts into precise relationships of time, place, likeness, definition, and accompaniment. To establish most of these relationships, the writer used relatively little words: *with, on, after, like,* and so on. How is that such tiny words can establish such precise connections among ideas?

PREPOSITIONS AND PREPOSITIONAL PHRASES

Little words like *with, on, after, like, to,* and *of*—as well as combinations like *because of, thanks to,* and *together with*—are called ***prepositions.*** This term comes from the Latin word *praepositus,* meaning "placed before." A preposition like *with* is "placed before" a **nominal** (that is, a noun or noun substitute) that becomes the **object** of the preposition: *with* **underwater exploration.** The preposition relates its object to another word or construction: **my experiences** *with underwater exploration.* The preposition and its object make up what is called a ***prepositional phrase.***

PREPOSITIONAL PHRASES AS MODIFIERS

With this definition in mind, underline each of the prepositional phrases in the student writer's sentence. You should find seven:

1 My experiences with underwater exploration began on television after dinner,
  2 with Jacques Cousteau and his intrepid divers,
    3 who floated like fish through the flickering blue-green ocean on my screen.

Notice that some of the prepositional phrases modify nominals, while others modify verbs:

Word(s) Modified	**Prepositional Phrase**	
	Preposition	***Object***
A. Nominals		
My experience	with	underwater exploration
the blue-green ocean	on	my screen
B. Verbs		
began	on	television
began	after	dinner
began	with	Jacques Cousteau and his intrepid divers
floated	like	fish
floated	through	the flickering blue-green ocean

Notice, too, that six of the seven prepositional phrases in the student's sentence are bound modifiers, not set off by punctuation. This is the case even when two of the phrases do not modify the words they follow. In the base clause, the prepositional phrase *after dinner* modifies the verb *began,* not the noun *television.* Likewise, at level 3 the phrase *through the flickering blue-green ocean* modifies the verb *floated,* not the noun *fish.* Because we can easily grasp which words each prepositional phrase modifies in these constructions, the writer adds no punctuation.

But this is not the case with the prepositional phrase at level 2, which is a free modifier. This phrase is set off from the base because we might be misled if it were not. Consider what this version of the sentence implies:

> My experiences with underwater exploration began on television after dinner with Jacques Cousteau and his intrepid divers. . . .

Had the student written her sentence this way, without punctuation, we would be led to believe she had dined with Cousteau and company. The comma cuts off this unwanted suggestion by separating the prepositional phrase from the word *dinner.* Whenever you face a possible misunderstanding like this, set the prepositional phrase off as a free modifier.

WHAT PREPOSITIONAL PHRASES ADD TO YOUR WRITING

As we have seen, prepositional phrases do not simply add information. They create *relationships* among ideas. These relationships fall into six broad categories:

1. Specifying direction or location
2. Indicating time relationships
3. Making comparisons
4. Adding details
5. Showing logical relationships
6. Revealing the actor in a passive construction

As we consider each category in turn, you can refer to this partial list of prepositions. Here are the most common **simple prepositions:**

about	beneath	in	through
above	beside(s)	inside	till
across	between	into	to
after	beyond	like	toward(s)
against	but (meaning *except*)	near	under
along	by	of	until
among	concerning	off	up
around	down	on	upon
at	during	outside	with
before	except	over	within
behind	for	past	without
below	from	since	

Prepositions made up of two or more words are called **compound prepositions:**

according to	by reason of	on account of
ahead of	by way of	out of
apart from	contrary to	owing to
as for	due to	rather than
as to	except for	together with
as well as	for the sake of	up at
aside from	in keeping with	up on
away from	in regard to	up to
because of	in spite of	with respect to
belonging to	inside of	
by means of	instead of	

Whether simple or compound, prepositions can help you establish exact relationships when you combine sentences.

1. Specifying Direction or Location

This first function of the prepositional phrase, specifying direction or location, allows us to combine related sentences into very precise descriptions of movement and space. For the most part, such combinations give us little trouble. Try combining these three sentences into one:

The last trumpet-shaped bloom had fallen.
It fell from the heaven tree.
The heaven tree was at the corner of the jail yard.

Write your version here:

____

____

____

Very likely, your version looks like this:

> The last trumpet-shaped bloom had fallen **from** *the heaven tree* **at** *the corner* **of** *the jail yard.*
>
> WILLIAM FAULKNER, *Sanctuary*

The first prepositional phrase in Faulkner's sentence modifies the verb *had fallen.* The phrase specifies the direction in which the bloom had fallen: **from** *the heaven tree.* The second and third prepositional phrases, **at** *the corner* **of** *the jail yard,* together specify the exact location of the tree itself. The second phrase, **at** *the corner,* modifies the nominal *heaven tree,* while the third identifies *the corner* **of** *the jail yard* precisely.

2. Indicating Time Relationships

Like specifying direction or location, the second function of the prepositional phrase requires little explanation. In speech and writing alike, we create such modifiers naturally. So far, however, we have studied prepositional phrases that follow the words they modify. As the following example reveals, writers often move prepositional phrases in front of the words they modify:

> Mrs. Tracy, **after** *the fourth cocktail,* noticed the gloom in the room anew.
>
> LOUISE BOGAN, "Conversation Piece"

Here the prepositional phrase **after** *the fourth cocktail* modifies the verb *noticed.* The phrase indicates the time when Mrs. Tracy noticed the gloom. Because the phrase precedes the word it modifies, it is set off as a free modifier. This would also be the case if Bogan had written the sentence this way:

> **After** *the fourth cocktail,* Mrs. Tracy noticed the gloom in the room anew.

Prepositional phrases that modify verbs are usually movable modifiers. You can achieve different stylistic effects by placing such modifiers in initial, medial, or final position.

It is also important to note that some words that indicate time—notably *before, after,* and *since*—can function either as prepositions (introducing *objects*) or as subordinators (connecting *clauses*). To grasp this, use the word *after* to combine these paired sentences:

A. We made love.
Then we talked about the tigers.

B. Father got well.
Then he seemed to want to forget the whole incident.

Write your versions here:

____

____

____

____

____

____

Although they both used the word *after*, two writers combined the pairs in different ways:

A. **After** *making love*, we talked about the tigers.
RICHARD BRAUTIGAN, *In Watermelon Sugar*

B. **After** *Father got well*, he seemed to want to forget the whole incident.
CLARENCE DAY, "Father Declines to Be Killed"

Richard Brautigan combined the sentences by creating a prepositional phrase. Here, as a preposition, *after* has the nominal *making love* as its object. (We shall consider noun substitutes like this more closely in Chapter 12.) On the other hand, Clarence Day used *after* as a subordinator to join the clause *Father got well* to the base. When you use words like *after, before,* and *since* to combine sentences, you often have the option of creating either a prepositional phrase or a subordinate clause. Which you choose will depend on your sense of style.

3. Making Comparisons

The third function of the prepositional phrase is especially important, since it is also one of the fundamental elements of style: making comparisons. The key prepositions here are, of course, *like* and *unlike*. Professional writers see similarities and differences everywhere, and they use such comparisons to sharpen their images and communicate their feelings. Combine the following paired sentences to show comparison or contrast:

A. The moon hung low in the sky.
The moon resembled a yellow skull.

B. Baseball players and jockeys often have noisy arguments.
Fighters seldom have noisy arguments.

Write your versions here:

____

____

____

____

____

____

Very likely, your versions look like these sentences:

A. The moon hung low in the sky **like** *a yellow skull.*
OSCAR WILDE, *The Picture of Dorian Gray*

B. **Unlike** *baseball players and jockeys,* fighters seldom have noisy arguments.
A. J. LIEBLING, "Mrs. Braune's Prize Fighters"

Wilde chose to create a bound modifier in the final position, while Liebling created an initial free modifier. As you can easily imagine, other combinations are possible. The important thing to note is that the two authors alike added comparisons—one a similarity, one a difference—to their sentences by creating prepositional phrases.

A Note on *As* and *Like*

As traditionalists have been lamenting for years, the distinction between the words *as* and *like* is blurry for most of us, especially when we speak or write informally. Nevertheless, in even moderately formal writing, the distinction persists. The word *like,* as we just saw, is a preposition. The word *as,* on the other hand, is a subordinator. Prepositions precede nominals: **like** *a yellow skull.* Subordinators connect clauses, **as** *this one does,* both of which have their own subjects and verbs. See if you can distinguish betweeen *as* and *like* when you combine these paired sentences:

A. Her brittle voice cracked.
Autumn leaves crack.

B. They enjoy literature.
Some men enjoy beer.

Write your versions here:

____

____

____

____

A student writer and a professional combined the sentences in these ways:

A. Her brittle voice cracked **like** *autumn leaves.*

STUDENT WRITER

B. They enjoy literature **as** *some men enjoy beer.*

ARNOLD BENNETT, "Why a Classic Is a Classic"

Both authors are correct in their choices. The student writer created a prepositional phrase in which the preposition **like** introduces an object, "autumn leaves." On the other hand, Arnold Bennett joined two full clauses together with the conjunction **as,** thus subordinating one clause to the other.

Because of linguistic forces that are stronger than grammar "rules," the *as–like* distinction seems to be wearing away. Still, on paper the distinction makes sense, and many people value it highly.

4. Adding Narrative and Descriptive Details

Like making a comparison, the fourth function of the prepositional phrase is among the most basic elements of good writing: adding details. The key word in this category is *with.* As we saw in the sentence that opened this chapter, *with* can modify either a nominal (**My experiences** *with underwater exploration* . . .) or a verb (**began** . . . *with Jacques Cousteau*. . .). When *with* modifies a nominal, it adds a descriptive detail. When *with* modifies a verb, it adds a narrative detail.

By using *with,* you can often reduce a full sentence to a short modifying phrase, thus saving words even as you add details. You can grasp this by combining these paired sentences:

A. She's a madam.
She has a master's in comparative lit.

B. Leopold Bloom ate the inner organs of beasts and fowls.
He relished them.

Write your versions here:

____

____

____

____

You can compare your combinations with these:

A. She's a madam, **with** *a master's in comparative lit.*
WOODY ALLEN, "The Whore of Mensa"

B. Leopold Bloom ate **with** *relish* the inner organs of beasts and fowls.
JAMES JOYCE, *Ulysses*

In the first instance, Woody Allen added a descriptive detail about the well-read madam by reducing a full clause to a prepositional phrase. In the second case, James Joyce added a narrative detail about how Leopold Bloom ate. The comma in Allen's sentence is a matter of style, not grammar, since the modification would be clear without the punctuation. Just what effect does the optional comma create?

5. Showing Logical Relationships

The fifth function of the prepositional phrase is perhaps the most important for *expository* writing, writing that explains facts, feelings, and opinions. Prepositions can show logical relationships between ideas. These relationships include causation, exception, substitution, and others, most of which are best expressed by **compound prepositions** like *because of, except for,* and *instead of.* For more of these, refer back to the list on page 134. Which prepositions might you use to combine the paired sentences below?

A. Shubert employees have a fear of assuming responsibility.
Shubert employees in general are the most literal-minded attachés of the American theater.

B. The bottle fly could smell almost nothing.
It could smell the female sex attractant.

C. The curse of great possessions became a living thought to me.
It was not a mere phrase.

Write your versions here:

Professional writers expressed logical relationships between the paired sentences in these ways:

A. **Because of** *their fear of assuming responsibility,* Shubert employees in general are the most literal-minded attachés of the American theater.

A. J. LIEBLING, "The Boys from Syracuse"

B. The bottle fly could smell almost nothing **except** *the female sex attractant.*

CARL SAGAN, *The Dragons of Eden*

C. The curse of great possessions became a living thought to me, **instead of** *a mere phrase.*

CLARENCE DAY, "Father Teaches Me to Be Prompt"

Creating such concise, logical combinations demands a thorough knowledge of the simple and compound prepositions, but the resulting precision makes the effort worthwhile.

6. Revealing the Actor in a Passive Construction

The final function of the prepositional phrase is to show the actor—the *doer*—in a passive construction. (We shall consider the passive construction itself in Chapter 13.) While active-voice verbs like *thanks* show their subject as an **actor,** performing an action ("John thanks Mary"), passive-voice verbs like *was thanked* show their subjects as **acted upon** ("Mary was thanked").

If you wish to include the actor as well as the person acted upon in a passive construction, you do so by means of a prepositional phrase ("Mary was thanked **by John**"). In passive constructions, **by** reveals who or what performed the action denoted by the verb. To understand this, try combining these paired sentences:

A. The need to make music, and to listen to it, is universally expressed. Human beings express the need.

B. The next morning the groans of hangover were decently stifled. The mists in the quad stifled the groans.

Write your versions here:

____

____

____

____

____

____

Professional writers combined the sentences to show agency:

A. The need to make music, and to listen to it, is universally expressed **by** *human beings.*

LEWIS THOMAS, "The Music of *This* Sphere"

B. The next morning the groans of hangover were decently stifled **by** *the mists in the quad.*

ALLAN SEAGER, "The Joys of Sport at Oxford"

In Thomas's sentence, the actor is human—"human beings," to be exact. In Seager's, the actor is nonhuman—"the mists in the quad." Whether the actor in a passive sentence is human or nonhuman, **by** allows you to reveal it clearly. Otherwise, your reader may well wonder who's *doing* what you say *has been done.*

PULLING IT ALL TOGETHER

The prepositional phrase is one of the most versatile structures in English, able to establish six essential relationships among words and ideas in a sentence. When you combine sentences by means of prepositional phrases, you add details and comparisons to your writing even as you eliminate needless words. In fact, prepositional phrases allow you to answer all six of the reporter's basic questions: *Who? What? When? Where? Why? How?* In this way, whether they are bound or free modifiers, prepositional phrases contribute to the **texture** of your writing.

In the sentence that opened this chapter, we saw how a student writer used prepositional phrases to create a vivid scene. We shall close the discussion by seeing how a professional writer manages similar effects. Consider, for instance, the way Ernest Hemingway constructed the final sentence of his powerful story "Indian Camp." Even before stating the main idea, Hemingway carefully established the time, place, and details of the scene:

> It was the early morning.
> They were on the lake.
> He sat in the stern of the boat.
> His father was rowing.
> He felt quite sure that he would never die.

Notice the rich texture of the combined version, which includes five prepositional phrases:

> **In** *the early morning* **on** *the lake* sitting **in** *the stern* **of** *the boat* **with** *his father rowing,* he felt quite sure that he would never die.

As the novelist and teacher John Erskine observed in "A Note on the Writer's Craft," "The modifier is the essential part of any sentence." Rich with modifying phrases that specify direction, indicate time, make comparisons, add details, show logical relationships, and reveal agency, the sentences you have studied in this chapter are living proof of Erskine's wisdom. By combining and creating prepositional phrases, you can produce equally impressive sentences in your own writing.

The Prepositional Phrase: Combinations

Combine each set of sentences below into one sentence that contains at least one prepositional phrase. You can compare your combinations with professional or student writers' sentences in the Appendix.

SAMPLE EXERCISE

"Boycott" is perhaps too strong a word.
The word stands for a fairly simple matter.
You do not go somewhere.

PROFESSIONAL WRITER'S VERSION

"Boycott" is perhaps too strong a word **for** *a fairly simple matter* **of** *not going somewhere.*

JOSEPH BRODSKY, "Playing Games"

1. The dinosaurs became extinct.
   Then mammals moved into daytime ecological niches.

2. A sickly light was slanting over the high walls into the jail yard.
   The light resembled yellow tinfoil.

3. The publisher and the ungrateful candidate had a resounding argument later.
   They argued at a dinner party.
   John Erskine gave the dinner party.

4. I had valuable contacts in vital supply centers.
   I had my former job in the saloon to thank for this.

5. Dick slapped the snow from his dark blue ski-suit.
   He used his cap.
   Then he went outside.

6. We violate probability.
   Our nature lets us do this.

7. Time went on.
   There was not much improvement on my part.

8. Shostakovich makes this setting a violent railing against fate.
   There are screaming unisons.
   The unisons are in the winds.
   There are sudden snaps and snarls.
   The snaps and snarls come from the percussion.

9. It was an affirmation.
   It was a moral victory.
   Innumerable defeats paid for the moral victory.
   Abominable terrors paid for the moral victory.
   Abominable satisfactions paid for the moral victory.

10. They came slowly up the road.
    They came through the colorless dawn.
    They resembled shadows.
    The night had left the shadows behind.

11. The entire station was uncomfortable to sit in.
    It had its broken mosaic tile walls.
    It had scummy and mostly empty gum machines.
    It had greasy fluorescent lamps.
    The lamps filled the station with cold light.
    The station was like a tomb.

12. The steelworkers' strike is still perching.
    It is over the doorway of No. 10.
    It resembles some large black bird.
    The bird will not go away.

13. Mr. Kaplan had distressing diction.
    He had wayward grammar.
    He had outlandish spelling.
    Mr. Parkhill was determined to treat him exactly as he treated every other pupil.

14. You change the language of art.
    You affect the modes of thought.
    You change thought.
    You change life.

15. It was in the moonlight.
    The child shone blue and flat.
    The child resembled the fresco.
    The fresco was of a cherub.
    The cherub was painted high across the dome.
    It was the dome of a cathedral ceiling.

Technology

Combine the sentences below into a paragraph that contains several prepositional phrases. You can compare your paragraph with a professional or student writer's version in the Appendix.

1. Technology has broken free of the cycles.
2. The cycles are natural.
3. Barry Commoner has pointed this out.

4. Technology has shifted people.
5. The technology is energy-intensive.
6. People have shifted from soap to detergents.
7. People have shifted from natural to synthetic fibers.
8. People have shifted from wood to plastic.
9. People have shifted from soil husbandry and land care to fertilizer.
10. Fertilizer is the means of increasing agricultural production.

11. The spread of chemicals has grown.
12. The chemicals are synthetic.
13. The growth is beyond measure.

14. Technology has shifted people.
15. This is in the West.
16. The people have shifted toward a new order.

Writing Suggestion 1: Has technology shifted you and your family toward a new order? Write a paragraph discussing the effect of modern technology on one part of your life. Is the shift for the better—or for the worse?

Writing Suggestion 2: Perhaps the major technological shift in recent years has been the so-called computer revolution. Write an essay analyzing how the computer revolution has already affected society around you. If you wish, speculate on what further effects we can expect in coming years.

Dr. Broad

Combine the sentences below into a paragraph that contains several prepositional phrases. You can compare your paragraph with a professional or student writer's version in the Appendix.

1. Dr. Broad entered the classroom on the hour.
2. He was in gown and mortarboard.
3. He opened his notebook.
4. He read aloud.
5. He paced between door and window.
6. The pacing was slow.

7. A dozen heads bent.
8. The heads included two Sikh turbans.
9. The turbans were immaculate.
10. The bending was earnest.
11. They bent to take down what he said.

12. He was nut-brown.
13. He was nearly bald.
14. He was like a healthy monk.
15. He read in an even tone.
16. He read at an even rate.
17. The rate was slightly too rapid.

18. He would take up Descartes, Spinoza, Locke, Hume, Leibniz, Kant, and Hegel.
19. He took them up in turn.
20. This was in the course of the three terms.

21. He gave an account of each thinker's life.
22. He gave an account of each thinker's work.
23. He gave an exposition of his principal arguments.
24. He gave an analysis of where he had gone wrong.

25. He was, in effect, dictating his own history of philosophy.
26. The philosophy was modern.
27. His history was critical.

28. Anyone kept up with him.
29. Anyone would possess it.

30. I could almost do it.
31. But I could not quite do it.

Writing Suggestion 1: The exercise above tells the story of a student's mixed reaction to a memorable teacher. Write a paragraph describing one of your own memorable teachers—and your reactions to him or her.

Writing Suggestion 2: Use a general encyclopedia and the specialized *Encyclopedia of Philosophy* to learn about one of Dr. Broad's subjects: René Descartes, Benedict (Baruch) Spinoza, John Locke, David Hume, Gottfried Leibniz, Immanuel Kant, or G. F. W. Hegel. Write a short essay summarizing the philosopher's main ideas. Be sure to acknowledge the sources of your material.

The Prepositional Phrase: Creations

Create at least one prepositional phrase in each sentence below. While most of the exercises ask you to create specific kinds of prepositional phrases, some leave you free to create any kind of prepositional phrase that seems appropriate. You can compare your creations with professional or student writers' sentences in the Appendix.

SAMPLE EXERCISES

A. 1 California, / , presents the most critical background of all the states.

2/ ______________________________ [signaled format]
(descriptive detail about **California**)

B. He had just entered a blind alley. [open format]

PROFESSIONAL WRITERS' VERSIONS

A. 1 California, / , presents the most critical background of all the states.
2/ **with** *its ever-increasing population*
EDWARD WEEKS, "Not So Rich as You Think: A Review"

B. **According to** *the map his friend had drawn for him,* he had just entered a blind alley **by** *the only entrance.*
KENZABURO OË, *A Personal Matter*

1. 2 ____ ,
(location)

1 a military parade had been in progress.

2. The United States must employ secret agents.

3. 1 Father and Margaret were united ______________________
(nonhuman agent)

____ .

4. 1 Definitions, / , tell us nothing about things.

2/ ____
(logical relationship: use *contrary to*)

5. I was aware of the ridiculousness of my situation.

6. 2 ____ ,
(narrative detail about **went out**)

1 he went out.

7. 2 ____ ,
(time)

2 ____ ,
(time)

1 these [outboard] motors made a petulant, irritable sound;

2 ____ ,
(time)

2 ____________________ when the afterglow lit the water,
(time)

1 they whined about one's ears ______________________ .
(comparison)

8. I remember the warm sun.

9. 1 His shoulders were very broad,

2 ____ ,
(comparison)

and

1 his arms were thickly knotted ______________________ .
(descriptive detail about **arms**)

10. These notions will affect everything.

Super-Cat City

Combine the sentences below into a paragraph that contains several prepositional phrases. You can compare your paragraph with a professional or student writer's version in the Appendix.

1. Imagine this.
2. You are strolling through a city at night.
3. It is a city of super-cats.

4. The business quarter is over yonder.
5. Its evening shops are blazing with jewels.

6. The great stockyards lie to the east.
7. From the east you hear those sad sounds.
8. You hear that low mooing as of innumerable herds.
9. The herds are waiting slaughter.

10. Beyond lie the aquariums.
11. The aquariums are silent.
12. Beyond lie the crates of mice.
14. The mice are fresh.

15. They raise mice instead of hens in super-cat land.

16. To the west is a park.
17. The park is beautiful.
18. But the park is weirdly bacchanalian.*
19. It has long groves of catnip.
20. There young super-cats have their fling.
21. There a few crazed catnip addicts live on till they die.
22. The addicts are unable to break off their orgies.
23. Their orgies are strangely undignified.

24. And here is the residence district.
25. You stand here.
26. The district is sumptuous.

27. Houses are everywhere.
28. The houses have spacious grounds.
29. There are no densely packed buildings.

30. The streets have been swept up.
31. Or they have been lapped up.
32. They are spotless.

* *bacchanalian:* The Bacchanalia was an ancient Roman festival devoted to the god Bacchus, whose worshippers indulged in drunken carousing.

33. Not a scrap of paper is lying around anywhere.
34. There is no rubbish.
35. There is no dust.

36. Few of the pavements are left bare.
37. Ours are left bare.
38. Those few are polished.

39. The rest have carpets.
40. The carpets are deep.
41. The carpets are soft.
42. The carpets are velvet.

43. No footfalls are heard.

Writing Suggestion 1: Although the exercise above is based on a fantasy, the fantasy has a rigorous logic of its own. If a super-cat city were to exist, it would surely have mouse stockyards, catnip groves, and velvet sidewalks. A fantasy is thus an illogical idea carried to its logical conclusion. Write a paragraph recounting a fantasy of your own. Begin with the word "Imagine."

Writing Suggestion 2: As best-sellers like Jim Davis's *Garfield at Large,* Simon Bond's *101 Uses for a Dead Cat,* and Philip Lief's *Cat's Revenge* reveal, in recent years Americans have had a love-hate affair with their cats. Using these and other books, as well as the endless posters, T-shirts, and other cat-commodities, write an essay explaining what values lie behind the cat craze. Why have our felines thrown us into such a frenzy?

The Prepositional Phrase: Sentence Acrobatics

Combine each set of sentences below into one or more "acrobatic" sentences. See if you can create at least one prepositional phrase as you do each exercise, but feel free to try out other constructions as well. Naturally, each problem invites more than one "correct" answer. Therefore, you must create original sentences that strike *you* as both correct and stylish.

You may enjoy comparing your combinations with the professional or student writers' versions in the Appendix. Look for both similarities and differences, but try to decide whose version is the more stylish—it may well be your own.

SAMPLE EXERCISE

The age of the modern encyclopedia began.
It began in August of the year 1751.
It began in France.
The first volume of the Encyclopédie was delivered to its subscribers.

STUDENT AND PROFESSIONAL WRITERS' VERSIONS

In *France,* **in** *August of the year 1751,* when the first volume of the Encyclopédie was delivered to its subscribers, the age of the modern encyclopedia began.

STUDENT WRITER

The age of the modern encyclopedia began **in** *August of the year 1751,* **in** *France,* **with** *the delivery of the first volume of the Encyclopédie to its subscribers.*

HANS KONING, "The Eleventh Edition"

1. Something or other lay in wait for him.
   It lay amid the twists and the turns of the months and the years.
   It lay like a crouching beast in the jungle.
2. Mrs. Allen did not punish her child.
   Mrs. Allen did not insult her child.
   Mrs. Allen listened to her daughter's story.
3. Jesus was in the kitchen.
   He sat behind the stove.
   He had his razor scar on his black face.
   The scar was like a piece of dirty string.
4. The Constableship had the prestige of military command.
   The command was second to the King.
   The Constableship had lucrative perquisites.
   The perquisites were attached to the business of assembling the armed forces.
5. Human beings are all born.
   They all have a genetic endowment.
   They can recognize language.
   They can formulate language.
   This is according to the linguistic school.
   The school is currently on top.
6. This is from the side.
   He's like the buffalo on the U.S. nickel.
   He's shaggy and blunt-snouted.
   He has the small clenched eyes and the defiant but insane look of a species.
   The species was once dominant.
   The species is now threatened with extinction.
7. The public may be the farmers.
   This is in respect to a railroad strike.
   The railroads serve the farmers.
   The public may include the very railroad men.

This is in respect to an agricultural tariff.
The railroad men were on strike.

8. She is like so many successful guerrillas.
The guerrillas are in the war.
The war is between the sexes.
Georgia O'Keeffe seems to have been equipped early.
She was equipped with the sense of who she was.
The sense is immutable.
And she was equipped with a fairly clear understanding.
She understood that she would be required to prove who she was.

9. Animals know their environment.
They know it by direct experience only.
Man crystallizes his knowledge.
He crystallizes his feelings.
He crystallizes them in phonetic symbolic representation.
He accumulates knowledge.
He passes it on to further generations of men.
He accumulates it and passes it on by written symbols.

10. This was during the whole of a day.
The day was dull, dark, and soundless.
The day was in the autumn of the year.
The clouds hung oppressively low in the heavens.
I had been passing.
I was alone.
I was on horseback.
I passed through a singularly dreary tract of country.
And at length I found myself.
The shades of the evening drew on.
I found myself within view of the melancholy House of Usher.

Fighto

Combine the sentences below into an essay that contains several prepositional phrases. You can compare your essay with a professional or student writer's version in the Appendix.

1. He was a foot long from head to toe.
2. He was covered with a film.
3. The film was clear.
4. The film was wet.
5. The film was slimy.

6. His only limbs were two hind legs and two forelegs.
7. The hind legs were powerful.
8. The hind legs were to propel him.
9. The forelegs were small.
10. The forelegs were to help him keep his balance.

11. We called the beast "Fighto."
12. This was because of his size.
13. This was because of his stature.

14. He was the only creature on earth.
15. The creature could be so beautiful and so ugly.
16. The creature was beautiful and ugly at the same time.

17. His two eyes were like tiny marbles.
18. They had a layer of skin.
19. The layer was thick.
20. The layer was stretched over them.

21. He had no eyelids.
22. He had just a cover over his eyes.
23. The cover was transparent.
24. The cover was protective.
25. The cover was like a pair of soft-lens contacts.

26. The two pureys rested atop his head.
27. His head was massive.
28. They were like a pair of ball bearings.
29. The ball bearings were on a lump of clay.
30. The clay was molded.

31. His nostrils protruded.
32. They were like his eyes.
33. But unlike his eyes they were hollow.
34. They were not crystalline.

35. His skin had a texture.
36. It was rough.
37. It was leathery.
38. It felt like a mixture.
39. The mixture was Jello and Vaseline petroleum jelly.
40. The Jello was unsolidified.

41. It had little bumps.
42. You touched them.
43. They gave way.
44. You removed your hand.
45. They returned to their original state.

46. His forelegs were small.
47. They seemed to have no use at all.
48. Their purpose was to hold him upright.

49. His hind legs were large.
50. The hind legs had three toes.

51. The hind legs had enough power.
52. The power was concentrated.
53. The power was to propel him three feet or more.
54. This was in a single bound.

55. His body was beautifully streamlined.
56. It was like a well-designed car.
57. But it had an aura about it.
58. The aura was pure ugliness.

59. All in all, he was like a monster.
60. The monster was miniature.
61. The monster was on the "Creature Double Feature."

62. The aroma was the odor of his habitat.
63. He carried the aroma.
64. It was a stench of the swamp.
65. The stench was permeating.
66. The stench was sticky.
67. The stench was musty.
68. The stench was damp.

69. He made little or no sound.
70. He swished through the tall wet grass.
71. He was attempting to elude our grasp.
72. He bumped into the walls of the bathtub.
73. He had been held captive in the bathtub.
74. This was after his apprehension.

75. The giant had a dark complexion.
76. The giant was gentle.
77. The complexion was green-brown.
78. The light hit the complexion.
79. The complexion glistened.

80. That beast was something from another world.
81. That beast was fantastic.

82. He was the monster from the world of the swamp.
83. The monster was giant.
84. The world was miniature.
85. Few if any of us ever know that world.

86. He was from the world of bull mummichogs.*
87. He was from the world of foliage.
88. The foliage eats men.

* *bull mummichog:* a minnowlike fish, often used as bait

89. He lived in a universe.
90. In the universe tiny things were big.
91. Big things were unrecognizable.

92. He was ugly in our universe.
93. Our universe is overgrown.
94. He was beautiful in his own right place.

Writing Suggestion 1: Once you have done the exercise above, you know exactly what kind of creature Fighto was. Locate a similar monster somewhere in your own habitat and write an essay about the creature and its world.

Writing Suggestion 2: In his essay "Walking," Henry David Thoreau wrote, "In wildness is the preservation of the world." This sentiment has since become a motto of the Wilderness Society and, more recently, of the Sierra Club. Whether or not you agree with Thoreau and his followers, write an essay in which you discuss the meaning of the saying.

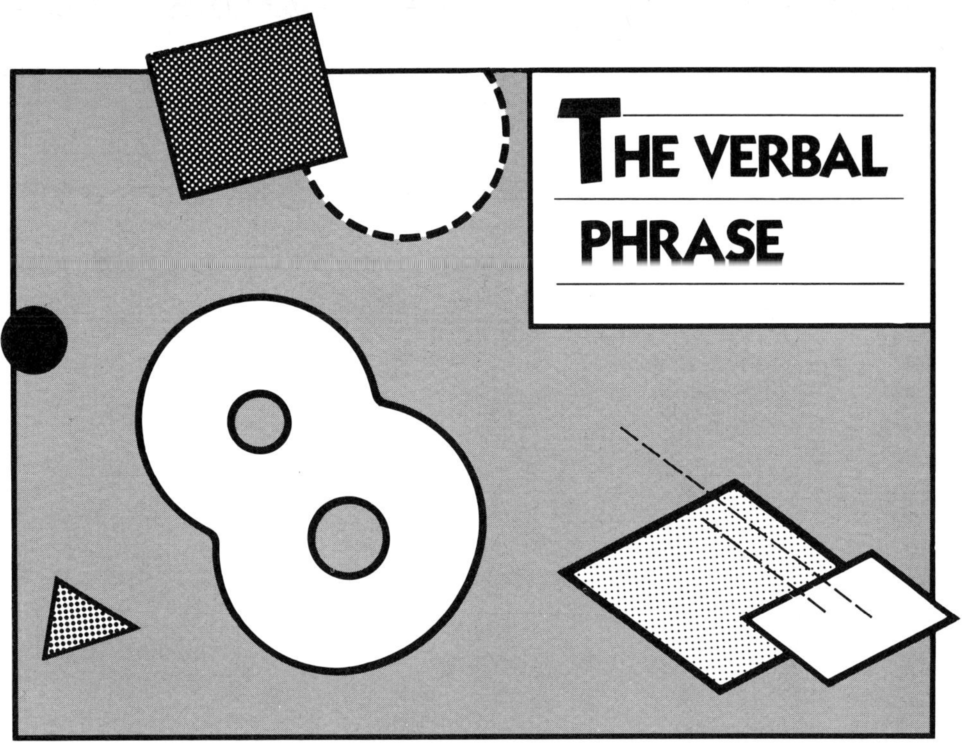

8 The Verbal Phrase

Intuitively I've always been aware of the vitally important pact which a man has with himself, to be all things to himself, and to be identified with all things, to stand self-reliant, taking advantage of his haphazard connection with a planet, riding his luck, and following his bent with the tenacity of a hound.

E. B. WHITE, "Freedom"

Though laden with wisdom, E. B. White's credo carries its weight lightly. His pithy declaration of independence opens with a personal conviction in the base clause:

> Intuitively I've always been aware of the vitally important pact which a man has with himself.

Having stated an intuitive truth, White specifies just what this pact with oneself entails:

> A man is to be all things to himself.
> A man is to be identified with all things.
> A man is to stand self-reliant.

Self-reliance is, indeed, the heart of the matter. Therefore, White explains the idea in detail:

> A man takes advantage of his haphazard connection with a planet.
> A man rides his luck.
> A man follows his bent with the tenacity of a hound.

Laid out in seven sentences, White's credo seems like heavy stuff, static and sententious. But when we read the single combined sentence as the author wrote it, the thought unfolds briskly:

1 Intuitively I've always been aware of the vitally important pact which a man has with himself,
  2 **to be** *all things to himself,* and
  2 **to be identified** *with all things,*
  2 **to stand** *self-reliant,*
    3 **taking** *advantage of his haphazard connection with a planet,*
    3 **riding** *his luck,* and
    3 **following** *his bent with the tenacity of a hound.*

Steadily moving to lower levels of generality, White makes his beliefs seem dynamic, not static. No wonder that, philosophical as the sentence is, it dances in our minds.

VERBS AND VERBALS

Each of the modifiers that White added to his base clause is a ***verbal phrase.*** Verbs are, of course, the basic predicates in every sentence we write or say. The complete verb in a given sentence may be one word (Jane *jogs*) or several words (Jane *has been jogging* for hours). What's important to note is that sentence verbs like these make complete statements. That is, by changing their forms, they reveal particular times or **tenses** (Jane *jogs* today, and she *will jog* tomorrow) and indicate whether their subjects are **singular** or **plural** (Jane *jogs* more than they *jog*).

But now look back at the first words in the modifiers at levels 2 and 3 in White's sentence: *to be, to stand, taking, riding, following.* These verb forms do not make complete statements. Unlike sentence verbs, they do not show tense or number. For these reasons, verb forms like *to be* and *taking* are called **verbals.**

Verbals cannot function as sentence verbs, but they can serve as modifiers. You can turn this limitation to advantage when you combine sentences. Like E. B. White, you can often reduce complete sentences to **verbal phrases** that modify words in the base clause. This strategy adds information to your writing even as it cuts down on words—quite an accomplishment.

INFINITIVE PHRASES

The verbal phrases that serve as modifiers are of two principal sorts. Look again at the level-2 modifiers in White's sentence:

2 **to be** *all things to himself,* and
2 **to be identified** *with all things,*
2 **to stand** *self-reliant,*

The word **to** or the phrase **in order to** before a verb form marks an **infinitive** (from the Latin *infinitus,* "unlimited"). An ***infinitive phrase,*** as we shall see in Chapter 12, can serve as a sentence subject:

> **To read** *a novel* is a difficult and complex art.
>
> VIRGINIA WOOLF, "How Should One Read a Book?"

Infinitive phrases can also serve as modifiers of words or sentences. In White's sentence, the three infinitive phrases all modify the noun *pact* in the base clause, commenting on this general term, specifying what it means.

As the modifier of a verb or of a whole sentence, however, an infinitive phrase can perform a distinctive and valuable function. It can express a goal, a purpose, a "want." For example, how might you combine these two sentences?

> We went back to the clubhouse.
> We wanted to watch the big race.

Write your version here:

____

____

____

You could subordinate one sentence to the other to express your goal:

> We went back to the clubhouse **because** we wanted to watch the big race.

On the other hand, you could simply *imply* your purpose by creating an infinitive phrase:

> We went back to the clubhouse **to watch** *the big race.*

This is just what Hunter S. Thompson did in his article "The Kentucky Derby Is Decadent and Depraved." Thompson created a bound infinitive phrase that tells *why* we went back to the clubhouse: "**to watch** *the big race.*" Since the infinitive phrase modifies the verb *went,* the modifier is adverbial. It expresses our *purpose.*

But infinitive phrases can also serve as free modifiers, commenting not on single words but on complete sentences. To grasp this, combine the two sentences below:

> I wanted to break the ice.
> I ventured a greeting in the few words of Japanese left over from Army service as a translator.

Write your version here:

____

____

____

Here's how the journalist Joseph Kraft combined the ideas in his "Letter from Baghdad":

2 **To break** *the ice,*
1 I ventured a greeting in the few words of Japanese left over from Army service as a translator.

While the infinitive phrase "**To break** *the ice*" still expresses purpose, here it functions as a free modifier of the sentence at large. Hence, it is set off from the base clause by a comma. Infinitive phrases of this sort are particularly useful in expository writing, writing that explains the *how* or *why* of something. As a final example of this, try to combine these two sentences:

You want to find out how your children perceive you.
Ask them to role-play being you.

Write your version here:

____

____

____

As before, you could subordinate one full sentence to the other:

If you want to find out how your children perceive you, ask them to role-play being you.

This is a legitimate sentence, one clearly showing a conditional relationship. Nevertheless, an infinitive phrase can create much the same meaning in fewer words:

2 **To find out** *how your children perceive you,*
1 ask them to role-play being you.

Jane O'Reilly wrote the sentence this way in her article "Doing Away with Sex Stereotypes." Used as a sentence modifier, the infinitive phrase is a simple and direct way of stating a goal.

PARTICIPIAL PHRASES

The three modifiers at level 2 in E. B. White's sentence are, then, infinitive phrases. Now consider the modifiers at level 3:

> 3 **taking** *advantage of his haphazard connection with a planet,*
> 3 **riding** *his luck,* and
> 3 **following** *his bent with the tenacity of a hound.*

The **-ing** ending on verbals like *taking, riding,* and *following* marks them as **present participles** (from the Latin *particeps,* "participating"). A ***participial phrase*** participates in both verbal and adjectival relationships with the noun or pronoun it modifies. Like all verbals, it indicates a state or action—from mere *being* to bold *taking, riding,* and *following.* And like all adjectivals (noun modifiers like "a *fresh* idea" or "the sentence *below*") it adds qualities of or details about the noun it modifies.

Again, as we shall see in Chapter 12, like infinitive phrases, present-participial phrases can serve as sentence subjects:

> **Reading** *the front page* made me feel a lot better.
> HUNTER S. THOMPSON, *Fear and Loathing in Las Vegas*

When participial phrases function in this way—as noun substitutes—they are called *gerunds.* More often, however, participial phrases serve as noun modifiers, as in the example from E. B. White.

Like infinitives, participles are verbals. Without an auxiliary or "helping" verb, participles cannot serve as sentence verbs. For example, *Jane* **jogging** is not a complete sentence, while *Jane* **was jogging** is one. Without the helping verb **was,** the verbal **jogging** does not make a complete statement. Like infinitives, participles in themselves do not show whether they modify singular or plural nouns. The helping verb (*is, are; was, were*) carries this information. But unlike infinitives, participles do show distinctions of tense. The participial modifiers in White's sentence are **present participles.** The marker of the present participle is the **-ing** ending: *taking, riding, following.* On the other hand, **past participles** are usually marked by an **-en** or **-ed** ending: *taken, ridden, followed.* (Some verbs like *sing, do,* and *sleep* have irregular past participles: *sung, done, slept.*) To practice creating past-participial phrase modifiers, try combining each pair of sentences below:

A. Tucson is situated in beautiful mesquite riverbed country.
Tucson is overlooked by the snowy Catalina range.

B. A briefcase swayed in his grip.
The briefcase was swollen with the weekend's reading.

Write your versions here:

____

____

____

____

____

____

As usual, more than one "correct" combination is possible for each pair. You can compare your versions with these:

A. Tucson is situated in beautiful mesquite riverbed country, **over-looked** *by the snowy Catalina range.*
JACK KEROUAC, *On the Road*

B. A briefcase, **swollen** *with the weekend's reading,* swayed in his grip.
KINGSLEY AMIS, *Lucky Jim*

In each sentence above, a past participle begins a verbal phrase that modifies a noun in the base. Can you point out which noun in each sentence is modified by the verbal phrase?

BOUND AND FREE PARTICIPIAL PHRASES

If you think back to earlier chapters, you will recall a key distinction that affects both meaning and punctuation. Modifiers may be either *bound* directly to the words they modify or set off as *free,* nonessential information. This distinction between modifiers that *define* their subjects and modifiers that merely *comment* on their subjects applies to verbal phrases as well as to relative and subordinate clauses. To understand this, try combining each pair of sentences below into one sentence that contains a present-participial phrase:

A. The door opens and a short middle-aged man walks in.
The man wears handmade sandals.

B. The house-master talked and talked.
He warmed to his subject.

Write your versions here:

____

____

____

____

Professional writers combined the sentences as follows:

A. The door opens and a short middle-aged man **wearing** *handmade sandals* walks in.

JOAN DIDION, "Where the Kissing Never Stops"

B. The house-master, **warming** *to his subject,* talked and talked.

CHRISTOPHER ISHERWOOD, *Lions and Shadows*

Joan Didion created a bound participial phrase that identifies the noun it modifies: "a short middle-aged man **wearing** *handmade sandals."* The phrase is essential information that *defines* the subject. Hence, it is not set off by any punctuation. On the other hand, Christopher Isherwood created a free participial phrase, "**warming** *to his subject,*" that simply *comments* on someone fully identified, "the house-master."

The same distinction applies to past-participial phrases as well. Once again, combine the sentences in the sets below, using participial phrases:

A. On the nearby water's edge a dozen fishing boats stood moored in berths.
The berths were scattered along a network of floating docks.

B. Jordan's fingers rested for a moment in mine.
Her fingers were powdered white over their tan.

Write your versions here:

____

____

____

____

____

____

Two writers, one a student, one a professional, combined the sentences in these ways:

A. On the nearby water's edge a dozen fishing boats stood moored in berths **scattered** *along a network of floating docks.*

STUDENT WRITER

B. Jordan's fingers, **powdered** *white over their tan,* rested for a moment in mine.

F. SCOTT FITZGERALD, *The Great Gatsby*

In the student's sentence, the past-participial phrase is a bound modifier of "berths," which it helps define fully. In Fitzgerald's sentence, on the other hand, the past-participial phrase is a free modifier, a *comment* on Jordan's fingers.

POSITIONING PARTICIPIAL PHRASES

As free modifiers, participial phrases can be placed before, within, or after the base clause of the sentence:

2 **Drenched** *to the bone,*
1 I arrived in a little Calabrian village.

NIKOS KAZANTZAKIS, *A Report to Greco*

1 A camp dog, / , barked petulantly.
2/ **seeing** *me in the road*

E. B. WHITE, "Walden"

1 A cloud began to cover the sun slowly,
2 **shadowing** *the bay in a deeper green.*

JAMES JOYCE, *Ulysses*

"DANGLING PARTICIPLES"

Despite this mobility, however, a participial phrase can be misplaced in a given sentence, often with comical results:

Putting *on his pants,* **a button** falls off.
Walking *down the Rue Lhomond one night in a fit of unusual anguish and desolation,* **certain things** were revealed to me.

If we read these sentences from Henry Miller's *Tropic of Cancer* literally, we run headlong into absurdities. The first seems to say that a *button* was putting on his pants. In the second sentence, *certain things* appear to have been walking down the Rue Lhomond in Paris. "Dangling participles," as these misplaced modifiers are called, modify the wrong word in the base clause—or no word at all. In Miller's sentences, the present-participial phrases wrongly modify the objects that are acted upon (**a button, certain**

things). Instead, they should modify the performers of the actions: **Carl** *put on his pants;* **I** *realized certain things.* Once we see this, we can revise the sentences:

> **Putting** *on his pants,* **Carl** tears off a button.
> **Walking** *down the Rue Lhomond one night in a fit of unusual anguish and desolation,* **I** realized certain things.

Now the participial phrases modify the words that they should, words that refer to the performers of the action: **Carl, I.** As these examples reveal, however, even a professional writer sometimes dozes off while composing.

WHAT PARTICIPIAL PHRASES ADD TO YOUR WRITING

As we have seen again and again, participial phrases enliven writing by adding **action details** to the base clause:

1 I hesitated,
  2 **twirling** *the ice in my drink.*
HUNTER S. THOMPSON, "The Kentucky Derby Is Decadent and Depraved"

Indeed, one detail seems to lead to another in good writing:

  2 For five years,
1 Grandmother waited on him,
  2 **feeding** *him with a spoon,*
  2 **changing** *the bed,* and
  2 **trying** *her best to look after their dying farm.*
BOBBIE ANN MASON, "Offerings"

1 The stories are endless,
  2 infinitely familiar,
  2 **traded** *by the faithful like baseball cards,*
  2 **fondled** *until they fray around the edges and blur into the apocryphal.*
JOAN DIDION, "7000 Romaine, Los Angeles 38"

As these examples show, participial phrases work especially well in series, creating a truly cumulative effect of added details.

Furthermore, like infinitive phrases, participial phrases can briskly indicate **cause-and-result** relationships. For instance, try to combine these pairs into single sentences that show cause and result:

A. He felt the sheets bunched at the foot of the mattress.
He remembered that he had made the bed in a hurry.

B. He retreated to the wilderness at last.
He nearly starved himself to death.

Write your versions here:

____

____

____

____

One option would be to place a subordinator like *when* or *because* before the first sentence in each pair, thereby creating a subordinate clause:

A. **When** he felt the sheets bunched at the foot of the mattress, he remembered that he had made the bed in a hurry.

B. **Because** he retreated to the wilderness at last, he nearly starved himself to death.

But note how the more economical participial phrases that professional authors created can do the job as well:

A. **Feeling** *the sheets bunched at the foot of the mattress,* he remembered that he had made the bed in a hurry.

BRENDAN GILL, "The Knife"

B. **Retreating** *to the wilderness at last,* he nearly starved himself to death.

ALEXANDER ELIOT, "The Brush of Legends"

Whether they show causation or simply add vital details, verbal phrases can enhance your writing. The infinitive phrase, past-participial phrase, and present-participial phrase alike enliven your sentence combinations even as they cut down the number of words and clauses you need to get your message across.

PULLING IT ALL TOGETHER

This chapter opened with an acrobatic sentence from E. B. White's essay "Freedom." With practice, you'll soon be creating such elegant, detailed sentences yourself. Imagine that you are writing about a particularly lively, action-packed topic: the advent of rock-and-roll music. You begin by jotting down a main idea:

So Elvis Presley came.

This is the story in a nutshell, but just what did Presley do?

> He strummed a weird guitar.
> He wagged his tail across the continent.
> He ripped off fame and fortune as he scrunched his way.

These action details bring Elvis into focus. A comparison can link him with another all-American boy:

> He was like a latter-day Johnny Appleseed.
> He sowed seeds of a new rhythm and style in the white souls of the white youth of America.
> The white youths' inner hunger and need was no longer satisfied with the antiseptic white shoes and whiter songs of Pat Boone.

As the details and comparisons accumulate, the coming of Elvis begins to seem more and more like a revolutionary event in American history. In fact, that's just how Eldridge Cleaver presented the facts in his essay "Convalescence." To capture the revolutionary energy of Elvis Presley's arrival, Cleaver packed all the data into a single dynamic sentence. Notice how participial phrases keep the action moving:

> So Elvis Presley came, **strumming** *a weird guitar and* **wagging** *his tail across the continent,* **ripping off** *fame and fortune as he scrunched his way,* and, like a latter-day Johnny Appleseed, **sowing** *seeds of a new rhythm and style in the white souls of the white youth of America,* whose inner hunger and need was no longer satisfied with the antiseptic white shoes and whiter songs of Pat Boone.

Thanks to its verbal-phrase modifiers, Cleaver's sentence captures the excitement of Elvis in action, *strumming, wagging, ripping,* and *sowing* his way across America.

The Verbal Phrase: Combinations

Combine each set of sentences below into one sentence that contains at least one verbal-phrase modifier. You can compare your combinations with professional or student writers' sentences in the Appendix.

A. INFINITIVE PHRASES

SAMPLE EXERCISE

You want to guard against the relentlessness of forgetting.
You must write down much of the information presented in class.

PROFESSIONAL WRITERS' VERSION

To guard *against the relentlessness of forgetting,* you must write down much of the information presented in class.

JOHN LANGAN AND JUDITH NADELL, *Doing Well in College*

1. He wanted to avoid the sin of being bareheaded.
   He covered his skull with both hands.
2. He used to beg in court at the age of six.
   His goal was to have his father set free.
3. The Iraqis' goal was to avoid dependence on any single country.
   The Iraqis deliberately diversified their foreign connections in both development and sales.
4. Their purpose was marking the occasion on this night.
   They were wearing collars and neckties.
5. He got out at the nearest Elevated station.
   He wanted to take a train for the office.
   He had the air of a man.
   The man had thoroughly wasted the morning.

B. PARTICIPIAL PHRASES

SAMPLE EXERCISE

He found me alone in the house.
I was reading by the kitchen table.

PROFESSIONAL WRITER'S VERSION

He found me alone in the house, **reading** *by the kitchen table.*

SHERWOOD ANDERSON, *Memoirs*

1. I was looking for clues to his personality.
   I found that Mr. Vincent would celebrate his seventy-sixth birthday in a few weeks.
2. His far-flung cane had brought him hither.
   He used the cane as a divining-rod at the last crossroads.
3. He stalked up and down a few feet.
   He smiled as his wooden spoon delivered mouthfuls.
   He veered back and forth on his toes.
   He stalked with youthful gait again for a moment.

4. And this letter to Monroe Rosenblatt was of importance.
   She had written it in her mind time and time again.
5. I was unbalanced with rage.
   I got to the exit just as an attendant brought in a carton.
   The carton contained two white kittens.
6. Every round was like a tiny concentration of high-velocity wind.
   Every round made the bodies wince and shiver.
7. He placed his fist just under Goldworm's sternum.
   He hugged sharply.
   He caused a side order of bean curd to rocket out of the victim's trachea and carom off the hat rack.
8. Roger Dewey and Daryl Freed were sitting on the floor.
   They were in earnest conversation.
   They bobbed heads at each other.
   They were like plastic birds.
   The plastic birds dipped for water.
9. They were asked to write.
   They would sit for minutes on end.
   They stared at the paper.
10. We caught two bass.
    We hauled them in briskly.
    We hauled them in as though they were mackerel.
    We pulled them over the side of the boat.
    We pulled them over in a businesslike manner.
    We used no landing net.
    We stunned them with a blow to the back of the head.

Peer Tutoring

Combine the sentences below into a paragraph that contains at least one verbal-phrase modifier. You can compare your paragraph with a professional or student writer's version in the Appendix.

1. We write.
2. Our goal is mainly to be judged.
3. This is in most academic settings.

4. We write.
5. Our goal is mainly to be understood.
6. This is in real life.

7. Peer criticism helps students.
8. The students experience writing as a real activity in this sense.
9. Tutors write peer critiques.

10. The tutors write for three audiences.
11. They must try to balance and satisfy the audiences' demands.

12. They want to help the author.
13. They are criticizing the author's work.
14. They must be clear.
15. They must be tactful.

16. They want to satisfy their own integrity.
17. They must be honest.
18. They must be truthful.

19. They want to meet the standards of the arbiter.
20. The arbiter is final.
21. The arbiter is the teacher.
22. The teacher will evaluate and grade their critical writing.
23. They must be thorough in details.
24. They must be tactful.
25. They must be helpful.
26. They must be truthful.

27. Peer criticism is the writing.
28. The writing is the hardest most students will ever do.

Writing Suggestion 1: By writing peer critiques, students help each other learn to write more effectively. Exchange versions of the exercise above (or any other writing assignment) with one or more of your peers and write critiques of each other's work. To make the most of the exchange, try to tell your peers what they do *best.*

Writing Suggestion 2: If you have been working with *Combining and Creating* for some time, your writing may well be changing. Review the writing you have been doing recently and then write a short essay in self-analysis. How has your writing changed, if at all? What do you feel are your strengths and weaknesses as a writer? What should you work on in the near future?

Peace Corps

Combine the sentences below into a paragraph that contains at least one verbal-phrase modifier. You can compare your paragraph with a professional or student writer's version in the Appendix.

1. John F. Kennedy stood on the steps of the student union.
2. The student union was the University of Michigan's.
3. Kennedy was a presidential candidate.
4. This was in the early hours of a cold morning.
5. The morning was in October 1960.

6. Kennedy addressed some 10,000 students.
7. He asked this.
8. "How many of you are willing to spend ten years in Africa or Latin America or Asia working for the U.S. and working for freedom?"

9. Some Michigan students sent Kennedy a list.
10. The list was of several hundred volunteers.
11. This was a few days later.

12. A federal agency was born.
13. It was born from this challenge.
14. It was born from this response.
15. The challenge was spontaneous.
16. The agency enjoyed popularity.
17. The popularity was unprecedented.
18. The agency enjoyed it for a decade.
19. The agency was the Peace Corps.

20. The Peace Corps was bolstered in Congress.
21. Stalwarts such as Senators Hubert H. Humphrey of Minnesota and Richard L. Neuberger of Oregon bolstered it.
22. The stalwarts were liberal Democrats.
23. The Peace Corps was a burst of idealism in an age.
24. In that age idealism was respectable.

25. Today the Peace Corps is racked.
26. Ideologies rack it from within.
27. The ideologies are conflicting.
28. Lack of support racks it from without.
29. The support is federal.

30. The corps is learning to live with a budget.
31. The budget is reduced.
32. The reduction is drastic.
33. The corps faces an arsenal of questions.
34. The questions are about its status as a government agency.
35. The questions are about its purpose.
36. The most important questions are about its viability as an aid program in the 1980s.

Writing Suggestion 1: Times—and students—have changed since that cold morning when John Kennedy challenged the students of the University of Michigan to undertake ten years of foreign service at low wages. If you are unfamiliar with the Peace Corps, go to your library and learn the facts on the agency. Then, in an essay, argue for or against the survival of the Peace Corps in the 1980s.

Writing Suggestion 2: Use John Kennedy's question as the basis for an opinion poll of your fellow students: "How many of you are willing to spend ten years in Africa or Latin America or Asia working for the U.S. and working for freedom?" Assemble the results of your poll and then write an essay analyzing your fellow students' response to Kennedy's question. Is the Peace Corps still a viable government agency? Is idealism still respectable?

The Verbal Phrase: Creations

Create at least one verbal phrase modifier in each sentence below. While most of the exercises ask you to create specific kinds of verbal phrases, some leave you free to create any kind of verbal phrase that seems appropriate. You can compare your creations with professional or student writers' sentences in the Appendix.

SAMPLE EXERCISES

A. 1 He jingles the coins in his pocket,

2 ______________________________ . [signaled format]
(present-participial phrase)

B. 2 ______________________________ , [signaled format]
(infinitive phrase)

1 a smallpox patient would be wrapped in red cloth in a bed hung with red hangings.

C. For a long while we just stood there. [open format]

D. He had them remain in the same distantly separate rooms as before. [open format]

PROFESSIONAL WRITERS' VERSIONS

A. 1 He jingles the coins in his pocket,
2 **thinking** *of the witty things he will say.*

DELMORE SCHWARTZ, "In Dreams Begin Responsibilities"

B. 2 **To prevent** *pockmarks,*
1 a smallpox patient would be wrapped in red cloth in a bed hung with red hangings.

BARBARA W. TUCHMAN, *A Distant Mirror: The Calamitous 14th Century*

C. For a long while we just stood there, **looking** *down at the profound and fleshless grin.*

WILLIAM FAULKNER, "A Rose for Emily"

D. **To maintain** *the order of the house,* he had them remain in the same distantly separate rooms as before.

YUKIO MISHIMA, *Thirst for Love*

1. 1 He raked the lawn with his fingers,

   2 ______________________________ .
   (present-participial phrase)

2. 2 ______________________________ ,
   (infinitive phrase)

   1 the gods use the desires and strivings of men.

3. I tumbled out of the hammock.

4. 1 A divided drove of branded cattle passed the windows,

   2 ______________________________ ,
   (present-participial phrase)

   2 ______________________________ ,
   (present-participial phrase)

   2 ______________________________ .
   (present-participial phrase)

5. He fled down to the steerage.

6. 2 ______________________________ ,
   (infinitive phrase)

   1 General Patton had to augment his battle costume with a pearl-handled revolver.

7. 2 ______________________________ ,
   (past-participial phrase)

   2 with ______________________________ ,
   (prepositional phrase)

   1 he was yet swayed and driven as an animal.

8. 1 He plunged along with his tiny camera,

   2 ______________________________ ,
   (present-participial phrase)

   and

   1 I followed,

   2 ______________________________ .
   (present-participial phrase)

9. One must first have a framework of open living.

10. 2 ____ ,
(past-participial phrase)

1 the aggregating clusters of medical scientists in the bright sunlight of the boardwalk at Atlantic City, / , have the look of assemblages of social insects.

2/ ____
(past-participial phrase)

Independence Days

Combine the sentences below into two paragraphs that contain several verbal-phrase modifiers. You can compare your paragraphs with a professional or student writer's version in the Appendix.

1. My Fourths of July all run together.
2. They are a parade of twilights.
3. In the twilights I sit expectantly on grassy hillsides.
4. I wait for enough darkness for the first big rocket.
5. In the twilights little children spin their magic sticks into hoops of fire and toss them as high as they can.
6. The magic sticks are dying.
7. The hot, white glow of sparklers is against the children's faces.
8. Their faces are half-thrilled, half-frightened.

9. Late arrivals pick their way through the tangle of seated forms.
10. They bend over now and then.
11. They look for the faces of friends in the light.
12. The light is fading.

13. Then there is the great whoosh.
14. The crowd is frozen in the brilliance of the first cascade of stars.
15. The crowd roars its delight at a bang.
16. The bang makes the hillside tremble.

17. This has always been for me among the most pleasant of our rituals.
18. Our rituals are patriotic.
19. Our rituals are tribal.

20. For on those evenings I and all the others become figures in one of those old cover illustrations.
21. The others are with me on the grass.
22. The figures are willing.
23. The illustrations are freckled.
24. The illustrations are by Norman Rockwell.

25. We become good, clean Americans all.
26. Our mouths are open at the booming of the rockets.
27. We are exhilarated by the thunder of the explosions.
28. We are warmed by the shower of sparks.
29. The sparks are red, white, and blue.
30. The sparks drip to the ground in the finale's huge firework flag.

31. We are stirred.
32. The incendiary symbolism stirs us.
33. The symbolism is of an old liberation.
34. We march home.
35. We are ragtag.
36. We march to fifes and drums.
37. The fifes and drums are inaudible.

Writing Suggestion 1: Write a few paragraphs discussing your own Independence Days—or any other holidays, secular or religious, you wish to consider. While you should certainly describe the public festivities, don't forget to discuss the personal meaning of the holiday as well.

Writing Suggestion 2: National holidays commemorate serious matters: the founding of a new country, the births of great leaders, the memory of fallen soldiers. Some lesser holidays, however, such as April Fools' Day and Halloween, celebrate lighter subjects. Write a short essay, serious or satirical, in which you propose a new holiday for us to celebrate. Whether your proposal is earnest or ironic, defend it as persuasively as you can.

The Verbal Phrase: Sentence Acrobatics

Combine each set of sentences below into one or more "acrobatic" sentences. See if you can create at least one verbal phrase as you do each exercise, but feel free to try out other constructions as well. Naturally, each problem invites more than one "correct" answer. Therefore, you must create original sentences that strike *you* as both correct and stylish.

You may enjoy comparing your combinations with the professional or student writers' versions in the Appendix. Look for both similarities and differences, but try to decide whose version is the more stylish—it may well be your own.

SAMPLE EXERCISE

The Prince wanted to signify his right to punish.
He twice rejected a good price.
The price was offered by towns.
The towns wanted to buy immunity.
The immunity would be from sack.

STUDENT AND PROFESSIONAL WRITERS' VERSIONS

To buy *immunity from sack,* towns offered a good price to the prince, who twice rejected the price **in order to signify** *his right to punish.*

STUDENT WRITER

To signify *his right to punish,* the Prince twice rejected a good price **offered** by towns **to buy** *immunity from sack.*

BARBARA W. TUCHMAN, *A Distant Mirror: The Calamitous 14th Century*

1. The whole point of the Ralegh story is this.
   A man's cloak was frequently the most valuable part of his wardrobe.
   A man's cloak cost hundreds of pounds.
2. The Count wanted to launch this concern.
   The Count spent a couple of weeks.
   He spent them promoting a bookmaker.
   The bookmaker was known as Boatrace Harry.
3. The worker viewed his weakness.
   The worker was weak in bargaining power.
   He was never in doubt.
   He had no doubt as to the appropriate solution.
4. The aim is to keep a nuclear reactor operating smoothly.
   The aim is to keep a nuclear reactor under control.
   A number of systems, subsystems, components, structures, and people have to work together.
   They must work in a coordinated way.
   They must work in a reliable way.
5. Freed and T.W. walked out of the living room.
   They were clowning.
   They had arms around each other's waists.
   They swayed their hips.
   The swaying had all the grace of cows.
   The cows were walking on ice.
6. This was on the date our Constitution was adopted.
   This was in most states.
   A man had to own a certain amount of property.
   He wanted to vote.
   He had to own a greater amount of property.
   He wanted to hold office.
7. Her legs resembled a child's tiny legs.
   The child's legs were burdened.
   The child's legs were under an immense winter coat.

Her legs were buried.
Her legs were beneath the volume of three petticoats.
Her legs carried her delicately across the dance floor.

8. They'd seen him.
He was rushing down the streets.
The rushing was eager.
The streets were winter.
He was bareheaded.
He carried his books to the pool hall.
Or he was climbing trees.
He wanted to get into the attics of buddies.
He spent days reading in the attics.
Or he spent them hiding from the law.

9. You watch television.
You'd think we lived at bay.
You'd think we lived in total jeopardy.
We are surrounded on all sides.
Germs surround us.
The germs seek humans.
We are shielded against infection.
We are shielded against death.
Only a technology shields us.
The technology is chemical.
The technology enables us to keep killing them off.

10. We had been having a spell of weather.
The spell was unseasonable.
We had been having hot days.
The days were close.
The fog shut in every night.
It scaled for a few hours at midday.
Then it crept back again at dark.
It drifted in first over the trees on the point.
Then it blew across the fields.
The blowing was sudden.
It blotted out the world.
It took possession of houses.
It took possession of men.
It took possession of animals.

Once More to the Lake

Combine the sentences below into a short essay that contains several verbal-phrase modifiers. You can compare your essay with a professional or student writer's version in the Appendix.

1. We went fishing the first morning.

2. I felt the same damp moss.
3. The moss covered the worms in the bait can.
4. I saw the dragonfly alight on the tip of my rod.
5. My rod hovered a few inches from the surface of the water.

6. It was the arrival of this fly.
7. Its arrival convinced me beyond any doubt.
8. Everything was as it always had been.
9. The years were a mirage.
10. There had been no years.

11. The small waves were the same.
12. The small waves chucked the rowboat under the chin.
13. We fished at anchor.
14. And the boat was the same boat.
15. It was the same color green.
16. The ribs were broken in the same places.
17. Under the floorboards were the same fresh-water leavings and débris.
18. The dead hellgrammite* was under the floorboards.
19. The wisps of moss were under the floorboards.
20. The rusty discarded fishhook was under the floorboards.
21. The dried blood from yesterday's catch was under the floorboards.

22. We stared at the tips of our rods.
23. Our stares were silent.
24. We stared at the dragonflies.
25. The dragonflies came and went.

26. I lowered the tip of mine into the water.
27. I lowered it tentatively.
28. I pensively dislodged the fly.
29. The fly darted two feet away.
30. The fly poised.
31. The fly darted two feet back.
32. It came to rest again a little farther up the rod.

33. There had been no years between the ducking of this dragonfly and the other one.
34. The other one was part of memory.

35. I looked at the boy.
36. He was silently watching his fly.

* *hellgrammite:* dobsonfly larva, used as fish bait

37. And it was my hands that held his rod.
38. It was my eyes watching.

39. I felt dizzy.
40. I didn't know which rod I was at the end of.

41. We caught two bass.
42. We hauled them in briskly.
43. We hauled them in as though they were mackerel.
44. We pulled them over the side of the boat.
45. We pulled them over in a businesslike manner.
46. We used no landing net.
47. We stunned them with a blow to the back of the head.

48. We got back for a swim before lunch.
49. The lake was exactly where we had left it.
50. It was the same number of inches from the dock.
51. There was only the merest suggestion of a breeze.

52. This seemed an utterly enchanted sea, this lake.
53. You could leave this lake to its own devices for a few hours.
54. And you could come back to it.
55. And you found that it had not stirred.
56. This body of water was constant.
57. This body of water was trustworthy.

58. In the shallows, the sticks and twigs were undulating.
59. The sticks and twigs were dark.
60. The sticks and twigs were water-soaked.
61. The sticks and twigs were smooth and old.
62. They undulated in clusters on the bottom.
63. The clusters were against the clean ribbed sand.
64. The track of the mussel was plain.

65. A school of minnows swam by.
66. Each minnow had its shadow.
67. Its shadow was small.
68. Its shadow was individual.
69. The shadows doubled the attendance.
70. The shadows were so clear and sharp in the sunlight.

71. Some of the other campers were in swimming.
72. They swam along the shore.
73. One of them had a cake of soap.
74. And the water felt thin.
75. It felt clear.
76. It felt unsubstantial.

77. Over the years there had been this person.
78. This person had the cake of soap.
79. There had been this cultist.
80. And here he was.

81. There had been no years.

Writing Suggestion 1: Consciously or unconsciously, when we revisit a place after an absence, we measure the place against our memory of it. Write an essay discussing a place you knew well and then revisited after a long time. Had the place changed? Had you changed? Had *both* changed?

Writing Suggestion 2: After you have written a version of *Once More to the Lake,* you will see that the exercise contains detailed observations of natural phenomena: the dragonfly on the rod, the twigs in the shallows, the minnows and their shadows. Try writing a similar account of natural phenomena you yourself have observed. Make your essay as specific, concrete, and vivid as the exercise above.

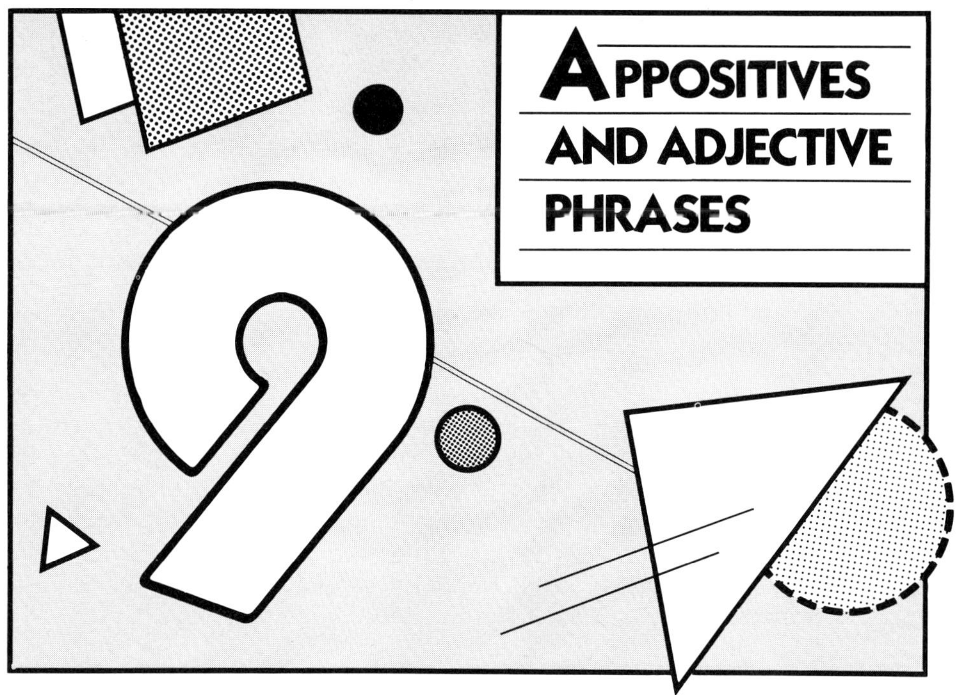

9 Appositives and Adjective Phrases

Dick Haddock, a family man, a man twenty-six years in the same line of work, a man who has on the telephone and in his office the crisp and easy manner of technological middle management, is in many ways the prototypical Southern California solid citizen.

JOAN DIDION, "Quiet Days in Malibu"

Even when Joan Didion sets out to describe the "typical" Southern Californian, she presents a three-dimensional portrait rather than a simple stereotype. Before drawing any conclusions about Dick Haddock, Didion offers us three factual details about the man. First, she comments on his home life:

> Dick Haddock is a family man.

Next she turns to his job history:

> Dick Haddock is a man twenty-six years in the same line of work.

Then she describes Haddock's personal manner:

> Dick Haddock is a man who has on the telephone and in his office the crisp and easy manner of technological middle management.

Finally, having stated these three definition-like details, the writer makes a general statement:

> Dick Haddock is in many ways the prototypical Southern California solid citizen.

When Didion arranges these parts into a whole, she creates a sentence that is at once suspenseful, coherent, and economical:

1 Dick Haddock, / , is in many ways the prototypical Southern California solid citizen.
2/ **a family man,**
2/ **a man twenty-six years in the same line of work,**
2/ **a man who has on the telephone and in his office the crisp and easy manner of technological middle management**

By placing three medial free modifiers between the subject, *Dick Haddock,* and the verb, *is,* in the base, Didion created suspense. We read through the details attentively, waiting for the verb that completes the sentence. By repeating the noun *man* in each of the medial modifiers, Didion made the sentence coherent. Finally, by adding the three modifiers to the base without adding any extra connective words like *and* or *that,* Didion made the sentence highly economical. What kind of combination allows her to pack so much information about Dick Haddock into such close quarters?

APPOSITIVES AND APPOSITION

Joan Didion created her elegant sentence by means of ***appositives.*** An appositive is a modifier, usually a noun or noun phrase, that defines, comments on, or repeats another noun elsewhere in the sentence.* The term **appositive** comes from the Latin word *appositus,* "placed nearby." When a noun or noun phrase is "placed nearby" another noun so as to define, comment on, or rename that noun, the modifier is said to be *in apposition to* the word it modifies.

In Didion's sentence, the three medial modifiers are in apposition to the noun *Dick Haddock,* the sentence subject. Each of the appositives comments on Haddock, telling more about what kind of *man* he is. Since *man,* the key word in each of the modifiers, is a noun like *Dick Haddock,* the appositives are **noun phrases.** Notice that the appositives in Didion's sentence are not only comments but noun repeaters. Each one repeats the noun *man,* thereby adding more and more information about Dick Haddock. It is this repetition that gives the sentence such tight coherence.

CREATING APPOSITIVES

As Joan Didion's sentence from "Quiet Days in Malibu" reveals, appositives add definition-like details that bring the subject into sharp focus. Consider, then, how you might combine these sentences:

Emma Boulanger was dusting the hall.
Emma Boulanger was the French housemaid.

* Occasionally, a noun substitute such as a **that**-*clause,* a *gerund phrase,* or an *infinitive phrase* serves as an an appositive. We shall take up these constructions fully in Chapter 12.

Linking the two ideas with **and** produces a sprawling compound sentence:

> Emma Boulanger was dusting the hall, **and** Emma Boulanger was the French housemaid.

No self-respecting housemaid would tolerate such clutter. A complex sentence that contains a free relative clause eliminates at least some of the repetition:

> Emma Boulanger, **who** *was the French housemaid,* was dusting the hall.

This is promising, but an appositive combination offers you a still more economical alternative:

> Emma Boulanger, **the French housemaid,** was dusting the hall.

This is exactly the option John Cheever chose when he wrote the sentence in his story "The Common Day."

As this example and the opening sentence by Joan Didion prove, appositives allow writers to add information to their sentences without creating new clauses—a significant saving on words. Equally important, appositives allow you to expand a base clause with telling observations at a lower level of generality. The observations may explain a general term, as in the following sentence:

1 Somebody's hat, / , lay forlorn on a small sideboard.
  2/ **his great-uncle's hat,**
  2/ **an old felt**

URSULA K. LE GUIN, "Two Delays on the Northern Line"

Or they may express the writer's feelings:

1 The moon came up nasty and full,
  2 **a fat moist piece of decadent fruit.**

MICHAEL HERR, *Dispatches*

By means of an appositive, Michael Herr implicitly compares the moon to a piece of overripe fruit. Such a comparison is called a **metaphor.** This figure of speech indirectly reveals the author's feelings about the situation he describes. Whether they add facts or feelings, appositives give your writing texture, the lively interplay of general and specific ideas.

APPOSITIVES BOUND AND FREE

Like the other modifiers we have studied, appositives may either be bound directly to the words they modify ("my sister **Miriam**") or marked off as free, nonessential information ("my sister**, Miriam,**"). The punctuation depends on the meaning. As a free modifier set off by commas, an appositive merely comments on a fully identified noun. Thus, "my sister, Miriam," implies that I have one and only one sister, Miriam. On the other hand, as a bound modifier, an appositive defines a noun that would not otherwise be fully identified. Thus, "my sister Miriam" implies that Miriam is only one of at least two sisters—my sister Miriam and my sister Jane.

This distinction between essential, defining appositives and nonessential, commenting ones applies to titles as well as to names. For example, how would you combine and punctuate these two sentences?

> Eudora Welty's first story appeared in a small literary magazine nearly 45 years ago.
> Eudora Welty's first story was "Death of a Traveling Salesman."

Write your version here:

____

____

____

In his essay "Songs of the South," reviewer Walter Clemons solved the problem this way:

> Eudora Welty's first story, **"Death of a Traveling Salesman,"** appeared in a small literary magazine nearly 45 years ago.

Quite rightly, Clemons set off the title as a free modifier. "Eudora Welty's first story" is, of course, fully identified; an author can have but one first story. Therefore, in this case, the added title is nonessential information: a comment. On the other hand, how would you combine and punctuate these two sentences?

> The sonnet is perhaps the best that Keats had yet written.
> The sonnet is "To My Brother George."

Write your version here:

____

____

____

When Walter Jackson Bate combined these ideas into a single sentence in his biography of the poet John Keats, he punctuated the sentence this way:

The sonnet **"To My Brother George"** is perhaps the best that Keats had yet written.

Bate correctly inserted no comma between the appositive and the noun it modifies. As the word "yet" implies, Keats wrote many sonnets. Thus, the title is essential information: a definition. Without it, we would not know which sonnet was being discussed. The same principle applies to works of art ("Leonardo's painting *La Gioconda*") and to musical compositions ("Verdi's opera *Aïda*"). The punctuation depends on whether the appositive *defines* the noun it modifies or simply *comments* on it.

INITIAL, MEDIAL, AND FINAL APPOSITIVES

In addition to being more economical than relative clauses, appositives are also more movable. Relative clauses always follow the words they modify:

America, **which** *leads the world in almost every economic category,* leads it above all in the production of schlock.

ROBERT CLAIBORNE, "Future Schlock"

Although the modifier in Claiborne's sentence is marked off as free, it cannot be moved. An appositive, on the other hand, may stand before or after the noun it modifies, depending on the effect the writer wants to create. The following sentences contain appositives in initial, medial, and final positions, respectively:

2 **A redskin most at home in white clown makeup,**
1 Fiedler has given many splendid performances over the years.

GORE VIDAL, "The Hacks of Academe"

1 The writer, / , had some difficulty in getting into bed.
2/ **an old man with a white mustache**

SHERWOOD ANDERSON, *Winesburg, Ohio*

1 He was accompanied by Shmuel Smetena,
2 **an unofficial lawyer,**
2 **a crony of both the thieves and the police.**

ISAAC BASHEVIS SINGER, "The Betrayer of Israel"

The only constraint here is that the appositive be "placed nearby"—before or after—the noun it modifies. Because of this relative flexibility of position, appositives can create movement within your writing as each modifier directs the reader's attention ahead or back to the word modified.

WHAT APPOSITIVES ADD TO YOUR WRITING

Appositives create a number of valuable effects. Foremost, they add **details** that define or comment on nouns elsewhere in the sentence. Such details bring the topic into sharp focus:

1 Joan Baez grew up in the more evangelistic thickets of the middle class,
  2 **the daughter of a Quaker physics teacher,**
  2 **the granddaughter of two Protestant ministers,**
    3 **an English-Scottish Episcopalian on her mother's side,**
    3 **a Mexican Methodist on her father's.**

JOAN DIDION, "Where the Kissing Never Stops"

Having introduced Joan Baez by name, Didion brings her subject into focus by adding four appositives that add details about family background. Indeed, as a good reporter, Didion refuses to stop at level 2. She presses on to level 3 by adding appositives that tell us exactly what *kinds* of Protestant ministers Baez has in her ancestry. The richly textured sentence thus brings the writer's topic, Joan Baez, into sharp focus.

Notice that the appositives in the sentence about Joan Baez, as in many of the sentences we have examined, themselves contain modifying phrases. Baez is not merely *the daughter.* She is *the daughter* **of a Quaker physics teacher.** Writers regularly expand an appositive noun phrase like *the daughter* by adding a prepositional phrase like **of a Quaker physics teacher** to it. In this respect, the preposition **with** is particularly useful, since it can be used to reduce a full clause to a short modifying phrase. To grasp this, try combining these three sentences:

The principal gave one of his laughs.
The principal was a small ventricose man.
The principal had a polished, rosy bald head.

Write your version here:

____

____

____

Here's how Kingsley Amis combined the details in his novel *Lucky Jim:*

The principal, *a small ventricose man* **with** *a polished, rosy bald head,* gave one of his laughs.

Amis combined the second and third sentences into a single appositive: a noun phrase modified by a prepositional phrase using **with.** This tactic at once saved words and added details—a neat accomplishment.

In addition to adding details that characterize a particular subject, appositives can specify the **parts of a whole.** For instance, in *Dispatches,* his account of the Vietnam war, Michael Herr first sums up the American strategy during late 1967:

That fall, all that the Mission talked about was control.

This is the whole story, but what of the parts? To the base clause Herr adds seven appositives that specify just what *kinds* of control the Mission discussed:

1 That fall, all that the Mission talked about was control:
2 **arms control,**
2 **information control,**
2 **resources control,**
2 **psycho-political control,**
2 **population control,**
2 **control of the almost supernatural inflation,**
2 **control of terrain through the Strategy of the Periphery.**

Finally, a series of appositives—or even a single appositive that underscores a key detail—can create **emphasis** in your writing. Michael Herr emphasized how much the American mission in Vietnam was concerned with *control* by repeating the noun in seven appositive phrases. But even a single repetition of a key word or phrase can create emphasis:

He made me see things—things.

JOSEPH CONRAD, *Heart of Darkness*

By repeating the single, enigmatic noun *things,* Joseph Conrad creates an air of mystery. We do not know what the *things* were, but we know that they were very important, thanks to the emphatic appositive.

PUNCTUATING APPOSITIVES

The appositive in Conrad's sentence is set off from the base by a dash. In most of the examples we have considered, the appositives have been set off by commas. In fact, when you create a free appositive, you have four options for punctuating it: the comma, the colon, the dash, and parentheses. Each of these options creates a different effect. Here's the full range:

I heard a trout jump in the river, a late jumper.

RICHARD BRAUTIGAN, *Trout Fishing in America*

> The day begins gloriously**:** a bright sky, a fresh wind, the houses newly washed.
>
> HENRY MILLER, *Tropic of Cancer*

> The car they drove was hers**—**a white Thunderbird convertible.
>
> ANN BEATTIE, "A Vintage Thunderbird"

> He told us what they [sea otters] weigh when they are born **(**three to five pounds**)** and when they grow up **(**a maximum of ninety-nine pounds for males, seventy-two for females**)**.
>
> EMILY HAHN, "Eleventh Hour"

The comma is, of course, the normal punctuation for setting off free modifiers. It's hardly an interruption at all. The colon serves a special function: it indicates a movement from the general to the particular or from the whole to the parts. The dash is dramatic. In the sentences by Conrad and Beattie, the dash accentuates a key detail. On the other hand, parentheses *de*-emphasize what they enclose. For this reason, reserve parentheses for truly parenthetical material (numbers, dates, technical terms) and—still more sparingly—for stage whispers (got it?). Last of all, square brackets allow you to insert your own comments, corrections, or clarifications into someone else's sentence, as in the above sentence by Emily Hahn.

ADJECTIVE PHRASES

Adjectives are descriptive words that modify nouns: a *blue* overcoat, a *delicious* meal. An ***adjective phrase*** is a modifier in which the key word is an adjective: a ***better* than average** program. In each of these examples, the adjective or adjective phrase precedes the noun it modifies. But adjectives and adjective phrases can occur in other positions as well. For example, they can be connected to the nouns they modify by linking verbs like *to be, to taste,* and *to seem:* The overcoat was **blue;** The meal tasted **delicious;** The program seemed **better than average.** In addition, like appositives, adjective phrases can occur as free modifiers "placed nearby" the nouns they modify: The *meal,* **hot and delicious,** steamed on the table; **Better than average,** the *program* held my attention all evening.

Creating Adjective Phrases

Since the formation of adjective phrases resembles the formation of appositives, we shall consider the two in relation to each other. Furthermore, writers regularly use appositives and adjective phrases together, since both constructions modify nouns. Where appositives add **details,** adjective phrases add **qualities.**

To grasp the similarities and differences between appositives and adjective phrases, try combining these two sentences:

> He was a memorable man.
> He was friendly and funny.

Write your version here:

___

___

___

If you use the second sentence as the base, you can create an appositive:

> He was friendly and funny, **a memorable man.**

This is a perfectly valid combination, one in which the noun phrase *a memorable man* stands in apposition to the sentence subject, *he.* But if you use the first sentence in the pair as the base, you can create an adjective phrase:

> He was a memorable man, **friendly and funny.**

This is how the master stylist E. B. White combined the sentences in order to characterize his college English teacher, Will Strunk. White reduced the second sentence to an adjective phrase, *friendly and funny,* which modifies the word *man.* Although the two versions are formed in similar ways, each contains a different kind of modifier.

Effective writing includes both **details** and **qualities.** Therefore, professional writers often employ appositives and adjective phrases in the same sentence in order to create a rich texture. For instance, how might you combine these four sentences into a comprehensive portrait of Franz?

> Franz met him at the tram stop.
> Franz was resident pathologist at the clinic.
> Franz was a Vaudois by birth.
> Franz was a few years older than Dick.

Write your version here:

___

___

___

The problem includes not only details (*pathologist, Vaudois*) but also a quality (*older*) of Franz. When F. Scott Fitzgerald pulled the ideas together in his novel *Tender Is the Night,* he wrote the combination this way:

1 Franz, / , met him at the tram stop.
2/ **resident *pathologist* at the clinic,**
2/ **a *Vaudois* by birth,**
2/ **a few years *older* than Dick**

The first two free modifiers at level 2 are noun phrases—appositives. Each adds a detail about Franz. The third free modifier also modifies Franz, but it is an adjective phrase in which the key word is *older.* This modifier adds a quality of Franz to the portrait. Since the two kinds of modifiers are formed in similar ways, we hardly distinguish between them when we combine sentences.

Initial, Medial, and Final Adjective Phrases

Again like appositives, adjective phrases can occur before, within, or after the base clause:

2 **Tubercularly thin,**
1 he sleeps on peacefully.

LOREN EISELEY, "The Brown Wasps"

1 The wind, / , intermittently swayed the bushes and trees.
2/ **mindless of direction**

JERZY KOSINSKI, *Being There*

1 The room smells of turpentine—
2 **heavy,**
2 **rich,**
2 **mysterious,**
2 **heady.**

JAMES STEVENSON, "Painting: A Journal"

The last example here illustrates that adjective phrases, like appositives, may be punctuated in several ways. While the comma is the usual choice, the dash remains an option as well, as does the colon and the double parenthesis. Again, each option creates a slightly different effect.

PAIRED ADJECTIVES

Writers often create single adjective-phrase modifiers like *mindless of direction* or adjective series like *heavy, rich, mysterious, heady.* Nevertheless, there seems to be a natural tendency to arrange adjectives in pairs:

2 **Shriveled and humped,**
1 she could fit into the palm of your hand.

NIKOS KAZANTZAKIS, *A Report to Greco*

1 Clay, / , began to be seen in the hole.
2/ **brown and damp**

JAMES JOYCE, *Ulysses*

1 She was about thirty-five years old,
2 **dissipated and gentle.**

JOHN CHEEVER, "The Sutton Place Story"

As these sentences illustrate, paired adjectives can occur in the initial, medial, or final position. The only restriction on them is the same as on any other adjective phrase or appositive: they must be "placed nearby" the nouns they modify. Thus, the medial modifier in Joyce's sentence could also be shifted into initial position:

Brown and damp, clay began to be seen in the hole.

But the modifier could not be moved to final position without creating confusion:

Clay began to be seen in the hole, **brown and damp.**

Here the adjectives **brown and damp** appear to modify not *clay* but *hole*—the noun nearest the modifying phrase. Since a **misplaced modifier** like this distorts your meaning, be sure appositives and adjective phrases are correctly placed nearby the words you intend them to modify.

PULLING IT ALL TOGETHER

Appositives and adjective phrases add details and qualities that modify nouns. Together, the two structures can create a rich *texture* in a sentence. That is, the modifiers add specifics that make the writing compelling and realistic. Imagine, for instance, that you are writing about the fabled desert city of Las Vegas. You begin with a general statement:

Las Vegas is the most extreme and allegorical of American settlements.

To explain this point, you then go over the same ground at a lower level of generality. First, you specify the *qualities* of the city:

Las Vegas is bizarre and beautiful in its venality and its devotion to immediate gratification.

Next, you add a *detail* that tells just what kind of place the Strip is:

Las Vegas is a place the tone of which is set by mobsters and call girls and ladies' room attendants with amyl nitrite poppers in their uniform pockets.

Each of these two observations presents a part of the whole sketched in the first general statement. In combination, the three sentences portray a city at once gorgeous and garish, sexy and seedy, fascinating and frightening:

> Las Vegas is the most extreme and allegorical of American settlements, **bizarre and beautiful** *in its venality and its devotion to immediate gratification,* **a place** *the tone of which is set by mobsters and call girls and ladies' room attendants with amyl nitrite poppers in their uniform pockets.*

This is the way Joan Didion combined the sentences in her essay "Marrying Absurd." This chapter opened with a sentence in which Didion created three appositives. In this closing example, she has created first an adjective phrase and then an appositive, each of which adds more information about Las Vegas: The modifiers work together to give Didion's analysis of the city a rich texture. Appositives and adjective phrases can do the same thing for your own writing.

Appositives and Adjective Phrases: Combinations

Combine each set of sentences below into one sentence that contains at least one appositive or adjective phrase. You can compare your combinations with professional or student writers' sentences in the Appendix.

SAMPLE EXERCISE

E. B. White is the youngest of six children.
E. B. White was born in Mt. Vernon, New York, on July 11, 1899.

PROFESSIONAL WRITER'S VERSION

The youngest of six children, E. B. White was born in Mt. Vernon, New York, on July 11, 1899.

WILLIAM SMART, *Eight Essayists*

1. Today's student is quick to learn through sight and sound.
   Today's student often experiences difficulty in reading and writing.

2. The circadian rhythm is known to go back at least to animals as humble as mollusks.
   The circadian rhythm is the daily cycling of physiological functions.

3. The president of the Boat Club was the coach.
   Tom Smith was the president of the Boat Club.

4. He was pig-eyed.
He was jowly.
He seemed to be enjoying himself.

5. This is what freedom means.
One is able to be a human being first.

6. They walked along.
They were two continents of experience and feeling.
They were unable to communicate.

7. Two kinds of person are consoling in a dangerous time.
Those who are completely courageous are consoling.
Those who are more frightened than you are are consoling.

8. He was a young man.
He was lean.
He was fair.
He was morose.
He had lanky hair.
He had a shuffling gait.

9. James Caan is almost the definition of a "gritty" actor.
He has rough skin.
He has jabbing movements.
He has nervous tics.
He has nervous sweat.

10. The work of Purcell's most widely known today is his opera.
This opera is *Dido and Aeneas.*
Dido and Aeneas has libretto by Nahum Tate.

11. There was a bathhouse in the town.
The bathhouse was an aluminum lean-to.
The lean-to had a hot spring piped into a shallow concrete pool.
And because of the hot baths the town attracted old people.
The old people were believers in cures and the restorative power of desolation.
The old people were eighty- and ninety-year-old couples.
The couples moved around the desert in campers.

12. My friend has told me all about Scandinavians and fish.
My friend is Knud Swenson.
Knud Swenson is the pianist.

13. This is a snail shell.
It is round.
It is full.
It is glossy.
A horse chestnut is round, full, and glossy.

14. Bridget went to answer the bell.
    Bridget was the waitress.
    Bridget was an awkward girl.
    Her mouth dropped wide open in crises.

15. Every year sees megalopolis relentlessly on its way to ecumenopolis.
    Megalopolis is the urban smear.
    The urban smear is staining the entire American northeast.
    The urban smear is blurring city boundaries everywhere.
    Ecumenopolis is a totally urbanized world.
    This is according to Constantinos Doxiadis.
    Constantinos Doxiadis is a planner.

Khrushchev

Combine the sentences below into a paragraph that contains at least one appositive. You can compare your paragraph with a professional or student writer's version in the Appendix.

1. Russia weighs its words.

2. A new edition of a dictionary was published.
3. The dictionary was the most widely used in Russia.
4. This was during Khrushchev's era.
5. It contained a single change from the previous edition.
6. The change was significant.

7. "Khrushch" is a kind of beetle.
8. "Khrushch" was no longer described as "deleterious to agriculture."

Writing Suggestion 1: "What's in a name?" complained Shakespeare's Juliet. Nevertheless, every so often we meet someone whose name seems particularly fitting. Such was the case with beetle-browed Nikita Khrushchev, Russia's premier from 1958 to 1964. Write a paragraph explaining how the name of someone you know reflects (or distorts) the actual person.

Writing Suggestion 2: All of us are familiar with desk dictionaries like the one mentioned in the exercise, but students should know about specialized dictionaries as well. At your school library, examine one of the dictionaries listed below. Write a brief report on the purpose, organization, and scope of the work, explaining its uses and limitations.

UNABRIDGED DICTIONARIES

Webster's Third New International Dictionary (1961)
Funk & Wagnalls New "Standard" Dictionary of the English Language (1964)

DICTIONARIES OF FOREIGN AND DIFFICULT TERMS

Byrne, Josefa Heifetz. *Mrs. Byrne's Dictionary of Unusual, Obscure, and Preposterous Words* (1974)

Mawson, C. O. Sylvester, and Charles Berlitz. *Dictionary of Foreign Terms* (2nd ed., 1975)

DICTIONARIES OF SYNONYMS, ANTONYMS, ACRONYMS, AND ABBREVIATIONS

Crowley, Ellen T. *New Acronyms, Initialisms, and Abbreviations:* 1976 Supplement to *Acronyms, Initialisms, and Abbreviations Dictionary* (5th ed.)

Chapman, Robert L. *Roget's International Thesaurus* (4th ed., 1977)

DICTIONARIES OF SLANG, IDIOMS, AND CLICHÉS

Makkai, Adam. *A Dictionary of American Idioms* (rev. ed., 1975)

Wentworth, Harold, and Stuart B. Flexner. *Dictionary of American Slang* (2nd ed., 1975)

ETYMOLOGICAL DICTIONARIES

Onions, C. T. *The Oxford Dictionary of English Etymology* (1966)

Morris Dictionary of Word and Phrase Origins (1977)

DICTIONARIES OF USAGE

Follett, Wilson. *Modern American Usage* (1969)

Morris, William, and Mary Morris. *Harper Dictionary of Contemporary American Usage* (1975)

Sakyamuni Descending from the Mountain

Combine the sentences below into a paragraph that contains at least one appositive or adjective phrase. You can compare your paragraph with a professional or student writer's version in the Appendix.

1. Sakyamuni is erect.
2. He is ecstatic.
3. He is half-dead.
4. His cloak is a wing.
5. The wing is drooping.

6. He did not have the wind's help.
7. He would never reach the valley below.

8. He is puppetlike.
9. He is skin and bone.

10. The bump on his head seems to exert a pull.
11. The bump is bald.
12. The pull is spiritual.

13. The pull keeps him upright in the push of the wind.
14. The push is helpful.

15. Where did he get that bump?

16. On the mountaintop.

17. It is itself a mountain of enlightenment.
18. The mountain is miniature.
19. The enlightenment is to come.

20. No head can contain in its casing the bliss.
21. No head can bury in its casing the bliss.
22. The head is human.
23. The casing is bony.
24. The bliss is of what Sakyamuni knows already.

Writing Suggestion 1: "Sakyamuni" is the Japanese name for the Buddha, the spiritual teacher who lived in ancient India and founded what we now know as Buddhism. "Sakyamuni Descending from the Mountain" is the title of a fourteenth-century scroll-painting of the Buddha returning from meditation in the wilderness, shortly before he became spiritually enlightened. Write a paragraph describing one of your favorite paintings or photographs in close detail.

Writing Suggestion 2: Use a general encyclopedia and the specialized *Encyclopedia of Philosophy* to learn the basic articles of the Buddhist faith. Write an essay in which you discuss what Westerners might learn from this Eastern philosophy.

Appositives and Adjective Phrases: Creations

Create at least one appositive or adjective phrase in each of the sentences below. While most of the exercises ask you to create specific kinds of modifiers, some leave you free to create any kind of appositive or adjective phrase that seems appropriate. You can compare your creations with professional or student writers' sentences in the Appendix.

SAMPLE EXERCISES

A. 1 Two friends, / , had stalls side by side in the market.

2/ ______________________________ [signaled format]
(free modifier of **friends**)

B. The barrage stretches on and on across the plain. [open format]

PROFESSIONAL WRITERS' VERSIONS

A. 1 Two friends, / , had stalls side by side in the market.

2/ **Farid and Mansour**

MOHAMMED MRABET, "Two Friends and the Rain"

B. The barrage stretches on and on across the plain, **distant, impenetrable.**

WILLIAM FAULKNER, "Crevasse"

1. 1 She crossed the wide street—

 2 ______________________ in ______________________ .
 (free modifier of **she**)

2. The pigeons went about picking up seeds.

3. 1 Is man what he seems to the astronomer,

 2 ____ ?
 (free modifier of **man**)

4. 1 A lovely hand, / , tentatively rose.

 2/ ____
 (free modifier of **hand**)

5. The tree was tremendous.

6. 1 Three young hoodlums from Brooklyn drifted in,

 2 ____ ,
 (free modifier of **hoodlums**)

 2 ____ ,
 (free modifier of **hoodlums**)

 2 ____ .
 (free modifier of **hoodlums**)

7. It is a difficult lesson to learn today.

8. 1 I walked over to the TV set and turned it on to a dead channel—

 2 ____ ,
 (free modifier of **dead channel**)

 3 ____ ,
 (free modifier of level 2)

 3 ____ .
 (free modifier of level 2)

9. 1 Two girls, / , came and sat on my right.

2/ ______________________ with ______________________ ,
(free modifier of **girls**)

2/ ______________________ with ______________________ ,
(free modifier of **girls**)

3/ like ______________________________________
(prepositional phrase)

10. Too many moralists begin with a dislike of reality.

Polynesia

Combine the sentences below into a paragraph that includes both appositives and adjective phrases. You can compare your paragraph with a professional or student writer's version in the Appendix.

1. There is one fragment of the Pacific.
2. The American believes he knows the fragment well.
3. The fragment is Polynesia.

4. He may not be quite certain of Sumatra.
5. He may not be quite certain of Mindanao.
6. He may not be quite certain about the difference between a *prau* and a gin pahit.
7. But Polynesia he knows.

8. This is the South Seas.
9. This is Paradise.
10. This is the Sunny Isles.

11. It is a place of soft winds.
12. It is a place of surfboards.
13. It is a place of outriggers.
14. It is a place of the pink bulk of the Royal Hawaiian Hotel.
15. It is a place of the scent of flowers.

16. It is a place.
17. In the place beachcombers watch their *vahines.**
18. Their *vahines* swim in the waves.
19. The beachcombers are defiantly drunk.
20. But the beachcombers are still white.
21. They are still superior.

22. In some way a vision of Polynesia creeps into the knowledge of all Americans.
23. The way is haunting.

* *vahines:* Polynesian women

24. The way is subtle.
25. It is a flawless vision.
26. It is a jeweled vision.

27. The defects of America are magically eliminated.
28. They are eliminated in Polynesia.

29. The place is warm.
30. The place is sunny.

31. It glows.

Writing Suggestion 1: Many people have long envisioned Polynesia—Hawaii, Samoa, Tahiti, and so forth—as a tropical paradise. Whether or not you have actually visited these islands, you likely have a mental image of them. Write an essay describing that vision.

Writing Suggestion 2: Travel not only enlarges one's world; it also puts one's home in a new perspective. If you have ever traveled to a new city, region, or country, write an essay explaining how your journey changed your view of your home.

Appositives and Adjective Phrases: Sentence Acrobatics

Combine each set of sentences below into one or more "acrobatic" sentences. See if you can create at least one appositive or adjective phrase as you do each exercise, but feel free to try out other constructions as well. Naturally, each problem invites more than one "correct" answer. Therefore, you must create original sentences that strike *you* as both correct and stylish.

You may enjoy comparing your combinations with the professional or student writers' versions in the Appendix. Look for both similarities and differences, but try to decide whose version is the more stylish—it may well be your own.

SAMPLE EXERCISE

Thoreau is unique among writers.
Those find him uncomfortable to live with.
Those admire him.
He is a regular hairshirt of a man.

STUDENT AND PROFESSIONAL WRITERS' VERSIONS

A regular hairshirt of a man, Thoreau is unique among writers. Even those who admire him find him uncomfortable to live with.

STUDENT WRITER

Thoreau is unique among writers in that those who admire him find him uncomfortable to live with—**a regular hairshirt of a man.**

E. B. WHITE, "A Slight Sound at Evening"

1. She looked back at him.
   She was erect.
   Her face was like a strained flag.

2. Only one anadromous fish still persists in any quantity.
   Anadromous means "running upward" in Greek.
   The fish is the steelhead.
   The steelhead is a subspecies of rainbow trout.

3. We were patient.
   We were cold.
   We were callous.
   Our hands were wrapped in socks.
   We waited to snowball the cats.

4. This is to my mind.
   Faith is a stiffening process.
   It is a sort of starch.
   The starch is mental.
   The starch ought to be applied as sparingly as possible.

5. The nights were beautiful.
   They were heavy.
   They were starry.
   They were those summer nights.
   On those summer nights you feel surrounded.
   All the warmth and fervor of life surround you.
   The fervor is primitive.

6. There was a speck above the island.
   The speck was a figure.
   The figure was dropping beneath a parachute.
   The dropping was swift.
   The figure hung.
   It had dangling limbs.

7. Elder Robert J. Theobold is twenty-eight years old.
   He was pastor of what was the Friendly Bible Apostolic Church.
   This was until October 12, 1968.
   The church was in Port Hueneme, California.
   He was born and bred in San Jose.
   He is a native Californian.
   His memory stream could encompass only the boom years.

8. The song is on the Rolling Stones' album.
The album is *Let It Bleed.*
The song is "You Can't Always Get What You Want."
The song features Mick Jagger.
Mick Jagger is the lead singer.
He is backed by the London Philharmonic Choir.

9. Patients have been described.
The patients have had prefrontal lobotomies.
They have been described as losing a "continuing sense of self."
This sense of self is the feeling.
I feel I am a particular individual.
I have some control over my life and circumstances.
This sense of self is the "me-ness" of me.
It is the uniqueness of the individual.

10. This was when Yochna turned twelve.
She was besieged.
Marriage brokers besieged her.
They offered matches.
But her father brought her a groom from Trisk.
Her father was Reb Piniele.
The groom was a yeshiva student.
He was an orphan.
He studied seventeen hours a day.

Write On!

Combine the sentences below into a paragraph that contains several appositives. You can compare your paragraph with a professional or student writer's version in the Appendix.

1. "The only reason for going to the bathroom is to read the graffiti."
2. This is according to one UCLA woman.

3. Her confession refers to the many sayings.
4. The reference is joking.
5. The sayings are amusing.
6. They are hastily scrawled.
7. They are on the school's restroom walls.

8. Yet her fascination also suggests something more.
9. Her fascination is with graffiti.
10. It is more than a taste for light reading.

11. The dictionary defines graffito as "an inscription, slogan, drawing, etc., crudely scratched or scribbled on a wall or other public surface."

12. This definition is simple.
13. Graffito is the singular form of the word.
14. The word is derived from *graffio.*
15. *Graffio* is Italian.
16. *Graffio* means "a scratch."

17. But a definition of graffiti is possible.
18. The definition is more penetrating.
19. The definition helps.
20. It explains the young woman's compulsion.

21. Graffiti are a form of "literature."
22. The form is ubiquitous.
23. The literature is popular.
24. Graffiti provide the reader with insights.
25. Graffiti provide the reader with peepholes.
26. The insights are brief.
27. The peepholes are tiny.
28. They are into the minds of individuals.
29. The individuals write not only for themselves.
30. They write for all of us.

31. Their graffiti are scrawled on the walls.
32. Their graffiti are scrawled on the stalls.
33. Their graffiti reveal four levels of adjustment.
34. The adjustment is social.
35. One level is hostility.
36. One level is anguish.
37. One level is cynicism.
38. One level is humor.

Writing Suggestion 1: Collect a dozen or more examples of local graffiti and try to sort them into the four categories proposed in the preceding exercise: hostility, anguish, cynicism, and humor. Using your examples, write a short essay analyzing what these scrawled messages tell us about their authors—and about ourselves.

Writing Suggestion 2: Restroom walls are not the only "public surfaces" on which people express their thoughts. Bumper stickers, buttons, and T-shirts offer ready-made graffiti in the form of trademarks and slogans. Collect examples of these commercial graffiti, classify them into categories, and write an essay presenting the results of your investigations.

The review exercises in this chapter will help you practice using **prepositional phrases, verbal phrases, appositives,** and **adjective phrases** along with other combinations.

Rock of Ages

Combine the sentences below into a paragraph that contains both bound and free modifiers. You can compare your paragraph with a professional or student writer's version in the Appendix.

1. Alcatraz Island is covered with flowers now.
2. It is covered with orange and yellow nasturtiums.
3. It is covered with geraniums.
4. It is covered with sweet grass.
5. It is covered with blue iris.
6. It is covered with black-eyed Susans.

7. Candytuft springs up.
8. It springs up through the concrete.
9. The concrete is cracked.
10. The concrete is in the exercise yard.

11. Ice plant carpets the catwalks.
12. The catwalks are rusting.

13. "WARNING! KEEP OFF! U.S. PROPERTY," the sign still reads.
14. The sign is big.
15. The sign is yellow.
16. The sign is visible for perhaps a quarter of a mile.

17. But since March 21, 1963, the warning has been only *pro forma.*
18. March 21, 1963, was the day they took the last thirty or so men off the island.
19. They sent them to prisons.
20. The prisons were less expensive to maintain.
21. The gun turrets are empty.
22. The cell blocks are abandoned.

23. It is not an unpleasant place to be.
24. The place is out there on Alcatraz.
25. Alcatraz has only the flowers.
26. Alcatraz has only the wind.
27. Alcatraz has only a bell buoy.
28. The bell buoy moans.
29. Alcatraz has only the tide.
30. The tide surges through the Golden Gate.

31. You like a place like that.
32. You have to want a moat.

Writing Suggestion 1: Abandoned places like Alcatraz can put any writer in a meditative mood. Write a paragraph discussing an abandoned place you know well. Try to recapture something of its past even as you describe its present state.

Writing Suggestion 2: Although Alcatraz Island, long known to convicts as "The Rock," is no longer used as a penitentiary, the issue of prison reform remains a much-discussed topic. Go to the library and use the *Readers' Guide to Periodical Literature* to locate a few recent articles on prison reform. After reading them, write an essay in which you discuss the principal issues in the prison-reform debate. What, if anything, should we do about our often antiquated and overcrowded prisons?

The Kool-Aid Wino

Combine the sentences below into a paragraph that contains both bound and free modifiers. You can compare your paragraph with a student or professional writer's version in the Appendix.

1. I was a child.
2. I had a friend.
3. He became a Kool-Aid wino.
4. This was as a result of a rupture.

5. He was a member of a family.
6. The family was very large.
7. The family was poor.
8. The family was German.

9. All the older children in the family had to work.
10. This was during the summer.
11. They worked in the fields.
12. They picked beans.
13. They were paid two-and-one-half cents a pound.
14. They wanted to keep the family going.

15. Everyone worked except my friend.
16. He couldn't.
17. He was ruptured.

18. There was no money for an operation.
19. There wasn't even enough money to buy him a truss.

20. He stayed home.
21. He became a Kool-Aid wino.

Writing Suggestion 1: This exercise concerns, to say the least, an exceptional child. Write a paragraph describing an exceptional child you have known.

Writing Suggestion 2: Although the Kool-Aid wino's drinking sounds relatively harmless, in recent years teen-age alcoholism has become a serious problem. Using both library research and personal interviews, write an essay analyzing the causes and effects of teen-age alcoholism today.

Review of Chapters 7, 8, 9: Sentence Acrobatics

Combine each set of sentences below into one or more "acrobatic" sentences. See if you can create prepositional phrases, verbal phrases, appositives, and adjective phrases as you do the exercises, but feel free to try out other constructions as well. Naturally, each problem invites more than one "correct" answer. Therefore, you must create original sentences that strike *you* as both correct and stylish.

You may enjoy comparing your combinations with the professional or student writers' versions in the Appendix. Look for both similarities and differences, but try to decide whose version is the more stylish—it may well be your own.

SAMPLE EXERCISE

Mrs. James Monroe took a crack at regal status.
She received guests on a dais.
She had something in her tousled hair.
It was suspiciously like a coronet.

STUDENT AND PROFESSIONAL WRITERS' VERSIONS

Taking *a crack* **at** *regal status,* Mrs. James Monroe received guests **on** *a dais* and had something **in** *her tousled hair*—**something** *suspiciously* **like** *a coronet.*

STUDENT WRITER

Mrs. James Monroe took a crack **at** *regal status,* **receiving** *guests* **on** *a dais* **with** *something suspiciously* **like** *a coronet* **in** *her tousled hair.*

GORE VIDAL, "President and Mrs. U. S. Grant"

1. The Thames had submerged the lower part of the landing stair.
   The Thames was pitted with rain.
   The Thames was high and sullen under a leaden sky.

2. One wants to help children.
   The children are mentally retarded.
   The children are physically handicapped.
   One must have patience.
   One must have sympathy.
   One must have maturity.

3. He was only a little boy.
   He was ten years old.
   He had hair like dusty yellow grass.
   He had shy polite gray eyes.
   He had a mouth.
   The mouth worked when he thought.

4. We continue to share the most tangled attitudes.
   We continue to share the most evasive attitudes.
   We share the attitudes with our remotest ancestors.
   The attitudes are about death.
   We share the attitudes despite the great distance we have come.
   We understand some of the profound aspects of biology.

5. The friars were an element of daily life.
   They were scorned.
   They were venerated.
   They were feared.
   They might have the key to salvation.
   This would be after all.

6. The sociable country postman had just given him a small parcel.
   The postman was passing through the garden.
   He took the parcel out with him.
   He left the hotel to the right.
   He crept to a bench.
   He had already haunted the bench.
   It was a safe recess in the cliff.

7. My father was a small man.
   He was frail.
   He was wearing a long robe.
   He had a velvet skullcap.
   The cap was above his high forehead.
   His eyes were blue.
   His beard was red.
   He put away pen and paper on his lectern.
   He put them away reluctantly.

8. Then he looked down at the log.
   He was standing beside Sam in the gloom of the afternoon.
   The afternoon was dying.
   The log was rotted.
   The log was overturned.
   It was gutted and scored with claw marks.
   And he looked down at the print.
   The print was in the wet earth beside the log.
   The print was of the enormous foot.
   The foot was warped.
   The foot had two toes.

9. The stereotype is lecherous.
   It is truculent.
   It is irrational.
   It is cruel.
   It is conniving.
   It is excitable.
   It dreams about lascivious heavens.
   It enforces oppressive legal codes.
   The enforcement is hypocritical.
   The stereotype of the Moslem is only partially softened.
   A Kahlil Gibran softens it.
   He puts it into sentimental doggerel.
   A Rudolph Valentino softens it.
   He does it with zest and good humor.

10. Their voices rang out.
    Then their voices died away.
    They left the street hot.
    They left the street empty.
    They left the street silent.
    It was silent except for the sound of some country music.
    The sound was thin.
    The music drifted along.
    It drifted like an old dog's leash.
    The leash trailed in the dust.

Home-Coming

Combine the sentences below into a paragraph that contains both bound and free modifiers. You can compare your paragraph with a professional or student writer's version in the Appendix.

1. It was on the day before Thanksgiving.
2. It was toward the end of the afternoon.
3. I had motored all day.
4. I arrived home.
5. I lit a fire.
6. The fire was in the living room.

7. The logs took hold briskly.
8. The logs were birch.

9. It was about three minutes later.
10. The chimney itself caught fire.
11. The chimney was not to be outdone.

12. I became aware of this development rather slowly.

13. I was rocking contentedly in my chair.
14. I was enjoying the stupor.
15. The stupor follows a day on the road.
16. I thought I heard the roar of a chimney swift.
17. The roar is dull.
18. The roar is fluttering.
19. It is a sound we are thoroughly accustomed to.
20. We live in this house.

21. Then I realized something.
22. There would be no bird in residence at this season of the year.
23. The bird resides in my chimney.

24. A glance up the flue made it perfectly plain.
25. The place was at last afire.
26. This was after twenty-two years of my tenure.

Writing Suggestion 1: Have you ever arrived home, after a long day, and discovered an unwelcome surprise anything like the one described in the exercise? If so, write a paragraph telling the tale of your own home-coming.

Writing Suggestion 2: The American novelist Thomas Wolfe wrote a book entitled *You Can't Go Home Again.* Have you ever returned to what was once your home—a house, a school, a town, a family—only to find things changed so drastically as to seem unfamiliar? If so, write an essay analyzing your experience. How had "home" changed during your absence? How had you changed? Can you ever go home again?

Beer Can

Combine the sentences below into a paragraph that contains both bound and free modifiers. You can compare your paragraph with a professional or student writer's version in the Appendix.

1. This seems to be an era of inventions and improvements.
2. The inventions are gratuitous.
3. The improvements are negative.

4. Consider the beer can.

5. It was beautiful.
6. It was as beautiful as the clothespin.
7. It was as inevitable as the wine bottle.
8. It was as dignified as the fire hydrant.
9. It was as reassuring as the fire hydrant.

10. It was a cylinder of metal.
11. The cylinder was tranquil.
12. The metal was resonant.
13. The resonance was delightful.
14. It could be opened in an instant.
15. It required only the application.
16. A gadget was applied.
17. The gadget was handy.
18. Every grocer dispensed the gadget.
19. The dispensing was free.

20. Who can forget the thrill of those two punctures?
21. The thrill was small.
22. The thrill was symmetrical.
23. The punctures were triangular.
24. Who can forget the *pffff*?
25. The *pffff* was dainty.
26. Who can forget the crest of suds?
27. The crest was little.
28. The suds foamed.
29. The foaming was eager.
30. The foaming was in the exultation of release.

31. Now we are given, instead, a top.
32. The top beetles with a "tab."
33. The "tab" is ugly.
34. The "tab" is shmoo-shaped.
35. The "tab" resists the fingers of the man.
36. The resistance is fierce.
37. The fingers are tugging.
38. The fingers are bleeding.

39. The man is thirsty.
40. The "tab" threatens his lips with a hole.
41. The hole is dangerous.
42. The hole is hideous.

43. We have discovered a way.
44. We want to thwart Progress.
45. Progress is usually so unthwartable.

46. *Turn the beer can upside down.*
47. *Open the bottom.*

48. The bottom is still the way.
49. The top used to be that way.

50. True, this operation gives the beer a jolt.
51. The jolt is unsettling.
52. The sight of a beer can might make people edgy.
53. The beer can is inverted.
54. The inversion is consistent.
55. This is not to say it might make people queasy.

56. The latter difficulty could be eliminated.
57. The manufacturers would design cans.
58. The cans looked the same.
59. It did not matter which end was up.
60. The cans were like playing cards.

61. What we need is Progress.
62. Progress has an escape hatch.

Writing Suggestion 1: As this exercise suggests, not all inventions and improvements are beneficial to humankind. Write an essay analyzing an invention or improvement that you consider to have been unnecessary, negative, or just plain silly.

Writing Suggestion 2: The exercise above describes a simple mechanical process—the opening of a beer can—in precise detail. Write an essay in which you describe in similar detail how another everyday process works. Before you begin your "how to" essay, write a list of at least ten commonplace operations that would make good subjects.

From every line there peers out at me the puckish face of my professor, his short hair parted neatly in the middle and combed down over his forehead, his eyes blinking incessantly behind steel-rimmed spectacles as though he had just emerged into strong light, his lips nibbling each other like nervous horses, his smile shuttling to and fro under a carefully edged mustache.

E. B. WHITE, *The Elements of Style*

E. B. White's beguiling description of his college English teacher, Will Strunk, reads with deceptive ease. The initial base clause gives White's general impression upon rereading Strunk's textbook:

> From every line there peers out at me the puckish face of my professor.

Next, to this sketch White adds four telling details, each detail evoking one of Strunk's puckish features:

> His short hair is parted neatly in the middle and combed down over his forehead.
> His eyes blink incessantly behind steel-rimmed spectacles as though he had just emerged into strong light.
> His lips nibble each other like nervous horses.
> His smile shuttles to and fro under a carefully edged mustache.

Suddenly, the portrait is complete, and Professor Strunk stands smiling before us:

1 From every line there peers out at me the puckish face of my professor,
  2 **his short hair parted neatly in the middle and combed down over his forehead,**
  2 **his eyes blinking incessantly behind steel-rimmed spectacles as though he had just emerged into strong light,**
  2 **his lips nibbling each other like nervous horses,**
  2 **his smile shuttling to and fro under a carefully edged mustache.**

But how did White manage so elegant a portrait with nothing stronger than commas to hold the parts in place?

USING ABSOLUTE PHRASES

E. B. White brought each of Professor Strunk's features into focus by means of an ***absolute phrase.*** This term is probably unfamiliar to you, although you have read hundreds of absolute phrases like White's with perfect ease. Creating absolute phrases is easy, too, once you get the hang of it. Consider, for instance, how you might combine these two sentences:

He sat for a long time.
His clothes were dripping.

Write your version here:

____

____

____

Because the first sentence describes the general situation, it makes a good base clause. You might use a subordinator to link the detail to the base:

He sat for a long time **while** his clothes were dripping.

On the other hand, if you value verbal economy, you might simply take out one word—*were*—and then make the connection:

He sat for a long time, **his clothes dripping.**

This is exactly the structure Sherwood Anderson used when he wrote the sentence in his *Memoirs.* Like E. B. White, Anderson created an absolute phrase.

The term "absolute phrase" is initially misleading, since *absolute* usually means something hard and fast, locked in place. Not so in this case. *Absolute* comes from the Latin verb *absolvere,* meaning "to loosen from," as in our English verb *absolve.* An absolute phrase, as the examples from White and Anderson show, is only loosely dependent on a base clause. In fact, the absolute phrase is practically a sentence itself. It has a noun phrase (*his clothes*) and a modifier (*dripping*). What it lacks is a complete verb, one that shows tense and number (His clothes *were dripping*). Because it lacks a complete verb, an absolute phrase cannot stand by itself as a sentence (*His clothes dripping . . .*), but it can serve as a free modifier:

1 He sat for a long time,
  2 **his clothes dripping.**

Here the absolute phrase at level 2 adds a specific detail to the general scene described in the base. Once you master several forms of the absolute, you can greatly increase the *texture* of your writing as you add more and more such details.

FORMS OF THE ABSOLUTE PHRASE

An absolute phrase consists of a noun or noun phrase plus a modifier, but it lacks a complete verb. Here is a table presenting nine possible forms of the absolute phrase, its full range:

BASE CLAUSE

She reached her left hand toward the doctor,

ABSOLUTE PHRASE

Noun Phrase	*Modifier*	
A. her fingers	**shaking.**	(present participle)
B. her fingers	**extended.**	(past participle)
C. her fingers	**pale.**	(adjective)
D. her fingers	**down.**	(adverb)
E. her fingers	**in a fist.**	(prepositional phrase)
F. her fingers	**like claws.**	(comparison using **like**)
G. her fingers	**to be examined.**	(infinitive)
H. her fingers	**a tangle.**	(noun phrase)
I. her fingers	**those of a pianist.**	(pronoun phrase)

What's missing from each of these pairs is, of course, the **to be** verb *were* that would turn the phrase into a full sentence. To create absolute phrases from complete sentences, writers either change a sentence verb like *runs* to a verbal like *running* or *to run,* or drop out a **to be** verb (*is, are; was, were*) altogether. Thus, E. B. White created an absolute phrase from the sentence "His eyes blink incessantly behind steel-rimmed spectacles" by changing the sentence verb *blink* to its verbal form *blinking.* On the other hand, Sherwood Anderson created an absolute phrase out of the sentence "His clothes were dripping" by simply dropping the **to be** verb *were.* In each case, the change resulted in both verbal economy and vivid detail.

WHAT ABSOLUTE PHRASES ADD TO YOUR WRITING

Absolute phrases can perform three valuable functions. First, they can add specific, concrete **details** to a general statement, as in the following example from a student writer:

1 The truck roared out of the garage bay,
  2 **siren wailing,**
  2 **bell clanging.**

or as in this parallel example from a professional author:

1 They bundled their books away,
  2 **pencils clacking,**
  2 **pages rustling.**

JAMES JOYCE, *Ulysses*

Second, as these examples suggest, absolutes can add **parts to a whole**—giving an idea flesh, muscle, and blood. This is true of E. B. White's description of his teacher's "puckish face," which includes Strunk's hair, eyes, lips, and smile, thanks to four well-turned absolute phrases. Here's how another professional author added a part to the whole by way of a quick absolute phrase:

1 One leg is crossed over the other,
  2 **her beautiful foot dangling.**

ANN BEATTIE, "The Lawn Party"

Finally, although it is only loosely connected to the base, an absolute phrase can suggest **cause and result**:

  2 **His birthday coinciding with the anniversary of his mother's death,**
1 I heard him saying *Kaddish* in the synagogue.

ELIE WIESEL, *Legends of Our Time*

Wiesel could, of course, have made the causal connection more explicit by using a different combination:

  2 **Because** *his birthday coincided with the anniversary of his mother's death,*
1 I heard him saying *Kaddish* in the synagogue.

Which version is better? Either one could be right in a particular context, but it was the absolute phrase that Elie Wiesel actually wrote. This combination establishes the cause-and-result relationship smoothly and economically, without any fanfare. Whether you are adding details, linking part to whole, or suggesting cause and result, absolute phrases can help you do the job gracefully.

INITIAL, MEDIAL, AND FINAL ABSOLUTE PHRASES

As we have seen again and again, much of modern writing is *cumulative,* with added modifiers following the base clause and thereby downshifting the sentence to lower levels of generality. Nevertheless, writers often create absolutes before the base or within it, in initial or medial position:

2 **Dinner done,** [initial position]
1 we fought over the check for a moment.
DONALD HALL, *Remembering Poets* ("Ezra Pound")

1 Chance, / , could not move.
2/ **his right leg raised above the bumper,**
2/ **his left one still trapped** [medial position]
JERZY KOSINSKI, *Being There*

1 The current was deepening,
2 **its flow becoming easier.** [final position]
A. ALVAREZ, *The Savage God*

Notice, too, that the absolute phrases in these sentences could be shifted to other positions as well. Because absolute phrases are only loosely connected to the base, they have great flexibility of position.

CREATING ABSOLUTE PHRASES

In the example above by A. Alvarez, the absolute phrase **its flow becoming easier** consists of a noun phrase (*its flow*) and a modifier (*becoming easier*). Here the modifier is a present-participial phrase, beginning with an **-ing** verbal. This is the most common form of the absolute phrase, but as the table on page 211 showed, it is by no means the only form. Remember that we can turn complete sentences into absolute phrases in two ways. Either we change a sentence verb (*becomes*) into a verbal (*becoming, to become*) or we drop out a **to be** verb (*is, are; was, were*). By following these rules, we can create a wide array of absolute phrases, each with a different kind of modifier.

To practice creating *all* forms of the absolute phrase, apply the rules presented above to the paired sentences below. Write out your absolute-phrase combinations below each pair:

A. Calvin was ahead.
The burning lamp swung low from his hand.

____

____

____

B. She looked up at him scornfully.
Her brown eyes were dilated under the dark eyebrows.

C. The photographer gave us the picture of me.
My hair was limp over the rail on the boat to Capri.

D. The meal was over.
We went to a café.

E. The pullets stood about in beachcombing attitudes.
Their feathers were in disorder.

F. He and Nicole looked at each other directly.
Their eyes were like blazing windows across a court of the same house.

G. Meanwhile the cardinal is in jail.
The sentence is to be pronounced tomorrow.

H. And then there is the particularly terrifying story of the careless construction worker who dangled fifty-two stories above the street until rescued.
His sole support was the Levi's belt loop through which his rope was hooked.

I. They ate in silence.
The only sound was that of the clicking knives and sweeping spoons.

J. The bull was watching the gypsy.
The bull's tongue was out.
The bull's barrel was heaving.

Now compare your combinations with the following versions. Note which kind of modifier you created in each absolute phrase you wrote:

A. 1 Calvin was ahead,
2 **the burning lamp swinging low from his hand.**

TONI MORRISON, *Song of Solomon*

Modifier: present-participial phrase (*swinging* low from his hand)

B. 1 She looked up at him scornfully,
2 **her brown eyes dilated under the dark eyebrows.**
KINGSLEY AMIS, *Lucky Jim*

Modifier: past-participial phrase (*dilated* under the dark eyebrows)

C. 1 The photographer gave us the picture of me,
2 **my hair limp over the rail on the boat to Capri.**
F. SCOTT FITZGERALD, *Tender Is the Night*

Modifier: adjective phrase (*limp* over the rail . . .)

D. 2 **The meal over,**
1 we went to a café.
HENRY MILLER, *Tropic of Cancer*

Modifier: adverb (over)

E. 1 The pullets stood about in beachcombing attitudes,
2 **their feathers in disorder.**
E. B. WHITE, "The Eye of Edna"

Modifier: prepositional phrase (*in* disorder)

F. 1 He and Nicole looked at each other directly,
2 **their eyes *like* blazing windows across a court of the same house.**
F. SCOTT FITZGERALD, *Tender Is the Night*

Modifier: comparison using *like* (*like* blazing windows . . .)

Note: Like is, of course, a preposition.

G. 1 Meanwhile the cardinal is in jail,
2 **the sentence to be pronounced tomorrow.**
LOWELL THOMAS, *CBS News,* February 7, 1949

Modifier: infinitive phrase (*to be pronounced* tomorrow)

H. 1 And then there is the particularly terrifying story of the careless construction worker who dangled fifty-two stories above the street until rescued,
2 **his sole support the Levi's belt loop through which his rope was hooked.**
CARIN C. QUINN, "The Jeaning of America"

Modifier: noun phrase (*the Levi's belt loop . . .*)

I. 1 They ate in silence,
2 **the only sound that of the clicking knives and sweeping spoons.**
ELIZABETH MADOX ROBERTS, *The Time of Man*

Modifier: pronoun phrase (*that* of clicking knives . . .)

J. 1 The bull, / , was watching the gypsy.
  2/ ***with* his tongue out,**
  2/ **his barrel heaving**

ERNEST HEMINGWAY, "The Undefeated"

Absolute phrase marked by *with* (*with* his tongue out . . .)

Note: With is indeed a preposition, but in this sentence it introduces an absolute phrase made up of a noun phrase (*his tongue*) and an adverb (*out*). To prove that the phrase is in fact an absolute, read it without the *with:* **his tongue out.** Writers often use *with* as a marker of the absolute phrase.

PULLING IT ALL TOGETHER

To exhibit the full range of the absolute, these exercises each included only one absolute phrase. In practice, one absolute often leads to another. Perhaps more than any other modifier, the absolute is a *generative* structure, an aid to discovery. As proof of this, and as a final illustration of the absolute in action, consider how two professional authors develop the figure of a man skiing. In his story "The Hartleys," John Cheever makes the very general observation, "Mr. Hartley was a good skier." His next sentence combines four details about the skier on the slope:

He was up and down the slope.
His skis were parallel.
His knees were bent.
His shoulders swung gracefully in a half circle.

Very likely, you can guess what Cheever did to combine these loosely related observations:

1 He was up and down the slope,
  2 **his skis parallel,**
  2 **his knees bent,**
  2 **his shoulders swinging gracefully in a half circle.**

Cheever created three absolute phrases in quick succession, each using a different kind of modifier: an adjective (*parallel*), a past participle (*bent*), and a present-participial phrase (*swinging gracefully in a half circle*). The result is a vivid snapshot of the skier. Cheever directs our attention upward, from the man's skis, to his knees, and finally to his shoulders.

Finally, consider how Ernest Hemingway developed similar details into a *motion* picture in his story "Cross-Country Snow." Try to combine these twenty loosely related sentences for yourself:

1. George was coming down in telemark position.
2. He was kneeling.

3. One leg was forward and bent.
4. The other was trailing.
5. His sticks were hanging.
6. They hung like some insect's legs.
7. The insect's legs were thin.
8. His sticks were kicking up puffs of snow.
9. This was as they touched the surface.
10. And finally the whole figure was coming around in a right curve.
11. The figure was kneeling.
12. The figure was trailing.
13. The right curve was beautiful.
14. The whole figure was crouching.
15. The legs were shot forward and back.
16. The body was leaning out against the swing.
17. The sticks were accenting the curve.
18. The sticks were like points of light.
19. All was in a cloud of snow.
20. The cloud was wild.

This is a long list of observations, but the author's combination is surprisingly easy to follow. Hemingway is careful to keep the details in chronological order even as he glances from one part of the moving figure to another. Notice, too, how the sentence, like the downhill run, ends climactically, in a flourish:

> George was coming down in telemark position, kneeling; **one leg forward and bent, the other trailing; his sticks hanging like some insect's thin legs,** kicking up puffs of snow as they touched the surface and finally **the whole kneeling, trailing figure coming around in a beautiful right curve,** crouching, **the legs shot forward and back, the body leaning out against the swing, the sticks accenting the curve like points of light,** all in a wild cloud of snow.

Hemingway's absolute phrases, seven of them in all, allow us to follow George all the way down the mountain—a complete story in a single sentence.

The Absolute Phrase: Combinations

Combine each set of sentences below into one sentence that contains at least one absolute phrase. You can compare your combinations with professional or student writers' sentences in the Appendix.

SAMPLE EXERCISE

Back and forth his head swiveled.
Desire was waxing.
Resolution was waning

PROFESSIONAL WRITER'S VERSION:

Back and forth his head swiveled, **desire waxing, resolution waning.**

MAX SHULMAN, "Love Is a Fallacy"

1. Luncheon was over.
   Dick returned to his villa.
2. Other firemen rushed around.
   Each was intent on his own assignment.
3. He looked good coming through the fog.
   The edges of his body were softened by mist.
   The contours were hidden in smoke.
4. The general's hands hung naturally at his sides.
   The general waited to be seated.
5. A woman in a turquoise-blue bathing suit was rising out of blue waves.
   Her mouth was in an unnaturally wide smile.
6. It is a splendid vision.
   Technology is the king.
   Jayne Mansfield is the queen.
7. He wore his full-dress uniform.
   The heavy braided white cap was pulled down rakishly over one cold gray eye.
8. His mouth was dry.
   His heart was down.
   Nick reeled in.
9. After the yard sale, they made themselves scarce.
   Floyd Senior went to his Boston apartment and his flight attendant.
   Edith went to the verge of a nervous breakdown in Cuttyhunk.
10. Her face was distorted with age.
    Her nose was a little crooked.
    Her cheekbones were prominent.
    One cheekbone was higher than the other.
    Her eyes were sunk into the sockets.
    Her forehead was large.

11. Was Spinelli trying to say that all life was represented here in his antipasto?
    The black olives were an unbearable reminder of mortality.

12. My train was to leave in ten minutes.
    I paced the platform nervously.

13. Grown people frowned at the three girls on the curbside.
    Two girls had their coats draped over their heads.
    The collars framed the eyebrows like nuns' habits.
    Black garters showed where they bit the tops of brown stockings.
    The stockings barely covered the knees.
    Angry faces were knotted like dark cauliflowers.

14. By the end of the novel, the two men are destined to be reunited over the corpse of this woman.
    Every possibility of a nontragic solution of the affair is exhausted.
    The men themselves are on the verge of destruction.

15. Clark McCormack had seemed to Everett the center of a vast social network.
    He seemed the pivot for dozens of acquaintances.
    All of them were constantly calling or dropping by the Deke house.
    One dropped by to bring Clark the stolen stencil for a mimeographed midterm.
    Another dropped by to drop off a box of Glenn Miller records in anticipation of a party.
    Others dropped by to leave their convertibles for Clark to use.
    The others were usually extraordinarily pretty girls.

Superstar

Combine the sentences below into a paragraph that contains at least one absolute phrase. You can compare your paragraph with a professional or student writer's version in the Appendix.

1. Viva leaned against the plaster wall.
2. The wall was white-washed.
3. She was in Andy Warhol's new loft studio.
4. His studio was "The Factory."
5. Her hair was cotton candy.
6. Her hair was bright blonde under the spotlights.

7. Her face and body were reminiscent of photographs.
8. Her face was fine-boned.
9. Her body was attenuated.
10. The photographs were sepia-tinted.
11. The photographs were of actresses of the early 1930s.
12. The photographs were found in an attic trunk.

13. She was wearing an Edwardian velvet coat.
14. She was wearing a white matelassé blouse.
15. She was wearing tapered black slacks.

16. "Do I look OK?"
17. She asked Paul Morrissey.
18. Paul Morrissey was Warhol's technical director.

19. "Like a star," he replied grandly.

Writing Suggestion 1: In 1968, Pop-artist Andy Warhol declared that, thanks to television, "In the future everyone will be world famous for fifteen minutes." An emaciated young woman called Viva was one of Warhol's first such "superstars"—instantaneously famous and instantly forgotten. Write a paragraph telling the story of a more recent "superstar," someone whose overnight fame was gone by early morning.

Writing Suggestion 2: Although college students purportedly spend much of their time reading and studying, many of them also devote a number of hours each week to television. Take an informal poll of your peers to determine their TV viewing patterns. Write up the results of your survey in a short essay. What kinds of television programs are students watching? Why do they watch them?

The Hunter

Combine the sentences below into a paragraph that contains several absolute phrases. You can compare your paragraph with a professional or student writer's version in the Appendix.

1. It was all over though.

2. The big cat lay.
3. He was tangled in the first willows.
4. His head and shoulder were raised.
5. His head and shoulder were against the red stems.
6. His legs were reaching.
7. His back was arched downward.
8. He was in the caricature of a leap.
9. But he was loose and motionless.

10. The eyes glared up through the willows.
11. The eyes were great.
12. The eyes were yellow.
13. The glare was baleful.
14. The willows were at the rock fort.
15. The rock fort was on top of the south wall.

16. The mouth was a little open.
17. The tongue hung down from it.
18. It hung behind the fangs.

19. The blood was still dripping from the tongue.
20. It dripped into the red stain.
21. It had already made the stain in the snow.

22. The black pelt was wet too.
23. It was wet high behind the shoulder.
24. It was wet one place, farther down, on the ribs.

25. Harold stood there.
26. Harold looked at it.
27. Harold felt compassion for the beauty.
28. The beauty was long.
29. The beauty was wicked.
30. The beauty was rendered motionless.
31. He felt even a little shame.
32. He was ashamed that it should have passed so hard.

Writing Suggestion 1: Like the hunter in the exercise above, many people have mixed feelings about killing animals for sport. Write an essay arguing for or against the pastime of recreational hunting, with details and examples supporting your argument.

Writing Suggestion 2: Because of the many successful and unsuccessful assassination attempts on public figures in recent years, many people have argued that firearms should be more strictly controlled. Use the *Readers' Guide to Periodical Literature* to find recent essays on this topic. Once you have determined the facts and the issues in the debate on gun control, write an essay that sets forth your own beliefs about the topic. Be sure to support your beliefs with factual evidence and logical arguments.

The Absolute Phrase: Creations

Create at least one absolute phrase in each sentence below. While most of the exercises ask you to create specific kinds of absolutes, some leave you free to create any kind that seems appropriate. You can compare your creations with professional or student writers' sentences in the Appendix.

SAMPLE EXERCISES

A. 1 Beyond the doctor's shoulder was the fire,

2 the fingers of flame ______________________
(present-participial phrase as modifier)

______________________________________,

3 the soft sound of their random flutter ______________
(noun phrase as

______________________________. [signaled format]
modifier)

B. The voices arose and fell about her apathy. [open format]

PROFESSIONAL WRITERS' VERSION

A. 1 Beyond the doctor's shoulder was the fire,
   2 the fingers of flame **making light prestidigitation against the sooty fireback,**
      3 the soft sound of their random flutter **the only sound.**

CONRAD AIKEN, "Silent Snow, Secret Snow"

B. The voices arose and fell about her apathy, **her mother's voice a refrain giving continual wisdom.**

ELIZABETH MADOX ROBERTS, *The Great Meadow*

1. 1 He ran, / , deep in the great sweep of men flying across the fields.

   2/ bayonet ________________________________
   (past participle as modifier)

2. 1 Mitchell sat there unblinking,

   2 the dimmed bulb on his table ________________________
   (noun phrase as modifier)

   ____ .

3. Her features were thick.

4. 1 The sewing room was large and light,

   2 the sun often ________________________________ ,
   (present-participial phrase as modifier)

      3 its rays ________________________________
      (present-participial phrase as modifier)

      ____ .

5. Against the wall there were two bunks.

6. 1 The oyster eaters, / , stood around the tables opening or eating or awaiting new supplies.

   2/ some of them ________________________________
   (prepositional phrase as modifier)

   and all of them ________________________________
   (prepositional phrase as modifier)

7. 2 With nothing else ________________________________ ,
   (infinitive as modifier)

   1 I began pacing around and around our cell.

8. 1 Temple leaned around the door,

 2 past his dim shape,

 2 her face ______________________________ .
 (adjective phrase as modifier)

9. It was a peasant's face.

10. 1 After a little while Mr. Gatz opened the door and came out,

 2 his mouth ______________________________ ,
 (adjective as modifier)

 2 his face ______________________________ ,
 (past-participial phrase as modifier)

 2 his eyes ______________________________ .
 (present-participial phrase as modifier)

Komodo Dragon

Combine the sentences below into a paragraph that contains at least one absolute phrase. You can compare your paragraph with a student or professional writer's version in the Appendix.

1. There are today a few remaining large reptiles on Earth.
2. The most striking of them is the Komodo dragon of Indonesia.
3. The Komodo is cold-blooded.
4. The Komodo is not very bright.
5. The Komodo is a predator.
6. The predator exhibits a fixity of purpose.
7. The fixity is chilling.

8. The Komodo has immense patience.
9. The Komodo will stalk a deer or boar.
10. The deer or boar is sleeping.
11. The Komodo will suddenly slash a hind leg.
12. The Komodo will hang on until the prey bleeds to death.

13. Prey is tracked by scent.
14. A dragon lumbers and sashays.
15. The dragon is hunting.
16. Its head is down.
17. Its forked tongue flicks over the ground for chemical traces.

18. The largest adults weigh about 135 kilograms.
19. 135 kilograms is 300 pounds.
20. They are three meters long.
21. Three meters is about ten feet.
22. They live perhaps to be centenarians.

23. The dragon digs trenches.
24. Its goal is to protect its eggs.
25. The trenches are from two to as much as nine meters deep.
26. Nine meters is almost thirty feet.
27. This is probably a defense against mammals.
28. The mammals eat eggs.

29. And it is probably a defense against themselves.
30. Adults are known occasionally to stalk a nest-hole.
31. They wait for the young to emerge.
32. The young are newly hatched.
33. The young provide a little delicacy for lunch.

34. The dragon hatchlings live in trees.
35. This is another clear adaptation to predators.

Writing Suggestion 1: Although the Komodo dragon is an actual creature, it has many of the characteristics of the imaginary dragons we read about in myths and fairy tales. Write a short essay discussing one or several mythical beasts—dragons, griffins, minotaurs, unicorns, and so forth. Try to explain why we find such imaginary creatures so fascinating.

Writing Suggestion 2: As humankind penetrates deeper and deeper into the wildernesses of the world, more and more living species are threatened with extinction. In America, our national bird, the bald eagle, has been added to the list of endangered species. Consult your library to learn which species, here or abroad, are in most danger of disappearing from the earth. Write an essay setting forth your findings. Should we make special efforts to prevent the extinction of certain species? Are some species expendable?

The Absolute Phrase: Sentence Acrobatics

Combine each set of sentences below into one or more "acrobatic" sentences. See if you can create at least one absolute phrase as you do each exercise, but feel free to try out other constructions as well. Naturally, each problem invites more than one "correct" answer. Therefore, you must create original sentences that strike *you* as both correct and stylish.

You may enjoy comparing your combinations with the professional or student writers' versions in the Appendix. Look for both similarities and differences, but try to decide whose version is the more stylish—it may well be your own.

SAMPLE EXERCISE

Their eyes were shining.
Their mouths were open.
They were triumphant.
They savored the right of domination.

STUDENT AND PROFESSIONAL WRITERS' VERSIONS

With their eyes shining and their mouths open, they triumphantly savored the right of domination.

STUDENT WRITER

Eyes shining, mouths open, triumphant, they savored the right of domination.

WILLIAM GOLDING, *Lord of the Flies*

1. He stops for a moment.
   He rubs his mustache.
   His pensive expression is an odd contrast to the Aloha shirt he's wearing.

2. She talked fast and fluently.
   She moved about a lot on the chair arm.
   Her legs kicked straight.
   It was as if they had been hammered on the knee.
   Her head jerked to restore invisible strands of hair.
   Her thumbs bent and straightened.

3. Evolution is still a game.
   The game is infinitely long.
   The game is tedious.
   The game is biologic.
   Only the winners stay at the table.
   The rules are beginning to look more flexible.

4. "Here in the corner you turn flat," he said.
   He demonstrated a quick spin on the heel.
   His knees were bent.
   His right shoulder was down.
   His shoulder acted as a pivot.

5. She was dressed to play golf.
   I remember thinking something.
   I thought she looked like a good illustration.
   Her chin was raised a little jauntily.
   Her hair was the color of an autumn leaf.
   Her face was the same brown tint as the fingerless glove on her knee.

6. It was at the corner of Serpukhovskaya.
   We kissed.
   Then we got into separate taxis.
   I was to spend an evening at home.
   She was to begin another chapter of her life.
   Her life was violent.
   Her life was complex.

7. Zurito sat there.
His feet were in the box-stirrups.
His great legs were in the armor.
The armor was buckskin-covered.
His legs gripped the horse.
The reins were in his left hand.
The long pic was held in his right hand.
His broad hat was well down over his eyes.
The purpose of the hat was to shade his eyes from the lights.
He was watching the distant door of the toril.

8. She had come silently.
She had come in a dream.
She had come to him after her death.
Her wasted body was within its loose brown graveclothes.
Her body gave off an odor of wax and rosewood.
Her breath was mute.
Her breath had bent upon him.
Her breath was reproachful.
Her breath was a faint odor of wetted ashes.

9. Temple was sitting on the bed.
Her legs were tucked under her.
She was erect.
Her hands were lying in her lap.
Her hat was tilted on the back of her head.
She looked quite small.
Her very attitude was an outrage to muscle and tissue of more than seventeen.
Her very attitude was more compatible with eight or ten.
Her elbows were close to her sides.
Her face was turned toward the door.
A chair was wedged against the door.

10. Her little bird body revealed itself on the scene.
It was either immobile or tense.
It was immobile in trembling mystery.
It was tense in the incredible arc.
The arc was her lift.
Her instep was stretched ahead in an arch.
The arch was never before seen.
The tiny bones of her hands were in ceaseless vibration.
Her face was radiant.
Diamonds glittered under her dark hair.
Her little waist was encased in silk.
The great tutu was balancing.
It was quickening.
And it was flashing over her legs.

Her legs were beating.
Her legs were flashing.
Her legs were quivering.
Every man and woman sat forward.
Every pulse quickened.

Eighty-Yard Run

Combine the sentences below into a paragraph that contains several absolute phrases. You can compare your paragraph with a professional or student writer's version in the Appendix.

1. The pass was high.
2. The pass was wide.
3. He jumped for it.
4. He felt it slap against his hands.
5. The slapping was flat.
6. He shook his hips.
7. He wanted to throw off the halfback.
8. The halfback was diving at him.

9. The center floated by.
10. The center's hands brushed Darling's knee.
11. The brushing was desperate.
12. Darling picked his feet up high.
13. He ran over a blocker.
14. He ran over an opposing lineman.
15. His running was delicate.
16. The blocker and lineman were in a jumble.
17. They were on the ground.
18. They were near the scrimmage line.

19. He had ten yards in the clear.
20. He picked up speed.
21. He breathed easily.
22. He felt his thigh pads.
23. The pads rose and fell against his legs.
24. He listened to the sound of cleats.
25. The cleats were behind him.
26. He pulled away from the cleats.
27. He watched the other backs.
28. They headed him off toward the sideline.
29. The whole picture was all suddenly clear in his head.
30. The men were in the picture.
31. The men closed in on him.
32. The blockers were in the picture.
33. The blockers fought for position.

34. The ground was in the picture.
35. He had to cross the ground.
36. For the first time in his life the picture was not a confusion of men, sounds, speed.
37. The confusion was meaningless.

38. He smiled a little to himself.
39. He ran.
40. He held the ball in front of him.
41. He held it lightly.
42. He held it with two hands.
43. His knees pumped high.
44. His hips twisted in the run of a back in a field.
45. The run was almost girlish.
46. The field was broken.

47. The first halfback came at him.
48. Darling fed him his leg.
49. Then Darling swung at the last moment.
50. He took the shock of the man's shoulder.
51. He did not break stride.
52. He ran right through him.
53. His cleats bit into the turf.
54. The biting was secure.

55. There was only the safety man now.
56. The safety man came at him.
57. He came warily.
58. His arms were crooked.
59. His hands were spread.

60. Darling tucked the ball in.
61. Darling spurted at him.
62. Darling drove hard.
63. Darling hurled himself along.
64. All two hundred pounds were bunched into attack.
65. The attack was controlled.

66. He was sure.
67. He was going to get past the safety man.

68. He did not think.
69. His arms and legs worked together.
70. The working was beautiful.
71. He headed right for the safety man.
72. He stiff-armed him.
73. He felt blood spurt from the man's nose onto his hand.
74. The spurting was instantaneous.

75. He saw his face go awry.
76. His head was turned.
77. His mouth was pulled to one side.

78. Darling pivoted away.
79. He kept the arm locked.
80. He dropped the safety man.
81. He ran toward the goal line.
82. The running was easy.
83. The drumming of cleats diminished behind him.

Writing Suggestion 1: Either as a player or as a spectator, you have likely witnessed an exciting moment in sports: a crucial play, a spectacular performance, or a close call. Write a paragraph describing such a moment, with absolute phrases filling in the play-by-play action.

Writing Suggestion 2: Once you have written a version of *Eighty-Yard Run,* use your paragraph as the basis for a parody—a humorous imitation. That is, preserve the word order and phrasing of your *Eighty-Yard Run* paragraph but substitute in a new subject. Thus, instead of football, you might write about supermarket shopping, dating, or politics. The first sentence of your *Eighty-Yard Run* paragraph might go like this:

> The pass was high and wide and he jumped for it, feeling it slap flatly against his hands, as he shook his hips to throw off the halfback who was diving at him.

The first sentence of your parody, "The Eighty-Thousand-Dollar Run," might read this way:

> The envelope was fat and heavy and he fumbled with it, feeling it slip suspiciously from his pocket, as he tipped his hat to thank the undercover agent who was bribing him.

Try to preserve the word order, phrasing, and rhythm of your original paragraph even as you create your parody.

That man-thing relationships are growing more and more temporary may be illustrated by examining the culture surrounding the little girl who trades in her doll.

ALVIN TOFFLER, ***Future Shock***

When futurologist Alvin Toffler proposes that man-thing relationships are growing more and more temporary, his writing is both assertive and lively. Indeed, in his sentence above, the grammatical subject is not simply a noun or pronoun. Instead, the subject is itself a sentence, a clause with its own subject and verb:

> Man-thing relationships are growing more and more temporary.

Introduced by **that,** this clause serves as the subject of the verb *may be illustrated.* We can even replace the entire clause with a single pronoun, **this:**

> **This** may be illustrated by examining the culture surrounding the little girl who trades in her doll.

But now consider the predicate in Toffler's sentence. How may **this** be illustrated?

> You examine the culture surrounding the little girl who trades in her doll.

With *you examine* reduced to the verbal *examining,* this sentence becomes the object of the preposition *by.* The entire phrase may be replaced by a noun like **something:**

> **This** may be illustrated by **something.**

The result of this analysis is a sentence-combining problem that contains three parts:

> Man-thing relationships are growing more and more temporary.
> This may be illustrated by something.
> You examine the culture surrounding the little girl who trades in her doll.

Once you grasp how complete sentences can be made to replace nouns like **something** and pronouns like **this,** Toffler's combination seems as easy as it is economical and assertive:

> **That** *man-thing relationships are growing more and more temporary* may be illustrated by **examining** *the culture surrounding the little girl who trades in her doll.*

Note that when the first and third sentences replace **this** and **something,** they do not become modifiers. Instead, they become integral parts of the sentence, substitutes for the words they replace. How you can create such substitutions when you combine sentences is the subject of this chapter.

CREATING NOUN SUBSTITUTES

As the sentence by Alvin Toffler revealed, writers regularly make clauses and phrases behave like nouns. That is, they create ***noun substitutes.*** In Toffler's sentence, the first noun substitute, a **that**-*clause,* served as the sentence subject. A second noun substitute served as the object of the preposition *by.* This was a participial phrase (*examining the culture . . .*) used as a nominal. A participial phrase so used is called a **gerund phrase.** We shall see that these are but two of four principal noun substitutes writers use to insert sentences within sentences.

That-Clauses

In Chapters 3 and 4, you learned to use the word **that** as a relative pronoun and as a subordinator. In Toffler's sentence, **that** performs yet another function. Placed before a complete sentence, **that** turns the sentence into a noun substitute called a **that**-*clause.* The **that**-*clause* can then replace a nominal like *this* or *something* when you combine sentences. To grasp how this process works, combine each pair of sentences below in the light of Toffler's example:

> A. Stratas is a great singer.
> This is beyond question.

B. As a child I thought something.
Any knots in my life must somehow be my fault.

C. The scientific test of "truth," like the social test, is strictly practical, except for this.
The "desired results" are more severely limited.

D. The basic fact about most verbal utterance is this.
It doesn't get through.

One sentence in each pair contains the word *this* or *something* to mark the spot where the other sentence might be inserted as a noun substitute. Thus, you can combine the sentences by turning one into a **that**-*clause* and then using it to replace *this* or *something* within the second sentence.

Write your versions here:

____

____

____

____

____

____

____

____

____

____

____

____

In the first pair, the **that**-*clause* replaces *this* and so becomes the subject of the combined sentence:

A. **That** *Stratas is a great singer* is beyond question.
WINTHROP SARGEANT, "Presence"

In the second pair, the **that**-*clause* replaces *something* and becomes the direct object of the verb *thought:*

B. As a child I thought **that** *any knots in my life must somehow be my fault.*

WILLIAM ALLEN, "Toward an Understanding of Accidental Knots"

In the third pair, the noun substitute becomes the object of the compound preposition *except for:*

C. The scientific test of "truth," like the social test, is strictly practical, except for **the fact that** *the "desired results" are more severely limited.*

S. I. HAYAKAWA, *Language in Thought and Action*

Note how we must use **the fact that** when a **that**-*clause* serves as the object of a preposition. As you will find, in some combinations the choice between **that** and **the fact that** is a matter of style, not rule. Finally, in the fourth pair, we can replace *this* with a **that**-*clause,* which becomes the complement of the **to be** verb *is:*

D. The basic fact about most verbal utterance is **that** *it doesn't get through.*

PETER ELBOW, *Writing Without Teachers*

Here, Peter Elbow might almost as easily have used **the fact that** instead of **that** alone. He rightly applied the principle of verbal economy, however, and opted for the shorter combination.

That-Clauses for Indirect Quotation

In English, we have two ways of expressing what someone says. On the one hand, we can give a **direct quotation.** For this, we use quotation marks to enclose the speaker's actual words:

"Gentlemen," he said, "we have cheated death."

BILL BARICH, "Steelhead"

On the other hand, we can express a person's words, thoughts, or feelings by means of **indirect quotation.** For this, we use a **that**-*clause* and no quotation marks. To grasp this strategy, try combining these paired sentences:

A. They said this.
They had come to see the fireplace.

B. He suggested something.
They have a walk to town before their nap and dinner.

Write your versions here:

____

____

____

____

____

____

The writers who originally created these sentences both used indirect quotation. That is, they relayed the message in their own words, without using quotation marks. The author of the first sentence simply created a **that**-*clause:*

A. They said **that** *they had come to see the fireplace.*
PENELOPE GILLIATT, "Break"

The author of the second sentence varied on this strategy:

B. He suggested *they have a walk to town before their nap and dinner.*
ALAN LELCHUK, "The Doctor's Holiday"

Notice how Alan Lelchuk deleted **that** from the combination. This variation is both grammatical and concise.

What's important in handling such matters is that you remember the difference between direct and indirect quotation. Direct quotation presents the speaker's actual words enclosed in quotation marks. Indirect quotation, on the other hand, allows you to sum up the message in your own words. Indirect quotation requires no quotation marks—only a **that** at most.

WH- Clauses

If you glance back over the sentences that you turned into **that**-*clauses,* you will find that all of them are statements of fact or opinion. What happens when the sentence that's to be turned into a noun substitute is a question? To discover the answer, try this combination:

What distinguished Buffon's *Epochs of Nature?*
It was the cumulative weight of his whole argument.

Write your version here:

____

____

____

If you drop the question mark from the first sentence, you can then use what remains as a substitute for *it* in the second sentence:

> **What** *distinguished Buffon's Epochs of Nature* was the cumulative weight of his whole argument.
>
> STEPHEN TOULMIN AND JUNE GOODFIELD, *The Discovery of Time*

By means of this relatively simple strategy, you can convert a question into a noun substitute. Specifically, you turn the question into a **WH**-*clause*. The name "**WH**-*clause*" comes from the fact that most question words begin with the letters **wh**, which makes them easy to remember:

what, whatever	whom
when, whenever	whose
where, wherever	why
which, whichever	how
who, whoever	

All these words can indicate questions. They can also introduce **WH**-*clauses*, which serve as noun substitutes when you combine sentences.

In the sentence above by Toulmin and Goodfield, the **WH**-*clause* replaced *it* and became the subject of the combined sentence. Like **that**-*clauses*, **WH**-*clauses* can also serve as objects and complements. You will grasp this if you combine these paired sentences:

A. I was sitting in my office cleaning the debris out of my thirty-eight and wondering something.
Where was my next case coming from?

B. A basic reason for such "insoluble" problems in society is this.
What might be called "institutional inertia?"

Write your versions here:

____

____

____

____

You can check your combinations against these:

A. I was sitting in my office cleaning the debris out of my thirty-eight and wondering **where** *my next case was coming from.*
WOODY ALLEN, "Mr. Big"

B. A basic reason for such "insoluble" problems in society is **what** *might be called "institutional inertia."*
S. I. HAYAKAWA, *Language in Thought and Action*

In Woody Allen's sentence, a **WH**-*clause* beginning with *where* replaces the word *something* and becomes the object of the verb *wondering.* In S. I. Hayakawa's sentence, a **WH**-*clause* beginning with *what* replaces the word *this* and becomes the complement of the **to be** verb *is.* Like **that**-*clauses,* **WH**-*clauses* offer you a concise and flexible way of putting sentences together.

As we have seen, **WH**-*clauses* are closely related to questions. The questions raised by **WH**-words like *who, what, when, where, why,* and *how* all call for answers that are more than a simple yes or no. You cannot answer "yes" to a question like "How are you feeling?" You can, however, answer "yes" to a question like "Are you feeling well?" Turning a yes-no question into a noun substitute is an easy matter, thanks to the words **whether** and **whether or not.** To grasp this, write out the following combination:

I often wondered something.
Would music made a good career for me?

Write your version here:

If you turned the question into a statement ("Music would make a good career for me") and then replaced *something* with **whether,** you came up with this noun substitute:

I often wondered **whether** *music would make a good career for me.*
STUDENT WRITER

As is often the case, **whether or not** would have worked almost equally well here. Furthermore, in less formal writing, the word **if** could also do the job:

> I often wondered **if** *music would make a good career for me.*

Which choice you make depends on your audience and purpose. What matters most is that by creating noun substitutes like these you can turn questions into statements for further discussion.

FROM CLAUSES TO PHRASES

Both **that**-*clauses* and **WH**-*clauses,* then, allow you to insert complete sentences—independent clauses with their own subjects and verbs—into other sentences. But as we have seen in earlier chapters, effective sentence combining is often a matter of reducing clauses to phrases and thereby saving on words. While we can turn a complete sentence into a noun substitute by creating a **that**-*clause* or **WH**-*clause,* we can also reduce a sentence to a phrase that serves as a noun substitute. You will recall that this was the case with the second noun substitute in the sentence that opened this chapter:

> That man-thing relationships are growing more and more temporary may be illustrated by **examining** *the culture surrounding the little girl who trades in her doll.*

Here a verbal, the present participle *examining,* begins a phrase that serves as a noun substitute, specifically as the object of the preposition *by.* When an **-ing** verbal like *examining* is used as a noun substitute, it is called a **gerund** (from the Latin word *gerundus,* "doing"). The object of the preposition *by* is thus a **gerund phrase.** While the phrase is indeed a noun substitute, it retains some of its force as a verbal and thereby enlivens Toffler's sentence.

A second kind of verbal phrase with which you are familiar is the **infinitive phrase.** In Chapter 8, we saw how infinitive phrases can serve as modifiers. Infinitive phrases can also serve as noun substitutes. For example, consider the subject in this sentence:

> **To make** *an organism* demands the right substances in the right proportion and in the right arrangement.
>
> GEORGE WALD, "The Origin of Life"

The subject in Wald's sentence is an infinitive phrase, **to make** *an organism.* The phrase is clearly a noun substitute, since we could replace it with a noun like *something* or a pronoun like *this.* Because noun substitutes like these are at once lively and concise, we shall study how you can create them when you combine sentences.

Gerund Phrases

A gerund is an **-ing** verbal serving as a nominal: **Writing** *is her hobby.* A **gerund phrase** is a noun substitute made up of a gerund plus all its modifiers: **Judy's *writing* about extrasensory perception** *is hypnotic.* Notice that this gerund phrase is almost a clause. That is, it has a subject, *Judy,* and a verbal, *writing.* You can grasp how gerund phrases are formed by combining these paired sentences:

A. Jack ran his lap in record time.
   This meant victory for us.

B. Except for something, I like the cold.
   Winter causes me to become housebound.

Write your versions here:

____

____

____

____

____

____

As before, the words *this* and *something* mark spots where noun substitutes might be inserted into one sentence in each pair. Therefore, we turn the verbs in the other sentences into gerunds:

Jack **running** his lap in record time
Winter **causing** me to become housebound

But because gerunds are noun substitutes, not verbs, we must also change the sentence subjects to possessive form:

Jack**'s running** his lap in record time
Winter**'s causing** me to become housebound

Now that one sentence in each pair has been transformed to a gerund phrase, we can make the combinations:

A. **Jack's running his lap in record time** meant victory for us.
STUDENT WRITER

B. Except for **winter's causing me to become housebound,** I like the cold.
E. B. WHITE, "The Winter of the Great Snows"

Like the other noun substitutes we have studied, gerund phrases can serve as sentence subjects, as objects of verbs or prepositions, and as complements of **to be** verbs. In the student writer's sentence above, the gerund phrase replaces the sentence subject *this.* In E. B. White's sentence, the gerund phrase replaces the noun *something* and becomes the object of the compound preposition *except for.*

As we just saw, when a sentence is converted into a gerund phrase, the sentence subject goes into possessive form: **Jack's running; winter's causing.** When the subject of the sentence is no one in particular, but rather *one, someone,* or an all-inclusive *you,* the subject can simply be dropped from the combination. For instance, try combining these two sentences by creating a gerund phrase:

> Someone works with very disturbed patients.
> This is painful.

Write your version here:

____

____

____

"Someone," the subject of the sentence to be turned into a gerund phrase, is hardly worth preserving. What's important is the gerund, the action word, which can open the combined sentence with a flourish:

> **Working** *with very disturbed patients* is painful.
>
> JANET MALCOLM, *Psychoanalysis: The Impossible Profession*

Thus, when you reduce a sentence to a gerund phrase, you create a versatile noun substitute even as you preserve the basic *action* of the sentence. No wonder the resulting combinations have both economy and vitality.

Infinitive Phrases

An **infinitive** is the **to** form of a verb: *to write, to run, to be.* **Infinitives** are verbals, and in Chapter 8 you studied how **infinitive-phrase** modifiers can help you express a goal or purpose. To review this process, combine these two sentences into one:

> You want to use a colloquial expression.
> Mrs. Quabarl was knocked off her perch.

Write your version here:

Notice that the author who originally wrote the sentence created a free infinitive phrase at level 2:

1 Mrs. Quabarl, / , was knocked off her perch.
2/ **to use** *a colloquial expression*
SAKI (H. H. MUNRO), "The Schartz-Metterklume Method"

The infinitive phrase in Saki's sentence modifies the base clause. But infinitive phrases can also serve as noun substitutes. For instance, consider the following combination:

A mathematician failed as a husband.
This had no bearing on his ability as a mathematician.

Write your version here:

The word *this* in the second sentence can be replaced by a noun substitute. To turn the first sentence into an infinitive phrase, we must perform two steps. First, we turn the verb *failed* into an infinitive:

A mathematician **to fail** as a husband

Next, we insert the word **for** in front of the subject:

For a mathematician **to fail** as a husband

Notice that like a gerund phrase, an infinitive phrase is *almost* a sentence. That is, it has a subject, *mathematician,* and a verbal, *to fail.* Now that we have reduced the sentence to this form, we can make the combination:

For a mathematician to fail as a husband had no bearing on his ability as a mathematician.

A. ALVAREZ, *Life After Marriage*

Again like a gerund phrase, an infinitive phrase preserves the basic *action* of the sentence from which it comes. For this reason, sentences containing infinitive phrases seem dynamic and assertive.

Furthermore, infinitive phrases resemble gerund phrases in yet another way. We saw that when the subject of a gerund was a general *one, someone,* or *you,* the subject could simply be dropped out, leaving the essential action. This is also the case with infinitive phrases. Consider the following combination:

> You do not expect something.
> You see dead animals in the open.

Write your version here:

____

____

____

If we turn the second sentence into a noun substitute, we can use it to replace the noun *something* in the first sentence. Therefore, we turn the second sentence into an infinitive phrase: **for you to see dead animals in the open.** But the subject of the first sentence is also *you.* To avoid needless repetition, we can eliminate the subject from the infinitive phrase: **to see dead animals in the open.** The resulting combination is natural and direct:

> You do not expect **to see dead animals in the open.**
>
> LEWIS THOMAS, "Death in the Open"

Even though the infinitive phrase here is a noun substitute, it presents an action. Like gerunds, infinitive phrases retain their verbal force when used as noun substitutes. For this reason, they can make your writing seem telling and assertive.

Gerund and Infinitive Phrases as Appositives

As noun substitutes, gerund and infinitive phrases can serve as sentence subjects, as objects of verbs or prepositions, and as complements of **to be** verbs. In addition, because they are nominals, they can stand in apposition to nouns elsewhere in the sentence:

> He almost finished a commercial course in high school before he got his first job, **being** *an order clerk for a chain of dairy-and-herring stores.*
>
> A. J. LIEBLING, "The Jollity Building"

It is a difficult lesson to learn today—**to leave** *one's friends and family and deliberately practice the art of solitude for an hour or a day or a week.*

ANNE MORROW LINDBERGH, *Gift from the Sea*

In A. J. Liebling's sentence, a gerund phrase stands in apposition to the noun "job," while in Anne Morrow Lindbergh's sentence, an infinitive phrase stands in apposition to the noun "lesson." If you are unsure just what an appositive is, review Chapter 9.

WH-Infinitive Phrases

These, then, are the four noun substitutes writers use to combine sentences: **that**-*clause,* **WH**-*clause,* **gerund phrase,** and **infinitive phrase.** In addition, some sentences invite a double combination that involves both a **WH**-word and an infinitive. For example, how might you combine these two sentences?

He does not know something.
Where should he look?

Write your version here:

____

____

____

The noun *something* in the first sentence and the **WH**-word *where* in the second invite you to create a **WH**-*clause* that combines the sentences:

He does not know **where he should look.**

This is a respectable combination, but you can carry it a step further still. The **WH**-*clause* "where he should look" needlessly repeats the sentence subject, *he.* Therefore, why not reduce the clause to a phrase by dropping out *he* and changing the verb *should look* to an infinitive?

He does not know **where to look.**

This is exactly what William Golding did when he wrote the sentence in his essay "Gradus ad Parnassum." Golding created a **WH-infinitive phrase** that combined his ideas in short order.

PULLING IT ALL TOGETHER

Noun substitutes allow writers to make sentences behave as if they were nouns: as subjects, objects, complements, and appositives. In addition, because noun substitutes have their own verbals, they can make writing active and assertive. We saw this in the sentence that opened this chapter. That sentence, from Alvin Toffler's *Future Shock,* combined a **that**-*clause* and a gerund phrase into a provocative assertion about our "throw-away" society:

> **That** *man-thing relationships are growing more and more temporary* may be illustrated by **examining** *the culture surrounding the little girl who trades in her doll.*

Thanks to the noun substitutes Toffler has created, his sentence carries its weight lightly, even as it raises profound issues.

To conclude our study of **that**-*clauses,* **WH**-*clauses,* gerund phrases, and infinitive phrases, let us turn to another topic: education. Specifically, imagine you have been teaching English to a group of immigrant adults. They are beginners, but they are eager to learn. The problem is that they lack English vocabulary for expressing what they think and feel. After a frustrating class, you write down two questions for yourself:

> What did students in the beginners' grade most need?
> What could they put to instant use?

Even as you raise these questions, answers leap to mind:

> It was a copious supply of words.
> It was English words.
> Words for something.

Words for what? Your brainstorming has helped you plan your next lesson:

> The words name ordinary objects.
> The words ask simple questions.
> The words describe everyday experience.

Having jotted down your thoughts and gradually discovered a solution to your problem, you combine your notes into a statement:

> **What** *students in the beginners' grade most needed,* **what** *they could put to instant use,* was a copious supply of words: English words, words for **naming** *ordinary objects,* **asking** *simple questions,* **describing** *everyday experiences.*

Your questions have become statements: noun substitutes, specifically **WH**-*clauses.* The words you will teach your students will help them speak out, as your gerund phrases imply. Your students will soon have words for *naming, asking,* and *describing.* Your sentence is an assertion, a plan for action. Will the plan work? To find out, you should read Leo Rosten's humorous story "Vocabulary, Vocabulary!" in *O K*A*P*L*A*N! My K*A*P*L*A*N!* since that's where the sentence originally appeared.

Noun Substitutes: Combinations

Combine each set of sentences below into one sentence that contains at least one noun substitute: a **that**-*clause,* **WH**-*clause,* gerund phrase, or infinitive phrase. You can compare your combinations with professional or student writers' sentences in the Appendix.

SAMPLE EXERCISE

The great thing about human language is this.
It prevents us from something.
We stick to the matter at hand.

PROFESSIONAL WRITER'S VERSION

The great thing about human language is **that** *it prevents us from* **sticking** *to the matter at hand.*

LEWIS THOMAS, "Information"

1. One reserves judgments.
   This is a matter of infinite hope.
2. Few people feel terribly discontented with their lot.
   This is a plausible explanation of the mood of the moment.
   The mood is highly nonrevolutionary.
3. He knew something.
   Where was everything when he wanted it?
4. One designs a highway.
   The highway minimizes ambiguity, error, and accidents.
   This increases everyone's sense of security.
5. He told her something.
   She should finish high school.
   Afterward she would have a scholarship.
   The scholarship would be waiting for her.
6. Did the Elizabethans cheat like mad at cards and dice at home?
   This is difficult to say.

7. Other writers then began to echo Simmons's suggestion.
   Simmons suggested women could support themselves by something.
   They cooked.
8. She didn't know something.
   What should she make of the man?
9. These issues matter to the political system.
   This means something.
   All the principal institutions and actors in the system are part of the budget process.
10. One corrects the Consumer Price Index.
    The Consumer Price Index is overestimated.
    This will slow down the spiral.
    The spiral is inflationary.
11. Our civic education does not even begin to tell the voter this.
    How can he reduce the maze of public affairs to some intelligible form?
12. Basically the family has fulfilled three social functions.
    It has provided a basic labor force.
    It has transmitted property.
    It has educated and trained children.
    It has educated and trained them into an accepted social pattern.
    It has educated and trained them in the work skills.
    Their future subsistence would depend upon the work skill.
13. For one shameless moment Mr. Parkhill wondered something.
    Could he reconcile it with his conscience?
    He did promote Mr. Kaplan to Advanced Grammar and Civics.
14. The end, nonetheless, was this.
    What had he expected?
    It failed to come to him.
15. One couples the concept of freedom to breed with the belief.
    One believes everyone born has an equal right to the commons.
    This is something.
    One locks the world into a course of action.
    The course is tragic.

Barriers

Combine the sentences below into a paragraph that contains at least one noun substitute. You can compare your paragraph with a professional or student writer's version in the Appendix.

1. People feel safer.
2. They are behind some kind of barrier.
3. The barrier is physical.

4. A situation is in any way threatening.
5. The situation is social.
6. There is an urge.
7. The urge is immediate.
8. The urge is to set up such a barricade.

9. A child is faced with a stranger.
10. The child is tiny.
11. The problem is usually solved.
12. The child hides behind its mother's body.
13. The child peeps out at the intruder.
14. The child wants to see something.
15. What will the intruder do next?

16. The mother's body is not available.
17. A chair will do.
18. Some other piece of furniture will do.
19. The furniture is solid.

20. The stranger insists on coming closer.
21. The face must be hidden too.
22. The face is peeping.

23. The intruder continues to approach.
24. The intruder is insensitive.
25. The intruder approaches despite these signals of fear.
26. The signals are obvious.
27. There is nothing for the child but this.
28. It screams.
29. It flees.

Writing Suggestion 1: Do you agree that barriers make people feel safer? Write a paragraph explaining your opinion. Whether you agree or disagree, try to prove your point by citing details and examples.

Writing Suggestion 2: Students of nonverbal communication have observed that "keeping your distance" is more than an empty phrase. In various cultures, people follow strict patterns of proximity to, and distance from, one another, depending on the relationships among them. Thus, the traditional Japanese wife walked a few steps behind her husband. Most American men greet male friends at arm's length, with a handshake, whereas men in other cultures regularly greet one another with a hearty embrace. As you go about your business, observe how people in different situations "keep their distance." Once you have sufficient data, write an essay analyzing the behavior you have observed. In what ways do people use physical proximity and distance to establish and maintain social relationships?

Brotherly Love

Combine the sentences below into a paragraph that contains at least one noun substitute. You can compare your paragraph with a student or professional writer's version in the Appendix.

1. Harold got hurt.
2. This was perhaps rather often.
3. The important thing to do was this.
4. Choke him.

5. We had tried something first.
6. We comforted him.
7. His wails would have brought Mother up on the run.

8. We also had found something by experience.
9. We choked him in silence.
10. This was a great mistake.
11. That silence itself would make Mother suspect something.
12. Something dreadful had happened.

13. We choked our little brother.
14. He was indignant.
15. We had to make sounds.
16. The sounds were joyful.

17. This must have given us the appearance of fiends.
18. The fiends were peculiarly hard-hearted.

Writing Suggestion 1: Keeping a younger brother, sister, or friend in line is no easy job for a child. Write a paragraph recounting a humorous incident in which you tried to persuade a younger friend or relative to see things your way.

Writing Suggestion 2: The exercise above presents a situation in which, to the boys' view, the end justified the means. Thus, to keep themselves out of trouble, the boys temporarily throttled their brother Harold. Whether a good, or supposedly good, end justifies an evil, or supposedly evil, means is a philosophical question of long standing. Can one, for example, justify the assassination of a dictator, the administration of an untested drug to a terminally ill patient, or the civil disobedience of an unjust law? Write an essay in which you set forth your own beliefs about any of these questions, or about any other situations in which ends and means seem to be in conflict.

Noun Substitutes: Creations

Create at least one noun substitute—a **that**-*clause,* **WH**-*clause,* gerund phrase, or infinitive phrase—in each sentence below. While most of the exercises ask you to create specific kinds of noun substitutes, some leave you free to replace an indefinite *this* or *something* with any kind of noun substitute that seems appropriate. You can compare your creations with professional or student writers' sentences in the Appendix.

SAMPLE EXERCISES

A. ______________ (infinitive phrase) is immoral. [signaled format]

B. **This** is a notorious fact. [open format]

PROFESSIONAL WRITERS' VERSIONS:

A. **To waste** *anything in America* is immoral.
JOHN KNOWLES, *A Separate Peace*

B. **That** *more than one kind of English is likely to be in use at the same time and place* is a notorious fact.
MARTIN JOOS, *The Five Clocks*

1. One simple, unrefuted fact about radioactive substances is ______________ (**that**-clause).
2. A century from now our great-grandchildren may marvel at **this.**
3. I went to bed still trying to figure out ______________ (yes/no question clause—use **whether**).
4. ______________ (gerund phrase) gave me a chance ______________ (infinitive phrase) about ______________ (**WH**-clause).
5. I vowed **something.**
6. We need only a single case as an example of ______________ (**WH**-infinitive phrase).
7. **Something** was not a weakling's work.

8. ______________________________ was only discovered
(**WH**-clause)

after we'd spent it, and nobody can be sure ______________
(**WH**-clause)

____.

9. **This** must have been far more nourishing than **something.**

10. ____
(**the fact that**-clause)

does not mean ___________________________________
(**that**-clause)

____.

News and Views

Combine the sentences below into a paragraph that contains several noun substitutes. You can compare your paragraph with a professional or student writer's version in the Appendix.

1. The newspaper is the only mass medium.
2. The medium acts as a source of information.
3. The source is daily.
4. The information is detailed.
5. The information is about the world.

6. The newspaper is unlike the electronic media.
7. The electronic media afford only brief profiles of news events.
8. The newspaper covers a wide array of news stories.
9. The coverage has supplemental facts.
10. The coverage has background information.

11. Newspapers have such great potential.
12. They relate information to the public.
13. Mass communication researchers have been investigating something.
14. They call it "the agenda-setting influence of the press."

15. The agenda-setting theory attempts this.
16. It explains something.
17. How do newspapers influence the reader's perception?
18. Newspapers highlight particular events.
19. What does the reader perceive as important in the world?

20. The basic premise is this.
21. Certain readers will consider an event important.
22. The event is simply in the newspaper.

23. The press then has the effect.
24. It sets an agenda of issues.
25. The issues are "important."
26. People think about the issues.
27. People discuss the issues.

28. Bernard Cohen has noted something.
29. Bernard Cohen is a communications specialist.
30. "The press may not be successful much of the time in telling people what to think, but it is stunningly successful in telling its readers what to think about."

Writing Suggestion 1: Do you agree that by emphasizing selected stories the press shapes our beliefs about what's important? How does this influence affect our lives? Write an essay analyzing "the agenda-setting influence of the press" on you and on others.

Writing Suggestion 2: In an essay entitled "The Medium Is the Message," communications scholar Marshall McLuhan argued that various media—newspapers, magazines, radio, and television—not only report events but shape them as well. Indeed, if you follow a news item in several media, you may be surprised at how different the "facts" seem in each medium. Select a recent event that was covered by several media—television, magazines, and newspapers, say—and examine how each medium portrayed the "facts." Write up your findings in a short essay.

Noun Substitutes: Sentence Acrobatics

Combine each set of sentences below into one or more "acrobatic" sentences. See if you can create at least one noun substitute as you do each exercise, but feel free to try out other constructions as well. Naturally, each problem invites more than one "correct" answer. Therefore, you must create original sentences that strike *you* as both correct and stylish.

You may enjoy comparing your combinations with the professional or student writers' versions in the Appendix. Look for both similarities and differences, but try to decide whose version is the more stylish—it may well be your own.

SAMPLE EXERCISE

What does the government really do?
It does not rule men.
It adds force to men.
The men rule their affairs.
The force is overwhelming.

STUDENT AND PROFESSIONAL WRITERS' VERSIONS

Instead of **ruling** *men,* **what** *the government really does* is **to add** *force—*overwhelming force—*to men ruling their affairs.*

STUDENT WRITER

What *the government really does* is not **to rule** *men* but **to add** *overwhelming force to men when they rule their affairs.*

WALTER LIPPMANN, *A Preface to Morals*

1. We have cast another group in the role of the enemy.
   We know something.
   They are to be distrusted.
   They are evil incarnate.
2. You live for the moment.
   This is the prevailing passion.
   You live for yourself.
   You do not live for your predecessors.
   You do not live for posterity.
3. He gave any money to mother.
   He asked her something.
   What was it for?
   He made a note of it.
   He made the note in his pocket notebook.
4. I knew something.
   I had to move forward.
   I had to continue on.
   I turned back now.
   This would be making a decision.
   I would regret the decision for the rest of my life.
5. What am I trying to do?
   I am trying to add together those elements.
   Some are horrible.
   Some are merely funny.
   All are significant.
   I suppose those elements are the forces of history.
   The history is off-campus.
6. We brush our teeth with Colgate toothpaste.
   This becomes something.
   It wards off calamities.
   The warding is dramatic.
   The warding is timely.
   The calamities are terrible.
   The calamities are personal.

They are like this.
One gets fired.
They are like this.
One loses one's girlfriend.

7. Profits are now appraised.
They are not appraised by the standards.
Are they earned?
Are they deserved?
Are they subject to the rule of possession?
The rule of possession has nine points.
They are appraised by the evidence.
Are they favorable for economic performance?

8. I am fairly certain.
She is the only member of the American Academy of Arts and Letters.
The member is female or male.
The member has thwarted an attempted rape.
She thwarted it by this.
She staged a fit of something.
She sneezed.

9. "There is no boon in nature."
One of the new philosophers had written this.
He wrote it in the first years of the industrial cities.
The writing was harsh.
A mercy had persisted.
It persisted through war.
It persisted through famine.
It persisted through death.
The mercy was sparse.
The mercy was like a mutation.
The mutation's time had not yet come.

10. I think this.
Man has contaminated the planet.
The contamination has been gradual.
The contamination has been creeping.
He has sent up dust into the air.
He has added strontium in our bones.
He has discharged poisons into rivers.
The poisons are industrial.
The rivers once flowed clear.
He has mixed chemicals with fog.
The fog is on the east wind.
This adds up to a fantasy.

The fantasy is of such grotesque proportions.
It makes everything seem pale.
It makes everything seem anemic.
Everything is said on the subject.
This is by contrast.

Mr. Gatsby

Combine the sentences below into two paragraphs that contain several noun substitutes. You can compare your paragraphs with a professional or student writer's version in the Appendix.

1. Already it was deep summer.
2. It was summer on roadhouse roofs.
3. It was summer in front of wayside garages.
4. New red gas-pumps sat out in pools of light in front of the garages.

5. I reached my estate at West Egg.
6. I ran the car under its shed.
7. I sat for a while on a grass roller in the yard.
8. The grass roller was abandoned.

9. The wind had blown off.
10. The wind left a night.
11. The night was loud.
12. The night was bright.
13. Wings beat in the trees.
14. There was a persistent organ sound.
15. The full bellows of the earth blew the frogs full of life.

16. The silhouette of a cat wavered across the moonlight.
17. The cat was moving.
18. I turned my head.
19. I wanted to watch it.
20. I saw something.
21. I was not alone.

22. Fifty feet away a figure had emerged.
23. He emerged from the shadow of my neighbor's mansion.
24. He was standing.
25. His hands were in his pockets.
26. He regarded the silver pepper of the stars.

27. Something in his movements suggested something.
28. His movements were leisurely.
29. Something in the position of his feet upon the lawn suggested something.
30. The position was secure.

31. It was Mr. Gatsby himself.
32. He had come out to determine something.
33. What share was his of our local heavens?

34. I decided this.
35. I should call to him.

36. Miss Baker had mentioned him at dinner.
37. That would do for an introduction.

38. But I didn't call to him.
39. He gave a sudden intimation.
40. He was content to be alone.

41. He stretched out his arms toward the water.
42. The water was dark.
43. He stretched them in a curious way.

44. I was far from him.
45. I could have sworn something.
46. He was trembling.

47. I glanced seaward.
48. My glance was involuntary.
49. I distinguished nothing except a single light.
50. The light was green.
51. The light was minute.
52. The light was far away.
53. The light might have been the end of a dock.

54. I looked once more for Gatsby.
55. He had vanished.
56. I was alone again in the darkness.
57. The darkness was unquiet.

Writing Suggestion 1: Watching people is often an unsettling but revealing way to learn about human nature. Make a point to observe someone from a distance for a short time. Write a paragraph or two describing, analyzing, and speculating on what you observe.

Writing Suggestion 2: The faraway green light across the bay has some special meaning for Mr. Gatsby. Because the green light suggests something beyond itself, it is a symbol. Write an essay in which you discuss some of the objects that hold symbolic meanings for you. Is there any actual connection between the symbols and the things symbolized?

It is one of the greatest paradoxes of modern democracy that the questions of greatest interest to the mass of mankind are not interesting.

WALTER LIPPMANN, "The South and the New Society"

In his essay "The South and the New Society," political scientist Walter Lippmann expounds one of the paradoxes of democracy in a sentence that is at once clear and emphatic. Notice that the most important point in Lippmann's sentence, the paradox itself, comes at the end of the sentence:

> The questions of greatest interest to the mass of mankind are not interesting.

This statement occurs in a **that**-*clause,* a noun substitute you studied in Chapter 12. Lippmann inserts this noun substitute into a sentence we may render thus:

> This is one of the greatest paradoxes of modern democracy.

In other words, Lippmann's statement is a combination of these two sentences:

> The questions of greatest interest to the mass of mankind are not interesting.
> This is one of the greatest paradoxes of modern democracy.

Thanks to your study of noun substitutes, you should have no trouble combining these sentences by creating a **that**-*clause:*

> **That** *the questions of greatest interest to the mass of mankind are not interesting* is one of the greatest paradoxes of modern democracy.

But while this combination is perfectly grammatical, it is not what Lippmann actually wrote, nor is it as effective as his version. Here, the **that**-*clause* serves as the subject of the sentence. In a typical English sentence like this one, we read from subject to verb to complement (a complement is a word, phrase, or clause that "completes" the meaning of the verb in a sentence). In this version of Lippmann's sentence, then, we must rush through the long **that**-*clause* as we seek out the verb and complement that allow us to grasp the author's complete idea. This arrangement thus distracts us from the initial **that**-*clause,* which contains the writer's main point.

Walter Lippmann avoided this problem when he composed the sentence. He did this by rearranging the parts of the sentence. By slipping the word **it** into the subject position and then moving the **that**-*clause* into final position, Lippmann made his point clearly and forcefully:

> **It** is one of the greatest paradoxes of modern democracy **that** *the questions of greatest interest to the mass of mankind are not interesting.*

Here the word **it** is merely a place holder that allows us to reach the verb and complement quickly. This rearrangement not only makes the entire sentence easier to understand but also moves the most important point to the most emphatic position: the very end of the sentence. In this chapter you will learn how to *recombine* sentences so as to make them as clear and emphatic as Lippmann's.

RECOMBINING STRATEGIES

Notice that when Walter Lippmann recombined his sentence by moving the **that**-*clause* from the beginning to the end, he added no new information to the sentence. What the rearrangement added was clarity and emphasis. By ***recombining sentences,*** you change the *focus* of your writing, thereby redirecting your reader's attention to what you think is most important in your sentence. Recombining is thus a matter of *style,* a matter of choice rather than rule. Sentence combining teaches you how to add texture to your writing by adding details, qualities, and comparisons. Recombining practice teaches you how to present your information effectively. To this end, we shall study four principal recombining strategies: *inversions, cleft patterns,* **there**-*patterns,* and *passives.*

INVERSIONS

A rearrangement is striking only when it alters a familiar pattern. The familiar pattern of the English sentence is *subject-verb-complement (or ob-*

ject). It is this pattern that fulfills our everyday expectations about word order:

A beautiful New England day (*subject*) spread (*verb*) around them. (*complement*)

From *subject* to *verb* to *complement* is thus the usual direction of movement in an English sentence. But author John Knowles did not follow this usual direction of movement when he actually wrote a version of the sentence above in his novel *A Separate Peace.* Instead, Knowles recombined the sentence this way:

Around them (*complement*) spread (*verb*) a beautiful New England day. (*subject*)

Knowles turned the familiar pattern around by creating an **inversion.** Instead of directing our attention from subject to verb to complement, Knowles woke us up by directing us from complement to verb to subject.

Inversion and Emphasis

The unexpected pattern gives us a mild surprise. But what is more important is that it changes the *focus* of the sentence. In addition to our expectations about normal word order, we have expectations about focus or *emphasis.* From long experience, we expect the most important information in a sentence to come at the end of the sentence, the next most important information to come at the beginning, and the least important information to be tucked away in the middle. Thus, by inverting his sentence, Knowles focused our attention on the most important element in his sentence, *a beautiful New England day.*

An inversion thus creates not only variety; it creates emphasis as well. And here is where a writer's sense of style becomes crucial. Sometimes the familiar subject-verb-complement pattern obscures rather than emphasizes a key element in a sentence. By creating an inversion, a writer can bring the key element into prominence. To grasp this, try combining these sentences twice. First, follow the familiar subject-verb-complement pattern:

The Cubans themselves were forgotten during the controversy.
Most of the Cubans had been badly frightened.

Write your version here:

____

____

____

If you turned the second sentence into a modifier, your version resembles this:

> 1 The Cubans themselves, / , were forgotten during the controversy.
> 2/ most of whom had been badly frightened

This combination preserves the normal sentence pattern in the base. Since it ends with *the controversy* and begins with *the Cubans,* this version emphasizes these elements in that order. But what if you wished instead to emphasize two different elements in the combination? See what effect you create when you recombine the sentences by means of an inversion in the base clause:

Write your version here:

____

____

____

Your version should look like this:

> 1 Forgotten during the controversy were the Cubans themselves,
> 2 most of whom had been badly frightened.

When the base clause is inverted, the modifier moves to final position. The recombination ends with *frightened* and begins with *forgotten.* Notice how the emphasis has changed from the facts of the matter—the Cubans and the controversy—to the feelings associated with the matter. This is exactly how the journalist James Conaway recombined the sentence in his article "Unwanted Immigrants: Cuban Prisoners in America," an essay with a strong emotional thrust. Conaway used an inversion to emphasize that the Cubans were *frightened* and *forgotten.*

Simply inverting the usual word order of a sentence, then, creates emphasis. But inversion also has its perils. As Wolcott Gibbs lamented in *More in Sorrow,* "Backwards ran sentences until reeled the mind." Overused or used carelessly, inversion can twist your prose into pretzels. Such is all too often the case in student journalism, where writers commonly mistake inversion for elegance:

> At the top of a long list of unusual appetizers is cottage cheese.
>
> STUDENT WRITER

Far from sounding elegant, this inversion sounds awkward. In addition, shifting a commonplace dish like cottage cheese to the emphatic final position hardly makes the appetizer list sound unusual. Given the material, the normal pattern of *subject-verb-complement* is more appropriate than the inversion:

Cottage cheese is at the top of a long list of unusual appetizers.

Simple and familiar as it is, this version at once sounds more natural than the inversion and puts emphasis on what is really the key element, *a long list of unusual appetizers.*

The *It*-Inversion

Simple inversion of normal word order adds neither new information nor new words to a sentence. What the recombination adds is emphasis. There is a second kind of inversion, however, that involves adding the word **it** to a sentence containing a noun substitute in the subject position. It was this pattern, you will recall, that Walter Lippmann used in the sentence that opened this chapter:

> **It** is one of the greatest paradoxes of modern democracy **that** *the questions of greatest interest to the mass of mankind are not interesting.*

This **it**-*inversion* pattern allowed Lippmann to move the long **that**-*clause* from initial to final position. This recombination not only put the emphasis where it should be but also made the sentence easier to read and understand.

You can review exactly how the **it**-*inversion* works by first combining and then recombining the two sentences below. Begin by creating a noun substitute that can replace the word *something* in the first sentence:

Something was plain.
Ted had all the virtues.

Write your version here:

____

____

____

Turning the second sentence into a **that**-*clause* and then slipping it into the first sentence puts the two together this way:

That *Ted had all the virtues* was plain.

But is this really the way you would write the combination? Probably not. The **that**-*clause* makes an unwieldy subject. The noun substitute would go better at the end of the sentence. Therefore, you recombine the sentence by means of an **it**-*inversion:*

> **It** was plain **that** *Ted had all the virtues.*

Clarence Day wrote the sentence this way in his story "Noble Boys." The **it**-*inversion* makes Day's sentence sound natural and puts the main idea into the emphatic final position. Note that the word **it** in Day's sentence is merely a place holder that allows the author to move the **that**-*clause* out of the subject position.

The reason why the **it**-*inversion* appeals to us is easy to grasp. When a sentence has a long noun substitute—a **that**-*clause,* say—as its subject, we have trouble remembering the subject as we read on:

> **That** *the ingenuity of man—or rather of the radicals—in dreaming up new social services is endless* is a basic tenet of the conservative faith in the United States.

On the other hand, we have no particular trouble remembering a long noun substitute when it comes after the sentence verb:

> **It** is a basic tenet of the conservative faith in the United States **that** *the ingenuity of man—or rather of the radicals—in dreaming up new social services is endless.*
>
> JOHN KENNETH GALBRAITH, *Economics and the Art of Controversy*

Like Walter Lippmann, John Kenneth Galbraith recombined his sentence by means of the **it**-*inversion.* The recombination was both clearer and more emphatic than the original version, in which a long initial **that**-*clause* impeded the reader's progress through the sentence.

Almost every sentence with a noun substitute in the subject position can profitably undergo an **it**-*inversion.* The combinations and recombinations below illustrate how the **it**-*inversion* applies to a **WH**-*clause,* to an infinitive phrase, and to a gerund phrase:

COMBINATION 1

Something was surprising.
How well did we get along in these weeks?

***WH*-CLAUSE**

How *well we got along in these weeks* was surprising.

***IT*-INVERSION**

It was surprising **how** *well we got along in these weeks.*

JOHN KNOWLES, *A Separate Peace*

COMBINATION 2

You are part of the improvement of the species.
This is a source of satisfaction.

INFINITIVE PHRASE

To be *part of the improvement of the species* is a source of satisfaction.

***IT*- INVERSION**

It is a source of satisfaction **to be** *part of the improvement of the species.*

LEWIS THOMAS, "Organelles as Organisms"

COMBINATION 3

You ride a motorcycle at 100 m.p.h. without a helmet.
This is suicidal.

GERUND PHRASE

Riding *a motorcycle at 100 m.p.h. without a helmet* is suicidal.

***IT*- INVERSION**

It is suicidal **riding** *a motorcycle at 100 m.p.h. without a helmet.*

STUDENT WRITER

In each case above, the writers chose to apply the **it**-*inversion* in order to shift a noun substitute from initial to final position within a sentence. But remember that the recombination is always optional rather than obligatory. Whether or not you apply it in a given instance is a matter of emphasis, clarity, and style.

CLEFT PATTERNS

As we have seen, the most emphatic positions within a sentence are the beginning and the end. While the inversion patterns allow you to shift important information to the end of the sentence, a second set of recombinations allows you to emphasize material at either end of the sentence. These are the **cleft patterns.** The term "cleft" comes from the fact that these patterns cleave or split a sentence into its two fundamental parts, the subject and the predicate, either of which may be emphasized.

Like the inversions, the first cleft pattern, the **what**-*cleft,* focuses our attention on the final element in a sentence. The recombination works by inserting the word **what** at the beginning of the sentence along with a form of **to be** after the verb. Here's a before-and-after pair of sentences illustrating how the **what**-*cleft* works:

BASIC SENTENCE PATTERN

Hopper really liked domestic architecture.

***WHAT*- CLEFT PATTERN**

What Hopper really liked **was** domestic architecture.

The **what**-*cleft* pattern thus emphasizes the final element in the basic sentence, *domestic architecture.* And as the complete sentence that art critic

Calvin Tomkins wrote reveals, domestic architecture was indeed a central theme in Edward Hopper's paintings:

1 **What** Hopper really liked **was** domestic architecture—
  2 Victorian houses,
  2 New York tenements,
  2 small-town façades,
  2 gas stations,
  2 lighthouses.

"Sun in an Empty Room"

The appositives added at level 2 suggest what kinds of domestic architecture interested the artist, but the **what**-*cleft* pattern in the base clause emphasizes the general point Tomkins wishes to stress.

The second cleft pattern, the **it**-*cleft,* creates an effect quite opposite to the effect the **what**-*cleft* creates. Instead of stressing the final element in a sentence, the **it**-*cleft* focuses attention on the initial element. This pattern involves adding **it is** or **it was** to the beginning of the sentence along with the word **who, that,** or **which** between the subject and the predicate:

BASIC SENTENCE PATTERN

The Queen worried them.
(subject) *(predicate)*

***IT*-CLEFT PATTERN**

It was the Queen **who** worried them.

ELIZABETH BURTON, *The Pageant of Elizabethan England*

As you can tell by reading the sentence aloud, the **it**-*cleft* pattern emphasizes *the Queen,* the subject of the basic sentence. Both the cleft patterns work by raising expectations about information to come. The **what**-*cleft* seems almost to raise a question: *What* did Hopper really like? We get the answer in the predicate: *domestic architecture,* that's what. The **it**-*cleft* raises our expectations with an initially puzzling pronoun: *It* was who? It was *the Queen*—Elizabeth I, to be exact—who worried them.

Naturally, which of the cleft patterns, if any, you use to recombine a given sentence depends on what you wish to emphasize in the sentence. If you wish to stress the final element, use the **what**-*cleft;* if you wish to stress the initial element, use the **it**-*cleft.* Furthermore, it is often possible to combine a cleft pattern with an inversion. This double recombination greatly expands the possibilities for emphasis in our sample sentences:

A. BASIC SENTENCE PATTERN

Hopper really liked domestic architecture.

***WHAT*-CLEFT PATTERN**

What Hopper really liked **was** domestic architecture.

***IT*-CLEFT PATTERN**
It was Hopper **who** really liked domestic architecture.

***IT*- CLEFT PLUS INVERSION**
It was domestic architecture **that** Hopper really liked.

B. BASIC SENTENCE PATTERN
The Queen worried them.

***WHAT*-CLEFT PATTERN**
What the Queen did **was** worry them.

***WHAT*-CLEFT PLUS INVERSION**
What worried them **was** the Queen.

***IT*- CLEFT PATTERN**
It was the Queen **who** worried them.

***IT*- CLEFT PLUS INVERSION**
It was they **whom** the Queen worried.

These recombinations show how a basic sentence pattern can be rearranged to focus attention on almost any element a writer wishes to emphasize.

Because the cleft patterns stress one element over another, they are especially useful for making contrasts. This is exactly the case with our two sample sentences, as a glance at their contexts reveals. In discussing Edward Hopper's paintings, Calvin Tomkins first noted that Hopper had little interest in painting the human form. Tomkins then used the **what**-*cleft* to make a telling contrast:

What Hopper really liked **was** domestic architecture.

Likewise, Elizabeth Burton began with a general statement that the Privy Council was worried. But they were not concerned about such mundane matters as spies or taxes. No, Burton used the **it**-*cleft* to stress:

It was the Queen **who** worried them.

As it happened, Queen Elizabeth I once had a royal toothache that nearly toppled the throne of England.

THERE-PATTERNS

The inversions and cleft patterns, then, recombine basic sentences and thereby change the style and focus of the sentences. This is also the case with a third set of recombinations, **there**-*patterns.* Like the inversions and the **what**-*cleft,* the **there**-*pattern* shifts the important information in a basic sentence to the most emphatic position, to the end. Indeed, this pattern shifts *both* the subject and the complement into the predicate, as this example reveals:

BASIC SENTENCE PATTERN

Nothing (*subject*) is (*verb*) at all absurd about the human condition. (*complement*)

***THERE*-PATTERN**

There is (*verb*) nothing (*subject*) at all absurd about the human condition. (*complement*)

Note that creating a **there**-*pattern* involves two simple steps. First, you move a **to be** verb (like *is*) to the beginning of the sentence, thereby shifting both the subject and the complement into emphatic predicate positions. Second, you add the word **there** to the very front of the recombination. Here, as is usually the case, the **there**-*pattern* sounds not only more emphatic than the original sentence but more natural as well. Thus, it is no surprise to learn that the recombination is what Lewis Thomas actually wrote in his essay "The Youngest and Brightest Thing Around."

Generally, any sentence that has an indefinite subject like *a man, some people,* or *nothing* can be profitably recombined by means of the **there**-*pattern.* Indeed, we almost always use a **there**-*pattern* when we wish to assert merely that something exists. For instance, in the paired sentences below, the basic pattern sounds awkward:

BASIC SENTENCE PATTERN

Half a million more automobiles are in Los Angeles than people are.

***THERE*- PATTERN**

There are half a million more automobiles in Los Angeles than **there** are people.

ISAAC ASIMOV, "Fascinating Facts"

As Asimov's sentence reveals, the **there**-*pattern* sounds so natural and familiar to us that we easily forget it is not a basic pattern but a recombination.

The **there**-*pattern* thus allows you to establish the mere existence of something in a natural-sounding way. In addition, a variation on this pattern can help you make the existence of something seem important. This recombination resembles the **it**-*cleft* in that it involves the addition of **who, that,** or **which** between the subject and predicate of the basic sentence. For this reason, we can call this recombination the **there**-*cleft* pattern:

BASIC SENTENCE PATTERN

A man came each day to work on the collapsed heating system.

***THERE*-CLEFT PATTERN**

There was a man **that** came each day to work on the collapsed heating system.

E. B. WHITE, "What Do Our Hearts Treasure?"

Again like the **it**-*cleft,* the **there**-*cleft* pattern works especially well when you seek to make a telling contrast, as this lively sentence from a student writer reveals:

> I didn't mind the shake, rattle, and roll of my brother's vintage Studebaker, but **there was** a low grinding noise **that** worried me whenever he shifted gears.

In the second clause of this compound sentence, the **there**-*cleft* emphasizes the troubling noise—and suggests there may be more trouble to come. The recombination thus focuses our attention on what will likely prove to be a key element in the story.

PASSIVES

The final recombination we shall consider is the **passive.** The passive has a bad reputation among teachers, who usually urge their students to write simple **active** sentences, like this one from H. M. Tomlinson's *A Lost Wood:*

London	frightened	him.
(subject)	*(verb)*	*(direct object)*

The passive recombination of Tomlinson's sentence is as follows:

He	was frightened	by	London.
(subject)	*(verb)*	*(preposition)*	*(object of preposition)*

Note just how the recombination changes the focus of Tomlinson's sentence. The original active version portrays the subject, *London,* acting on the direct object, *him.* In the passive version, the new subject, *he,* is acted upon *by London.* The active verb *frightened* shows the subject acting; the passive verb *was frightened* shows the subject acted upon. The difference between the two versions is a difference of focus. Both versions are grammatically correct, but each one calls attention to a different element in the sentence, either the actor or the acted-upon. Whether you write one version or the other is a matter of style and choice, conscious or unconscious.

And it is the unconscious or thoughtless choice of the passive that makes teachers boil. Such choice, if we can call it choice at all, often puts the focus where it does not belong, as in this sentence from a business executive's letter of resignation:

> After six months of deliberation, *the decision has been made by myself to retire from my job.*

Here, the passive recombination garbles the message. Who spent six months in deliberation? Not the decision but the executive. A simple active version of the sentence would make better sense:

> After six months of deliberation, *I have made the decision to retire from my job.*

Because this version portrays the subject, *I,* as actively making a decision, it not only clarifies the message but makes the executive appear decisive.

Nevertheless, there are times when the passive recombination improves an otherwise unfocused sentence. Consider this simple statement:

People universally **concede** poetry to be the loftiest of the verbal arts.

What's the key element here? Surely not people, but poetry. The sentence is thus out of focus. Therefore, the semanticist (and U.S. senator) S. I. Hayakawa recombined the sentence this way in his book *Language in Thought and Action:*

Poetry **is** universally **conceded** to be the loftiest of the verbal arts.

By changing the active verb *concede* into the passive *is conceded,* Hayakawa focused the sentence on *poetry,* the key element. In addition, since the concession is universal, Hayakawa simply dropped the word *people* out of the combination. Lewis Thomas did much the same thing in this passive sentence from "The Medusa and the Snail":

Self-enlightenment **can be taught** in college courses.

Taught by whom? Presumably by college teachers. When the doer of the action is obvious or repetitive, writers often simply drop it out of passive sentences.

But it is this very elimination of the original subject or actor that causes much of the uproar over the passive. Teachers rightly point out that an unscrupulous writer will recombine the active assertion "The candidate *arranged* the burglary" into the passive evasion "The burglary *was arranged.*" It is true that our ability to recombine sentences allows us not only to emphasize important matters but to de-emphasize them as well. Fortunately, as critical readers, we can call the bluff of the passive by demanding, "WAS ARRANGED BY WHOM?" The trick is to understand how the recombination works.

PULLING IT ALL TOGETHER

Used consciously and conscientiously, then, *inversions, cleft patterns,* **there**-*patterns,* and *passives* can add special effects to your writing. These recombinations allow you to change the focus and emphasis in basic sentence patterns.

In the sentence that opened this chapter, we saw how a political scientist, Walter Lippmann, recombined a paradoxical sentence to make the paradox clear and emphatic. To conclude, let us turn to a different field, medical biology. In his essay "Germs," Dr. Lewis Thomas argues that far from living at the mercy of hostile microorganisms, we humans for the most part live in harmony with the bacteria around and within us. Trouble arises when our own bodies mistake a benign "germ" for an enemy:

> Our arsenals for fighting off bacteria are so powerful, and involve so many different defense mechanisms, that we are in more danger from them than from the invaders. We live in the midst of explosive devices; we are mined.

Having set forth these facts, Thomas then draws a telling conclusion. We may consider his bold one-sentence paragraph as a sentence-combining problem with two parts:

> We cannot abide the information.
> The bacteria carry the information.

If the author had sought a matter-of-fact effect here, he might simply have combined the sentences by creating a relative clause:

> We cannot abide the information **that** *the bacteria carry.*

But while this version is grammatically correct, it is out of focus. The key idea here is that we cannot abide the *information.* In the basic pattern above, the word *information* is buried in the least emphatic position, in mid-sentence. Therefore, to bring the sentence into focus, Thomas used three of the recombinations we have studied. First, he inverted the sentence in order to bring *the information* into the emphatic initial position:

> *The information* that the bacteria carry we cannot abide.

He also recombined the relative clause from active to passive form by changing *the bacteria carry the information* into *the information is carried by the bacteria.* This recombination further focused our attention on the key element, *the information:*

> The information *carried by the bacteria* we cannot abide.

In addition, Thomas used the **it**-*cleft* pattern, which emphasizes the first part of the sentence:

> **It is** the information carried by the bacteria **that** we cannot abide.

This is the emphatic one-sentence paragraph as Thomas actually wrote it. Simple as it appears, the sentence is carefully focused on the elements the author seeks to stress. It is thus by *recombining sentences* that we turn statements into assertions.

Recombining Sentences: Recombinations

Study the sample problems below and then apply the appropriate inversion, cleft, **there-**, or passive recombinations to the sentences that follow the samples. You can compare your recombinations with professional or student writers' sentences in the Appendix.

A. Inversions

SAMPLE EXERCISES

The strong tide of human woe flows beneath the sparkling surface of these dilemmas. [simple inversion]

That *chemical insecticides must never be used* is not my contention. [**it**-*inversion*]

PROFESSIONAL WRITERS' VERSIONS

Beneath the sparkling surface of these dilemmas flows the strong tide of human woe.

E. B. WHITE, "Some Remarks on Humor"

It is not my contention **that** *chemical insecticides must never be used.*

RACHEL CARSON, *Silent Spring*

1. The root of the matter lies there.
2. What I ought to do was perfectly clear to me.
3. To overestimate the degree to which the invention of cellular respiration released the forces of living organisms is difficult.
4. A man's voice sounded over on Main Street, laughing.
5. That a single man in possession of a good fortune must be in want of a wife is a truth universally acknowledged.

B. Cleft Patterns

SAMPLE EXERCISES

You needed a map that would never be outdated because political configurations were settled. [**what**-*cleft*]

Only shallow people require years to get rid of an emotion. [**it**-*cleft*]

PROFESSIONAL WRITERS' VERSIONS

What you needed **was** a map that would never be outdated because political configurations were settled.

KENZABURO OË, *A Personal Matter*

It is only shallow people **who** require years to get rid of an emotion.

OSCAR WILDE, *The Picture of Dorian Gray*

6. "You have ideas; you need money," he said.
7. A large mirror climbed the wall in scrolls almost to the ceiling.
8. Both of us were too dumb to understand that although great passions may be possible without actually liking each other, marriages aren't.

9. Nietzsche was to have the most decisive influence on de Chirico.
10. The leisure time, community organization, and specialization of labor in the first cities permitted the emergence of the arts and technologies we think of as the hallmarks of civilization.

C. *There*-Patterns

SAMPLE EXERCISES

A tension is in American education today over what schools ought to be about. [simple **there**-*pattern*]

Some people undergo a complete change of nature when it comes time to get someone else out of bed. [**there**-*cleft*]

PROFESSIONAL WRITERS' VERSIONS

There is a tension in American education today over what schools ought to be about.

JUDITH S. SIEGEL AND EDWIN J. DELATTRE, "Blackboard Jumble"

There are some people **who** undergo a complete change of nature when it comes time to get someone else out of bed.

ROBERT BENCHLEY, "Awake, Awake!"

11. Nothing is more important for a narcissist than a smooth surface.
12. Some people cannot resist the desire to get into a cage with wild beasts and be mangled.
13. Four men were sitting at one of the tables, drinking coffee.
14. Nothing in the teachings of Jesus or St. Francis justifies us in thinking that the opinions of fifty-one percent of a group are better than the opinions of forty-nine percent.
15. No universal geniuses exist; only universal fools exist.

D. Passives

SAMPLE EXERCISES

The General Accounting Office is now investigating the costs. [passive]

Someone bribed the border patrol in advance. [passive]

PROFESSIONAL WRITERS' VERSIONS

The costs **are** now **being investigated by** the General Accounting Office.

ADA LOUISE HUXTABLE, "The Rayburn Building"

The border patrol **was bribed** in advance. [Note that the indefinite subject **someone** has been dropped from the recombination.]

ISAAC BASHEVIS SINGER, "Yochna and Shmelke"

16. Increasing complexity has accompanied biological evolution.
17. Someone is installing prison fixtures in the restrooms of city parks.
18. The work of linguistic scientists, parallel to the work the psychiatrists do, has not yet noticeably eased English-usage guilt-feelings.
19. Prominent Iranians made attempts to organize political support for Bani-Sadr.
20. The increasingly narrow definition of combat and the increasingly technological aspects of war make the issue of women in combat problematic.

A Note on the English Character

Combine the sentences below into a paragraph that contains at least one recombining pattern. You can compare your paragraph with a professional or student writer's version in the Appendix.

1. National faults exist.
2. National diseases exist.
3. Perhaps one can draw a parallel between them.

4. The national diseases of England should be cancer and consumption.
5. This has always impressed me.
6. Cancer and consumption are slow.
7. They are insidious.
8. They pretend something.
9. They are something else.
10. The diseases proper to the South should be cholera and plague.
11. Cholera and plague strike at a man.
12. He is perfectly well.
13. They may leave him a corpse by evening.

14. Mr. and Mrs. John Dashwood are consumptives.
15. Their consumption is moral.

16. They collapse.
17. Their collapse is gradual.
18. They do not realize something.
19. What is the disease?

20. Nothing is dramatic about their sin.
21. Nothing is violent about their sin.

22. You cannot call them villains.

Writing Suggestion 1: This exercise draws a parallel—an *analogy*—between a nation's physical ailments and its moral shortcomings. If you believe that such parallels are valid, write a paragraph comparing the national diseases and national faults of some other country besides England. If you reject the analogy as invalid, write a paragraph explaining why the parallel is false.

Writing Suggestion 2: Using: *A Note on the English Character* as a model, write "A Note on the American Character." Try to define and illustrate the national traits you believe are uniquely American.

Pros and Cons

Combine the sentences below into a paragraph that contains at least one recombining pattern. You can compare your paragraph with a professional or student writer's version in the Appendix.

1. Nothing is new about this.
2. Prisoners do some work.
3. The work is honest.

4. It was as long ago as the early nineteenth century.
5. Someone saw industry as the inmate's ticket to redemption.
6. The redemption was moral.
7. Someone judged wardens by their bottom lines.

8. By 1828 Sing Sing claimed something.
9. It was economically self-sufficient.
10. The self-sufficiency was by virtue of this.
11. The inmates cut stone.
12. The inmates were blacksmiths.
13. The inmates did other activities.

14. Private companies sought something.
15. They would limit the competition.
16. The competition was from so much cheap labor.

17. Congress came to the companies' aid.
18. This was during the Depression.
19. Congress severely curtailed the right to sell goods.
20. The goods were made in prison.
21. The goods were sold across state lines.

22. Work programs began to shut down.

23. Many of those barriers remain.
24. The barriers are legal.
25. Prison industries are making a comeback.
26. The reasons for this are sociological.
27. The reasons for this are financial.

Writing Suggestion 1: Should prisoners be required to work while serving time? Should they be paid for their labors? Write an essay arguing for or against the development of prison industries.

Writing Suggestion 2: This exercise alludes to the great economic depression of the 1930s. Use your school library to learn what the Depression was. What is the difference between a depression and a recession? Write an essay in which you compare and contrast the two economic conditions.

Recombining Sentences: Creations

The ten sentences below are drawn from the work of professional writers. As you will see, each sentence involves at least one of the recombining patterns that you have studied: the inversion, cleft, **there-**, or passive.

Study each sample closely and then create a sentence of your own that imitates the professional writer's sentence. Try to re-create the pattern of the model sentence in your own words.

SAMPLE EXERCISE

2 Once the offer **was made,** [passive]
1 Haig was on the next plane to Washington.
SANFORD J. UNGAR, "Alexander Haig: Pragmatist at State"

STUDENT WRITER'S VERSION

2 Once the pitch **was thrown,**
1 I was on my way to second base.
STUDENT WRITER

1. 1 **Inland from the sea on the dry coastal plain lay the town,** [simple inversion]
2 open,
2 spread out under the huge high sky.
PAUL BOWLES, "Under the Sky"

2. 1 **It** is unrealistic **to suppose** *that we buy our beer and toothpaste freely.* [**it**-*inversion*]
CHARLES REMBAR, "For Sale: Freedom of Speech"

3. 1 **What** he had asked of her **had been** simply at first not to laugh at him. [**what**-*cleft*]
HENRY JAMES, "The Beast in the Jungle"

4. 1 **It is** improbable people like E. B. White **who** lift up the hearts of a nation in time of war and show us why we must nourish artists as we do gunboats. [**it**-*cleft*]
TRB (RICHARD L. STROUT), "The Great White Way"

5. 2 Although **there** were no police at the concert site,
1 **there** were security guards. [**there**-*pattern*]
RALPH J. GLEASON, "Aquarius Wept"

6. 1 **There are** people **who** cannot conceive of a nation not driven by fear. [**there**-*cleft*]

WALTER LIPPMANN, *Drift and Mastery*

7. 1 This signal mark of honor **was greeted** with the greatest satisfaction and delight **by** everyone. [passive]

ELIZABETH BURTON, *The Pagaent of Elizabethan England*

8. 2 Before such women as Louise **can be understood** and their lives **made** livable,
1 much **will have to be done.** [passive]

SHERWOOD ANDERSON, *Winesburg, Ohio*

9. 2 High above him beside the funnel,
3 to escape the risk of infection,
1 **stood an Anglican parson,** [simple inversion]
2 one of the passengers.

ALLAN SEAGER, "This Town and Salamanca"

10. 2 His singing **would be much missed by** the choir and congregation at St. Stephen's Church, [passive]
1 the paper said,
and
1 **there** were two lines of appreciation from the Vicar George Wyatt Edmonton. [**there**-*pattern*]

MARGARET DRABBLE, *The Realms of Gold*

Small Town, U.S.A.

Combine the sentences below into a paragraph that contains several recombining patterns. You can compare your paragraph with a professional or student writer's version in the Appendix.

1. You grow up in a small town.
2. You do not have a number.
3. You have a name and rank.
4. Everybody knows your name and rank.
5. You have a history too.

6. You do not understand this.
7. How did Edgar Lee Masters write *Spoon River Anthology?*
8. But you understand this.
9. How did he get his material?
10. How did he come to know the secret lives of so many so well?

11. A small-town rearing consists, by and large, of this.
12. You get to know everybody.
13. You get to be known.
14. Everybody knows you.

15. You get to feel that familiarity.
16. The familiarity is intimate.
17. The familiarity is communal.
18. The familiarity is both support and intrusion.
19. The support is affectionate.
20. The intrusion is unrelenting.

21. Someone craves privacy.
22. This has often primarily impelled the flight.
23. The flight is from intimacy to anonymity.
24. The anonymity is the city's.

25. The bonding is formidable.
26. The bonding occurs when one's very history is community property.
27. The bonding is oppressive to certain temperaments.

28. That bonding makes most true small-towners suspicious.
29. They are more suspicious than city folk.
30. They are more suspicious of strangers.
31. The bonding is that sense.
32. They sense this.
33. They utterly are of a place.
34. They utterly belong to a place.

Writing Suggestion 1: Which kind of living do you prefer, the small town or the big city? Write an essay comparing the two ways of life and, if you wish, arguing for the superiority of one over the other.

Writing Suggestion 2: Demographics is the statistical science that deals with the density, distribution, and vital statistics of populations. Use your school library, especially the almanacs and government documents, to make up a demographic description of your home city. How many and what kinds of people live in your area at present? How might the population change in the future? Write up your findings in an essay.

Recombining Sentences: Sentence Acrobatics

Combine each set of sentences below into one or more "acrobatic" sentences. See if you can use recombining patterns as you do each exercise, but feel free to try out other constructions as well. Naturally, each problem invites more than one "correct" answer. Therefore, you must create original sentences that strike *you* as both correct and stylish.*

* *Note:* Because all recombinations—including passives—have been returned to their basic forms in these problems, the exercises are challenging. Nevertheless, if you have worked your way through the preceding material, you should be able to handle the "Acrobatics" here.

You may enjoy comparing your combinations with the professional or student writers' versions in the Appendix. Look for both similarities and differences, but try to decide whose version is the more stylish—it may well be your own.

SAMPLE EXERCISE

The number of meals does not necessarily measure gluttony.
The quantity of food measures gluttony.
One eats the food at each meal.
He seems to forget this.

STUDENT AND PROFESSIONAL WRITERS' VERSIONS

It is not the number of meals but the quantity of food one eats at each meal **that** measures gluttony, he seems to forget.

STUDENT WRITER

What he seems to forget **is** that gluttony **is** not necessarily **measured by** number of meals but **by** quantity of food **eaten** at each meal.

ELIZABETH BURTON, *The Pageant of Elizabethan England*

1. One says something.
   Modern medicine began with the era of antibiotics.
   This overlooks a staggering amount of basic research.
2. No one knows this.
   Was Debbie a good student or not?
   She worked such long hours after school.
   She had little time left for studying.
3. This coat needs something.
   One strips the coat off.
   The coat is smothering.
   The need is constant.
   One strips it off in life.
   One strips it off in relationships.
4. Everyone takes something for granted.
   A row will always exist.
   The row involves labor.
   The row concerns farmers.
5. He pretended something.
   She was an old friend.
   This was vain.
   All the communities were wanting.
   In spite of this he saw something.
   She would have suited him as an old friend.

6. No one recorded the precise time.
   At the time a majority of Americans looked up.
   They decided something.
   Their government had ceased to be a friend.
   It had ceased to be a helper.
   It had become a hindrance.

7. Some things happen to us.
   We cannot bear these things.
   The result is this.
   The result is paradoxical.
   We carry these things.
   We carry them on our backs.
   We carry them the rest of our lives.

8. This is in the Eden metaphor.
   No evidence of murder exists.
   This is before the Fall.
   But those fractured skulls may be evidence.
   Our ancestors killed many mammals.
   The skulls are of bipeds.
   The bipeds were not on the evolutionary line to man.
   The mammals were like men.
   Our ancestors killed them even in Eden.

9. Marinetti expressed the futurist ethos.
   This was before World War I.
   The ethos had its cult of speed.
   It had a cult of male potency.
   It had a cult of antifeminism.
   It had a cult of violent struggle.
   The futurist ethos supplied the framework.
   The framework was oratorical.
   The framework was for Mussolini's rise to power.
   The futurist ethos set the stage for his appearance.

10. This is true.
    Someone had perfected the atomic bomb.
    This was only after someone had eliminated Germany from the war.
    Japan was the only possible proving ground for the bomb as an actual weapon.
    Many in Japan would think something.
    Many elsewhere in the Orient would think something.
    We had been willing to use a weapon of this terribleness against Japan.
    We might not have been willing to use it against a white enemy.

Laying Waste

Combine the sentences below into an essay that contains several recombining patterns. You can compare your essay with a professional or student writer's version in the Appendix.

1. Humankind is fouling its own habitat.
2. The fouling is systematic.
3. This has been apparent for quite some time now.
4. Humankind litters its natural household with debris.
5. The debris is lethal.
6. The debris endangers life itself.

7. Modern chemical industries spew out great masses of waste every day.
8. Some of it is deadly beyond measure.

9. The simplest way to dispose of those residues, of course, is this.
10. You discharge them directly into the environment.
11. You spill the vapors out into the atmosphere.
12. You pour the liquids into nearby bodies of water.
13. You dump the solids onto empty parcels of land.

14. We use such methods so widely.
15. We often take a certain comfort from the thought.
16. We think many of the most hazardous of these wastes are sealed away in underground dump sites.
17. The most hazardous of these wastes are chemical solvents, toxic substances, radioactive materials.
18. We assume this.
19. In the underground dump sites they stew impotently in their own juices for a few years.
20. They gradually lose their bite.

21. We call this process "disposal."
22. It is a dangerously inapt word in many ways.

23. We dispose.
24. This means something.
25. We get rid of.
26. We discard.
27. We do away with.

28. And that is exactly it.
29. We find it hard.
30. We should do it.

31. The chemicals are among the best-built products of our shoddy age.
32. We bury the chemicals beneath our feet.

33. They are tough chains of molecules.
34. The molecules will not easily degrade.
35. The molecules will not easily break down.

36. Time has little effect on them.

37. The sun will not purify them.

38. All the waters in the world will not dissolve them.
39. All the waters in the world will not wash them clean.

40. We store them in the ground.
41. We inject them into the body of the earth itself.
42. In the body of the earth they can seep to the surface.
43. Or they can bleed through the walls of their subterranean pits.
44. They bleed into the underground waterways.
45. All life depends on the underground waterways.

46. We find the right words.
47. The words describe this situation.
48. We find the right notes.
49. The notes sound a general alarm.
50. This is sometimes difficult.
51. The vocabularies and images are so remote from everyday human experience.
52. We must draw on the vocabularies and images for the purpose.

53. The chemicals leak into our living spaces.
54. The chemicals have long laboratory names.
55. The names defy pronunciation.
56. The names sound as sanitary as the ingredients in toothpaste.

57. We often express their power to do harm in fractions so minute.
58. One part per billion, say, can be a dangerous dosage.
59. The mind does not know something.
60. What should it make of them?

61. We have deposited them in so many dump sites throughout the country.
62. A map identifies their locations.
63. The map would look like an explosion of dots.

64. How, then, is one to convey the nature of the problem?

65. How is one to organize all of those odd statistics into a story?
66. How is one to organize all of those technical details into a story?

67. Every now and then an incident occurs.
68. It occurs in one of those places on the map.
69. The places have names like Minamata and Grassy Narrows.
70. The places have names like Seveso and the Love Canal.

71. They are eruptions.
72. They are boils on the surface of an earth.
73. The boils are angry.
74. The earth is infected.

75. But they allow something.
76. Someone tells a story.
77. They involve manageable numbers of people.
78. They involve casualty figures.
79. The figures fall within the range of the normal human imagination.
80. They involve plots.
81. Someone can follow the plots.

Writing Suggestion 1: Go to the library and read about the effects of toxic chemicals in Minamata, Grassy Narrows, Seveso, or the Love Canal. A good place to start would be the *Readers' Guide to Periodical Literature,* although a book like Michael H. Brown's *The Poisoning of America by Toxic Chemicals* (New York: Pantheon Books, 1980) would also provide extensive information. Write an essay reporting your findings—and your thoughts on them.

Writing Suggestion 2: Probably the most talked-about toxic waste in recent years has been "radwaste," the radioactive by-products of atomic energy plants. At present, many of these by-products are in temporary storage, awaiting the day when scientists find a way to dispose of them permanently. Do you believe we are right in running nuclear power plants when we have, at present, no permanent way of disposing of their toxic wastes? Is the risk justified? Write an essay in which you argue your opinion, using details and examples to support your views.

The review exercises in this chapter will help you practice using **absolute phrases, noun substitutes,** and **recombining patterns** along with other combinations.

Crazy Thoughts

Combine the sentences below into a paragraph that contains both bound and free modifiers. You can compare your paragraph with a professional or student writer's version in the Appendix.

1. My father was fair.
2. His sidelocks were dark.
3. His beard was red.
4. The red was like tobacco.

5. He had a short nose.
6. He had blue eyes.

7. A strange thought occurred to me.
8. He resembled the czar.
9. The czar's picture hung in our cheder.*

10. I knew this well enough.
11. A comparison like that was a sacrilege.

* *cheder:* Jewish school for young children

12. The czar was a vicious man.
13. My father was pious.
14. My father was a rabbi.

15. But my brain was full of thoughts.
16. The thoughts were crazy.

17. People knew something.
18. What was I thinking?
19. They would put me in prison.

20. My parents would disown me.

21. Someone would excommunicate me.
22. I would be like the philosopher.
23. The philosopher was Spinoza.
24. My father spoke of Spinoza at the Purim* dinner.

25. That heretic had denied God.

26. He said this.
27. The world was not created.
28. The world had existed for eternity.

Writing Suggestion 1: Like the son in the exercise above, all of us now and again have "crazy thoughts" that come floating into our minds. Take ten minutes—and ten minutes only—to write the craziest thoughts you can think of right now. Share your writing with your classmates if you dare.

Writing Suggestion 2: Write a full description of your own father or mother. While you should certainly include a physical description of your parent, be sure to sketch his or her background, beliefs, and character as well.

Three Heresies

Combine each set of sentences below into a paragraph that contains both bound and free modifiers. You can compare your paragraphs with a professional or student writer's versions in the Appendix.

A.
1. This is in the tale about the emperor's clothes.
2. The tale is classic.
3. The emperor's clothes are finely woven.
4. A child discovers something.
5. The emperor is unclothed.

6. That makes him a naked emperor.

* *Purim:* Jewish holiday commemorating the deliverance of the Persian Jews by Queen Esther from a massacre plotted by Haman

7. For modern man the point of this story should not be this.
8. The emperor is naked.
9. The point should be this.
10. The emperor is a liar.

B.
1. A person understands another less.
2. His urge is greater.
3. He wants to classify him.
4. The classification is in terms of nationality.
5. It is in terms of religion.
6. It is in terms of occupation.
7. It is in terms of status.
8. The status is psychiatric.

9. Acquaintance renders such classification quite unnecessary.
10. The acquaintance is intimate.
11. The acquaintance is with another person.

12. We categorize people.
13. We classify people.
14. This is not a means of something.
15. We know them better.
16. It is a means of something.
17. We make sure of this.
18. We will not know them too well.

19. We classify another person.
20. In short, this renders acquaintance with him quite unnecessary.
21. It renders acquaintance with him impossible.
22. The acquaintance is intimate.

C.
1. This is in human relations.
2. The relations are intimate.
3. The relations are lasting.
4. Autonomy and proximity vary inversely.
5. The autonomy is psychological.
6. The proximity is physical.

7. Those want something.
8. They maximize both.
9. The wanting is foolish.
10. It may be in marriage.
11. It may be in friendship.
12. They will have neither.

13. Those are satisfied.
14. They have one or the other.
15. They have some of each sometimes.
16. Their satisfaction is wise.

17. Married people used to be this way.
18. Friends now tend to be this way.
19. They may have one or the other.
20. They may have sometimes some of each.

Writing Suggestion 1: Although we generally use the term "heresies" for religious opinions that are at odds with the established church, one can maintain a "heretical" opinion on any topic where conventional wisdom holds sway. Think over the received ideas that you have rejected and then write a paragraph stating a "heresy" of your own.

Writing Suggestion 2: Heresies—unorthodox opinions—arise not only in religion but in science, politics, and the arts as well. Indeed, scientists like Charles Darwin and Albert Einstein, political theorists like Jean Jacques Rousseau and Thomas Jefferson, and artists like Paul Cézanne and Pablo Picasso were all considered "heretics" at times. Write an essay discussing a "heretic" whom you consider especially important in the making of our culture. You can write on any of the people listed above or on any other "heretic" you choose.

Review of Chapters 11, 12, 13: Sentence Acrobatics

Combine each set of sentences below into one or more "acrobatic" sentences. See if you can use absolute phrases, noun substitutes, and recombining patterns as you do the exercises, but feel free to try out other constructions as well. Naturally, each problem invites more than one "correct" answer. Therefore, you must create original sentences that strike *you* as both correct and stylish.

You may enjoy comparing your combinations with the professional or student writers' versions in the Appendix. Look for both similarities and differences, but try to decide whose version is the more stylish—it may well be your own.

SAMPLE EXERCISE

Psychoanalysts believe in the Oedipus complex.
The belief is universal.
They disagree about something.
The disagreement is wide.
Is the Oedipus complex indeed the central experience of childhood?
Is it indeed the greatest problem of early life?

STUDENT AND PROFESSIONAL WRITERS' VERSIONS

Psychoanalysts universally believe in the Oedipus complex, but **what** they widely disagree about **is whether** *the Oedipus complex is indeed not only the central experience of childhood but also the greatest problem of early life.*

STUDENT WRITER

While belief in the Oedipus complex is universal among psychoanalysts, **there** is wide disagreement about **whether** *it is indeed the central experience of childhood and the greatest problem of early life.*

JANET MALCOLM, *Psychoanalysis: The Impossible Profession*

1. Two great identical snakes are on a Levantine libation cup of around 2000 B.C.
   They coil around each other in a double helix.
   The helix represents the original generation of life.

2. A sea of faces ringed around us.
   Some were hostile.
   Some were amused.
   A magnificent blonde stood in the center.
   She was facing us.
   She was stark naked.

3. Technologies are producing changes.
   Changes in social institutions do not adequately match the changes in technologies.
   People are under strain.
   People are under tension.

4. You want to teach reading.
   Rote learning is the wrong way.
   Someone recognized this.
   The recognition was over seventy years ago.

5. Doctors discovered the separation or lateralization of cortical functions.
   They discovered this on individuals.
   The individuals had brain damage.
   Doctors must demonstrate something.
   The conclusions apply to normal humans.
   This is important.

6. The Gallup polls are reports of this.
   What are people thinking?
   A plurality of people think one way.
   Someone sampled the people in the poll.
   This has no bearing upon something.
   Is the one way sound public policy?

7. Nicole's suit slid into the restaurant.
   Her suit was sky blue.
   The restaurant was dark.
   It was smoky.
   It smelled of the foods on the buffet.
   The foods were rich.

The foods were raw.
Nicole's suit was like a stray segment of the weather outside.

8. He stood.
He had folded his arms.
A cat was in each sleeve.
He resembled the Prophet Muhammad.
This was when Muhammad preached from the tallest minaret in Mecca.
Someone saw Muhammad carry his white cat.
Muhammad called the cat Muezza.
The cat was asleep in the sleeve of his robe.
Someone wrote it.

9. The beach sounds are jazzy.
Percussion is fixing the mode.
The surf is cracking and booming in the distance.
A little nearer dropped barbells are clanking.
Steel gym rings are ringing.
The rings are flung together.
Palm fronds are rustling above me.
They are like steel brushes.
The brushes are washing over a snare drum.
Troupes of sandals are splatting and shuffling on the sandy cement.
Their beat is varying.
Syncopation is emerging and disappearing.
It emerges and disappears with changing paces.

10. He had uttered a mad wish.
He himself might remain young.
The portrait would grow old.
His beauty might be untarnished.
The face on the canvas would bear the burden of his passions and his sins.
The lines of suffering and thought might sear the painted image.
He might keep all the bloom and loveliness of his boyhood.
The bloom was delicate.
His boyhood was then just conscious.

Some Self-Analysis

Combine the sentences below into a paragraph that contains both bound and free modifiers. You can compare your paragraph with a professional or student writer's version in the Appendix.

1. I have long wondered something.
2. Just what was my strength as a writer?

3. Enthusiasm for a subject often fills me.
4. The enthusiasm is tremendous.
5. I write about the subject.
6. This will seem an attempt.
7. The attempt will seem sorry.

8. I possess a sincerity.
9. This is above all.
10. My sincerity is driving.
11. Sincerity is that prime virtue of any worker.
12. The worker is creative.

13. I write only this.
14. What do I believe?
15. It is the absolute truth.
16. I must ruin the theme.
17. I do so.

18. It is in this respect.
19. I feel far superior to those people.
20. Those people are glib.
21. They are in my classes.
22. They often garner better grades than I do.

23. They are frauds.
24. This is too often.
25. The frauds are pitiful.
26. They are artificial.
27. They are insincere.

28. They have a line.
29. The line works.

30. They do not write.
31. The writing is from the depths.
32. The depths are of their hearts.

33. Pain never bore anything of theirs.

34. Many a piece of writing has outlived the product.
35. The piece was incoherent.
36. The piece was sincere.
37. The product was polished.

Writing Suggestion 1: Write a paragraph analyzing your own writing process. Consider your strengths and weaknesses, but try to seek out what sets you apart from other writers you have observed.

Writing Suggestion 2: Write an essay analyzing the style of any of the master writers whose work appears in *Combining and Creating*. To do this, you will need to read an extended piece of writing by the author, perhaps a story, essay, or book. Once you have completed this research, explain what techniques make the writer's style distinctive and effective.

The Undefeated

Combine the sentences below into several paragraphs that contain both bound and free modifiers. You can compare your paragraphs with a professional or student writer's version in the Appendix.

1. The bull stood.
2. The bull was alone.
3. The bull was in the center of the ring.
4. The bull was still fixed.

5. Fuentes was tall.
6. His back was flat.
7. He walked toward the bull.
8. His walk was arrogant.
9. His arms were spread out.
10. The two slim, red sticks were held by the fingers.
11. One was in each hand.
12. The points were straight forward.

13. Fuentes walked forward.

14. A peon was back of him.
15. The peon was to one side of him.
16. The peon had a cape.

17. The bull looked at him.
18. The bull was no longer fixed.

19. His eyes watched Fuentes.
20. Fuentes now stood still.

21. Now Fuentes leaned back.
22. He called to the bull.

23. Fuentes twitched the two banderillos.
24. The light on the points caught the bull's eye.
25. The points were steel.

26. His tail went up.
27. He charged.

28. He came straight.
29. His eyes were on the man.

30. Fuentes stood still.
31. He leaned back.
32. The banderillos pointed forward.

33. The bull lowered his head.
34. He wanted to hook.
35. Fuentes leaned backward.
36. His arms came together.
37. His arms rose.
38. His two hands touched.
39. The banderillos were two descending red lines.
40. And he leaned forward.
41. He drove the points into the bull's shoulder.
42. He leaned far in over the bull's horns.
43. He pivoted on the two upright sticks.
44. His legs were tight together.
45. His body curved to one side.
46. He curved his body to let the bull pass.

47. "Olé!" from the crowd.

48. The bull was hooking.
49. The hooking was wild.
50. The bull was jumping.
51. The bull jumped like a trout.
52. All four feet were off the ground.

53. The red shaft of the banderillos tossed.
54. The bull jumped.

Writing Suggestion 1: Although many North Americans consider bullfighting a cruel and dangerous sport, it is hardly less violent than more popular pastimes like hunting, auto racing, and boxing. Write a short essay analyzing the lure of violent sports. What do our sports tell us about ourselves?

Writing Suggestion 2: Once you have written a version of the exercise above, use your version of *The Undefeated* as the basis for an imitation. Observe the action in a familiar sport such as tennis, baseball, or hockey. Try to describe a crucial play in the kind of detail you used in your version of *The Undefeated.* As in the exercise, in your original writing try to capture the excitement and drama of the contest.

APPENDIX
Professional and Student Writers' Versions of the Exercises

Chapter 1: COMBINING AND CREATING SENTENCES pages 15–22

Combining and Creating Sentences: Combinations

1. When a man has decided to murder another, he does not play to the gallery.
   JOHN KENNETH GALBRAITH, *Economics and the Art of Controversy*

2. On the farms the hens brooded, but no chicks hatched.
   RACHEL CARSON, *Silent Spring*

3. All four brothers were lively by nature—athletic, red-haired men.
   CLARENCE DAY, "Father Visits the War"

4. He got out quietly, as though some mischief had been done him and he had his dignity to remember.
   EUDORA WELTY, "Death of a Traveling Salesman"

5. They walked along, two continents of experience and feeling, unable to communicate.
   WILLIAM GOLDING, *Lord of the Flies*

6. By eight in the evening, my husband would be studying, my daughter would be in bed, and I'd be drinking my third glass of rosé.
   STUDENT WRITER

7. A trade union can by mass action in a strike break an opposition so that the union official can negotiate an agreement.
   WALTER LIPPMANN, *Public Opinion*

8. One is free, like the hermit crab, to change one's shell.
   ANNE MORROW LINDBERGH, *Gift from the Sea*

9. It was early afternoon and the grounds and buildings were deserted, since everyone was at sports.
   JOHN KNOWLES, *A Separate Peace*

10. While she was drinking, holding the cup in both hands, she began to make the sound again.
    WILLIAM FAULKNER, "That Evening Sun"

11. People had gone to bed Thursday night in their habitual state of uncertainty; the governmental crisis in London which was bringing Winston Churchill to power was still the chief subject of preoccupation.
    A. J. LIEBLING, "The Knockdown: Paris Postscript"

12. Young men and women sat everywhere, on a bench, on the floor, smoking, trying to be heard above the general din.

ISAAC BASHEVIS SINGER, "Schloimele"

13. If our current problems are allowed to persist for the next ten to twenty years, they will destroy our standard of living, threaten our international alliances, and jeopardize our domestic tranquility.

LESTER C. THUROW, "Getting Serious About Tax Reform"

14. A school of minnows swam by, each minnow with its small individual shadow, doubling the attendance, so clear and sharp in the sunlight.

E. B. WHITE, "Once More to the Lake"

15. Whereas multiple regression is a shotgun, all the variables in the predictor set affecting each other and the criterion, path analysis is a rifle, designating inexorable lines of influence, assumed to be causal.

ROBERT L. DIAL, "Multivariate Analysis in Sentence-Combining Research"

Milton Barker

Milton Barker, the car checker, stood at the window, looking out at the freight yard. It was mid-April. A thin rain was blowing in from New York Harbor in little gusts and showers, filling the usual melancholy of the yard with further desolation. The dirt and cinders between the ties had turned to gray mud, and the smoke from a switching engine, idle in one of the leads, was flattened down by the rain and trailed off along the ground. The intricate steel towers that held the machinery for handling the car floats stood up dimly against the sky. Ben Rederson, the old switchman, went by with a lighted lantern, although it was only three o'clock in the afternoon.

WOLCOTT GIBBS, "The Courtship of Milton Barker"

Salao

He was an old man who fished alone in a skiff in the Gulf Stream and he had gone eighty-four days now without taking a fish. In the first forty days a boy had been with him. But after forty days without a fish the boy's parents had told him that the old man was now definitely and finally *salao,* which is the worst form of unlucky, and the boy had gone at their orders in another boat which caught three good fish the first week. It made the boy sad to see the old man come in each day with his skiff empty and he always went down to help him carry either the coiled lines or the gaff and harpoon and the sail that was furled around the mast. The sail was patched with flour sacks and, furled, it looked like the flag of permanent defeat.

ERNEST HEMINGWAY, *The Old Man and the Sea*

Meditation on a Camel Pack

Three of the four elements are shared by all creatures, but fire was a gift to humans alone. Smoking cigarettes is as intimate as we can become with fire without immediate excruciation. Every smoker is an embodiment of Prometheus, stealing fire from the gods and bringing it on back home. We smoke to capture the power of the sun, to pacify Hell, to identify with the primordial spark, to feed on the marrow of the volcano. It's not the tobacco we're after but the fire. When we smoke we are performing a version of the fire dance, a ritual as ancient as lightning.

Does that mean that chain smokers are religious fanatics? You must admit there's a similarity.

The lung of the smoker is a naked virgin thrown as a sacrifice into the god-fire.

TOM ROBBINS, *Still Life with Woodpecker*

Brown Paper Bag
He crossed the sandy road slowly, shuffling along and shaking his head as he muttered to himself. He carried a brown paper bag that was wrinkled to fit the shape of a bottle. In the predawn light, the gray scruff on his face made him look ageless; he could have been twenty or sixty. He reached the other side of the road, the smell of the saltwater filling his nostrils, the cries of the seagulls loud in his ears. He stood staring at the ocean, awkwardly raised the bag to his lips, and watched the gray-green waves slap the shore. Suddenly, as if he saw something in the fog, he took a half-step forward into the water that swirled from the last wave. But the cold water gripping his worn-out shoe seemed to startle him, and he stepped back, wearily and unsteadily, to the shore, where he bent down and removed his wet shoe. Placing the shoe beside him, he sat down and dried his foot with the inside of his tattered coat. He sat motionless for a long while, clutching the brown paper bag and staring out at the sea.

STUDENT WRITER

Chapter 2: COORDINATING CONNECTIVES pages 37–50

Coordinating Connectives: Combinations

1. The Big Bang may be the beginning of the universe, **or** it may be a discontinuity in which information about the earlier history of the universe was destroyed.
   CARL SAGAN, *Dragons of Eden*
2. I think democracy a most precious thing, **not** because any democratic state is perfect, **but** because it is perfectible.
   A. J. LIEBLING, "Rape Is Impossible"
3. All the other farmers had to contribute to these benefits by paying the processing taxes. **Thus** a dairyman paid a tax on cotton, wheat, hogs, and corn.
   WALTER LIPPMANN, *The Good Society*
4. I felt like shouting **and** running, **but** shouting was useless, **and** there was no place to run.
   STUDENT WRITER
5. It will not mean the end of nations; it will mean the true beginning of nations.
   E. B. WHITE, "Sootfall and Fallout"
6. They made one another very happy, **and** finally they fell into a perfect sleep.
   MOHAMMED MRABET, "The Canebrake"
7. Magic in the sense of something "inciting wonder" is also here to stay; **or** if it is not, man will have been vastly diminished by its loss.
   HOWARD ENSIGN EVANS, "In Defense of Magic: The Story of Fireflies"
8. The silence is not actually suppression; **instead,** it is all there is.
   ANNIE DILLARD, "Teaching a Stone to Talk"
9. But Paris was a very old city **and** we were young **and** nothing was simple there, **not** even poverty, **nor** sudden money, **nor** the moonlight, **nor** right and wrong, **nor** the breathing of someone who lay beside you in the moonlight.
   ERNEST HEMINGWAY, *A Moveable Feast*

10. The resources of a planet are limited, at each stage of the arts. **Also,** there is only a limited space on a planet.

CLARENCE DAY, *This Simian World*

11. There was **neither** time **nor** desire to consider moral **or** ethical issues.

VICTOR FRANKL, *Man's Search for Meaning*

12. Even Letitia Baldrige, the Establishment arbiter of etiquette, in 1978 pronounced the use of marijuana and hashish to be "marginally socially acceptable." **Meanwhile,** the street cost of all illegal drugs is sky-high.

JOHN BROOKS, *Showing Off in America*

13. He had a violent temper **and** kept a hatchet at his bedside for burglars **and** would knock a man down instead of going to law, **and** once I saw him hunt a party of men with a horsewhip.

WILLIAM BUTLER YEATS, *Autobiographies*

14. They stood for democracy, **not** from any reasoned conclusion about the proper ordering of human society, **but** simply because they had grown up in the middle of democracy **and** knew how it worked.

BRUCE CATTON, "Grant and Lee: A Study in Contrasts"

15. The artist knows he must be alone to create; the writer, to work out his thoughts; the musician, to compose; the saint, to pray.

ANNE MORROW LINDBERGH, *Gift from the Sea*

Petey's Predicament

I sat down in a chair **and** pretended to read a book, **but** out of the corner of my eye I kept watching Petey. He was a torn man. First he looked at the coat with the expression of a waif at a bakery window. **Then** he turned away **and** set his jaw resolutely. **Then** he looked back at the coat, with even more longing in his face. **Then** he turned away, **but** not with so much resolution this time. Back and forth his head swiveled, desire waxing, resolution waning. Finally he didn't turn away at all; he just stood **and** stared with mad lust at the coat.

MAX SHULMAN, "Love Is a Fallacy"

Inside Dope

Drug use is no different from any other form of human behavior, in that a great variety of distinct motives can cooperate to produce it. The particular weight of each of these motives **and** the way they are combined differs in each individual. **Furthermore,** drug use is affected **not only** by motives **and** forces *within* the individual, **but** by what is happening *outside* of him in his interpersonal environment, **and** in the wider social **and** political world. **Thus,** any effort to delineate "types" of motivations that enter into drug use is bound to be an oversimplification. For example, there are many individuals who share common characteristics with drug users **but** who do not use drugs because drugs are not available on their campus. **Similarly,** there are individuals who have little in common with other drug users **but** who **nonetheless** use drugs.

KENNETH KENISTON, "Heads and Seekers"

Coordinating Connectives: Creations

1. We are told that the enormous and expanding use of pesticides is necessary to maintain farm production.

Yet

is our real problem not one of overproduction?

RACHEL CARSON, *Silent Spring*

2. I must have been a chronically suspicious small boy, **for** *I remember thinking to myself that Father needed a great deal of watching.*
CLARENCE DAY, "Mother Gives Father a Surprise"

3. Jack lifted his head **and** *stared at the inscrutable masses of creeper that lay across the trail.*
Then
he raised his spear **and** *sneaked forward.*
WILLIAM GOLDING, *Lord of the Flies*

4. Possibly a war can be fought for democracy; *it cannot be fought democratically.*
WALTER LIPPMANN, *The Phantom Public*

5. The young movie actress was **neither** *as vulgar* **nor** *as unattractive as Seryozha had described her.*
ANDREA LEE, *Russian Journal*

6. I was an observer and a scientist.
Nevertheless,
I had seen the rainbow attempting to attach itself to earth.
LOREN EISELEY, *The Unexpected Universe*

7. The environment was empty, *the antagonist hidden,* **and** *I drifted into solo adventures.*
WILLIAM S. BURROUGHS, *Junkie*

8. For the most part, blacks and whites differ profoundly in their ideas **not only** *about the desires and the needs of the other group* **but also** *about which of the black leaders is best suited to erect an umbrella they can all live under.*
ROGER WILKINS, "Transition"

9. I would have to win a scholarship. **Otherwise,** *college would be out of the picture for me.*
STUDENT WRITER

10. It is thought to be an unnecessary cruelty to deny the patient the most successful treatment for his condition.
Consequently,
there can no longer be a control group of schizophrenics that is not given tranquilizers.
CARL SAGAN, *The Dragons of Eden*

The Stormy Season

I have only to break into the tightness of a strawberry, **and** I see summer—its dust **and** lowering skies. It remains for me a season of storms. The parched days **and** sticky nights are undistinguished in my mind, **but** the storms, the violent sudden storms, **both** frightened **and** quenched me. **But** my memory is uncertain; I recall a summer storm in the town where we lived **and** imagine a summer my mother knew in 1929. There was a tornado that year, she said, that blew away half of Lorain. I mix up her summer with my own. Biting the strawberry, thinking of storms, I see her. A slim young girl in a pink crepe dress. One hand is on her hip; the other lolls about her thigh—waiting. The wind swoops her up, high above the houses, **but** she is still standing, hand on hip. Smiling. The anticipation **and** promise in her lolling hand are not altered by the holocaust. In the summer tornado of 1929, my mother's hand is unextinguished. She is strong, smiling, **and** relaxed while the world falls down about her. So much for memory. Public fact becomes private reality, **and** the seasons of a Midwestern town become the *Moirai* of our small lives.
TONI MORRISON, *The Bluest Eye*

Coordinating Connectives: Sentence Acrobatics

1. Last year, organized crime was directly responsible for more than one hundred murders, **and** *mafiosi* participated indirectly in several hundred more, **either** by lending the killers carfare **or** by holding their coats.

   WOODY ALLEN, "A Look at Organized Crime"

2. In short, game theory is concerned with rules only to the extent that the rules help define the choice situation **and** the outcomes associated with the choices. **Otherwise,** the rules of games play no part in game theory.

   ANATOL RAPOPORT, *Two-Person Game Theory*

3. The financial burden of being sued—**not only** the judgment that one might have to pay **but also** the cost of the defense—inhibits free expression, **and so** the Supreme Court rewrote the law of libel.

   CHARLES REMBAR, "For Sale: Freedom of Speech"

4. A pale, gray light falls from the window above us; we sit in the dimness like wood lice under a rock.

   VICTOR SERGE, *Men in Prison*

5. In the sheltered simplicity of the first days after a baby is born, one sees again the magical closed circle, the miraculous sense of two people existing only for each other, the tranquil sky reflected on the face of the mother nursing her child. It is, **however,** only a brief interlude **and** not a substitute for the original **and** complete relationship.

   ANNE MORROW LINDBERGH, *Gift from the Sea*

6. Dorothea Brooke absorbs the afternoon like a buried seed absorbing the sunlight, **neither** consciously aware of it **nor** mindful of the internal changes it is causing.

   STUDENT WRITER

7. Dora was having trouble with her income tax, **for** she was entangled in that curious enigma which said the business was illegal **and then** taxed her for it.

   JOHN STEINBECK, *Cannery Row*

8. **Whether** it be war **or** revolution, **whether** they fight under one flag **or** another, no matter what their slogan, their aim remains the same—to perpetrate evil, cause pain, shed blood.

   ISAAC BASHEVIS SINGER, "Pigeons"

9. He became conscious of the weight of his clothes, kicked off his shoes fiercely, **and** ripped off each stocking with its elastic garter in a single movement. **Then** he leapt back on the terrace, pulled off his shirt, **and** stood there among the skull-like coconuts with green shadows from the palms **and** the forest sliding over his skin.

   WILLIAM GOLDING, *Lord of the Flies*

10. From here they had challenged kings, despoiled the Church, departed for **and** died on crusades, been condemned **and** excommunicated for crimes, progressively enlarged their domain, married royalty, **and** nurtured a pride that took for its battle cry *"Coucy à la merveille!"*

    BARBARA W. TUCHMAN, *A Distant Mirror: The Calamitous 14th Century*

Playing Housewife

I played housewife for eight months.

After five years of full-time work as an RN, I looked forward to the chance to be a homebody. I'd worked days, evenings, nights, weekends, holidays, **and** every birthday. I'd mopped puddles of urine from the floor, wrestled with alcoholics, **and** cuddled screaming babies. I'd taken care of women with slit wrists, infants with birth defects, **and** men with cancer eating away their manhood. I expectantly awaited peace **and** freedom, time for myself. I made lists of the projects I would accomplish: paint the bedroom, finish the needlepoint kit, play with Jennifer. . . .

For the first two months I stuck to my lists religiously. Soon, **however,** I'd crossed off everything but "play with Jennifer," **and** she was always playing with the girl next door **or** the boy down the street.

Life settled into a routine. After frying eggs **and** squeezing juice for my husband's breakfast **and** packing a peanut butter **and** jelly lunch for my daughter, I went back to bed until eleven o'clock. After a bubblebath, I watched "As the World Turns" **and** "The Edge of Night" until four. By eight in the evening, my husband would be studying, my daughter would be in bed, **and** I'd be drinking my third glass of rosé. On Saturday mornings I did the ritual—vacuuming, dusting, **and** toilet-bowl cleaning while Jennifer watched cartoons **and** Allen slept in. **Then** I watched the dog shed hair on the carpet, the dust resettle, **and** the Ty-D-bol man drown.

Whenever I ran out of Ban Roll-on, I had to ask my husband for the necessary $1.79. I learned 369 ways to make hamburger into nutritious, sometimes even delicious, meals. Dinner at McDonald's was an infrequent treat. We went only to Walt Disney movies; we couldn't afford a sitter. When we went to a party, I'd cringe in the corner in my two-year-old dress. At first I tried to get into the conversation, **but** after I shared such tidbits as "Ellen is Dan's mother," "Alex married his half sister," **and** "David is dying of cancer," I ran out of current events. I realized that sitting quietly in the corner was easier.

Our sex life should have been terrific. I had twelve hours of sleep each day **and** all afternoon to think up dazzling new techniques. My husband will verify, **however,** that not once was I sheathed in Saran Wrap when I met him at the door. The most exciting event of my day occurred at 4:30, when I decided **whether** to have green beans **or** corn with dinner. Frankly, neither one turned me on. **And** anyway, all the couplings **and** gropings of afternoon TV left me exhausted. I found the housewife game lacking in physical, intellectual, **and** sexual stimulation **and** in monetary reward; after eight months, I looked forward to bedpans, bandages, **and** bottoms.

I didn't want to play anymore.

STUDENT WRITER

Chapter 3: THE RELATIVE CLAUSE pages 62–73

The Relative Clause: Combinations

1. Mrs. Gaffney and Mrs. Betz nudged Mrs. Farrell, **who** *left her mouth open to giggle quickly with them.*

   LEANE ZUGSMITH, "The Three Veterans"

2. He was a sallow-faced man, **whose** *hair, moustache and sharply pointed beard were all tinged with gray.*

   FRED UHLMAN, *Reunion*

3. He had expected that Yakichi would make them separate, **which** *would have caused him little pain.*

   YUKIO MISHIMA, *Thirst for Love*

4. A strength **that** *astounded him* surged through Rabbi Naphtali.

   ISAAC BASHEVIS SINGER, "A Cage for Satan"

5. Few American industries have suffered so spectacular a decline as wrestling, **which** *had its happiest days during the early years of the general depression.*
A. J. LIEBLING, " 'Pull His Whiskers!' "

6. We backed up to an old gray man **who** *bore an absurd resemblance to John D. Rockefeller.*
F. SCOTT FITZGERALD, *The Great Gatsby*

7. There was once a town in the heart of America **where** *all life seemed to live in harmony with its surroundings.*
RACHEL CARSON, *Silent Spring*

8. Everyone has a moment in history **which** *belongs particularly to him.*
JOHN KNOWLES, *A Separate Peace*

9. Renunciation is a luxury *in* **which** *all men cannot indulge.*
WALTER LIPPMANN, *The Phantom Public*

10. I recently met somebody **whose** *eating memories of a childhood in Iowa are dominated by a barrel of oysters kept in the cellar.*
CALVIN TRILLIN, "A Stag Oyster Eat Below the Canal"

11. I took along my son, **who** *had never had any fresh water up his nose and* **who** *had seen lily pads only from train windows.*
E. B. WHITE, "Once More to the Lake"

12. The store *in* **which** *the Justice of the Peace's court was sitting* smelled of cheese.
WILLIAM FAULKNER, "Barn Burning"

13. The following afternoon, **when** *Irene returned to the apartment from a luncheon date,* the maid told her that a man had come and fixed the radio.
JOHN CHEEVER, "The Enormous Radio"

14. But for the figure of his grandfather, **whom** *he was afraid he would never find in the darkness,* he thought the world must be altogether empty.
SHERWOOD ANDERSON, *Winesburg, Ohio*

15. There is a front porch with white wooden columns **which** *support a white wooden balcony* **that** *runs along the second floor.*
EDMUND WILSON, "The Old Stone House"

Comrade Laski

Michael Laski, also known as M. I. Laski, is a relatively obscure young man with deep fervent eyes, a short beard, and a pallor **which** *seems particularly remarkable in Southern California.* With his striking appearance and his relentlessly ideological diction, he looks and talks precisely like the popular image of a professional revolutionary, **which** *in fact he is.*
JOAN DIDION, "Comrade Laski, C.P.U.S.A. (M.-L.)"

Westerners

The solitude *in* **which** *westerners live* makes them quiet. They telegraph thoughts and feelings by the way they tilt their heads and listen; pulling their Stetsons into a steep dive over their eyes, or pigeon-toeing one boot over the other, they lean against a fence with a fat wedge of snoose beneath their lower lips and take the whole scene in. These detached looks of quiet amusement are sometimes cynical, but they can also come from a dry-eyed humility as lucid as the air is clean.
GRETEL EHRLICH, "Wyoming: The Solace of Open Spaces"

The Relative Clause: Creations

1. The man **who** *stood at the door* was very young and very thin.
   SALLY BENSON, "Profession: Housewife"
2. This job also offered us access to a master key to all the rooms, **which** *turned out to be the root of all our evil.*
   STUDENT WRITER
3. He has the sort of face **that** *seems to want to swallow its own chin.*
   PENELOPE GILLIATT, "As Is"
4. I went to a carnival in Los Angeles **which** *had a side show called South Sea Mysteries.*
   EUGENE BURDICK, *The Blue of Capricorn*
5. Residues of these chemicals linger in the soil *to* **which** *they may have been applied a dozen years before.*
   RACHEL CARSON, *Silent Spring*
6. My eyes met with those of a girl about eighteen, **whose** *horse resided in the stall next to mine.*
   STUDENT WRITER
7. What English he learned he picked up from truck drivers, **who** *delivered the meat and the poultry.*
   HARRY GOLDEN, *Only in America*
8. The village's only real attraction, **which** *explains the tourist season,* is the hot spring water.
   JAMES BALDWIN, "Stranger in the Village"
9. He came from a village in a part of Extramadura **where** *conditions were incredibly primitive, food scarce, and comforts unknown and he had worked hard ever since he could remember.*
   ERNEST HEMINGWAY, "The Capital of the World"
10. There was once a French-Canadian **whose** *name I cannot at present recall* but **who** *had a window in his stomach.*
    A. J. LIEBLING, "Preface," *The Telephone Booth Indian*

Old Folks at Home

Old Henry and his wife Phoebe were as fond of each other as it is possible for two old people to be **who** *have nothing else in this life to be fond of.* He was a thin old man, seventy when she died, a queer, crotchety person with coarse gray-black hair and beard, quite straggly and unkempt. He looked at you out of dull, fishy, watery eyes **that** *had deep-brown crow's-feet at the sides.* His clothes, like the clothes of many farmers, were aged and angular and baggy, standing out at the pockets, not fitting about the neck, protuberant and worn at elbow and knee. Phoebe Ann was thin and shapeless, a very umbrella of a woman, clad in shabby black, and with a black bonnet for her best wear. As time had passed, and they had only themselves to look after, their movements had become slower and slower, their activities fewer and fewer. The annual keep of pigs had been reduced from five to one grunting porker, and the single horse **which** *Henry now retained* was a sleepy animal, not over-nourished and not very clean. The chickens, *of* **which** *formerly there was a large flock,* had almost disappeared, owing to ferrets, foxes, and the lack of proper care, **which** *produces disease.* The former healthy garden was now a straggling memory of itself, and the vines and flower-beds **that** *formerly ornamented the win-*

dows and dooryard had now become choking thickets. A will had been made **which** *divided the small tax-eaten property equally among the remaining four,* so that it was really of no interest to any of them. Yet these two lived together in peace and sympathy, only that now and then old Henry would become unduly cranky, complaining almost invariably that something had been neglected or mislaid **which** *was of no importance at all.*

THEODORE DREISER, "The Lost Phoebe"

The Relative Clause: Sentence Acrobatics

1. The battery was commanded by a captain named O'Neill, **whose** *family had emigrated to France from Ireland in the seventeenth century.*

   A. J. LIEBLING, "First Act at Gafsa"

2. The island **where** *I live* is peopled with cranks like myself.
   [*Note:* In this sentence, **where** functions as a relative.]

   ANNIE DILLARD, "Teaching a Stone to Talk"

3. He was one of those men *in* **whom** *the force* **that** *creates life is diffused, not centralized.*

   SHERWOOD ANDERSON, *Winesburg, Ohio*

4. The superintendent of the jail, **who** *was standing apart from the rest of us,* raised his head at the sound, moodily prodding the gravel with a stick.

   GEORGE ORWELL, "A Hanging"

5. The most famous lithotomist of all time was not a doctor but an itinerant thug named Jacques Baulot, **whose** *medical career began in 1680 as a servant to Pauloni,* a strolling lithotomist and curer of ruptures.

   RICHARD SELZER, "Stone"

6. The man born into this American society of ours confronts a world **which** *differs radically in its character from that world into* **which** *his ancestors were born.*

   WALTER LIPPMANN, "The South and the New Society"

7. One Sunday, **when** *the rest of her family had gone to a barbecue,* Connie relaxed at home, listening to music and daydreaming about the good times she had had with the boys.
   [*Note:* In this sentence, **when** functions as a relative.]

   STUDENT WRITER

8. Liberals must insist on wage settlements at the high end of the scale **that** *will reduce inflation and encourage renewed economic growth,* **which** *is the best real hope for the poor and for the well-being of our political institutions.*

   PAUL A. LONDON, "Inflationary Secrets"

9. The huge and unprecedented phenomenon of blue jeans, **which** *spread from the United States to the rest of the world in the 1970s,* was in its early phases largely a phenomenon of declassing.

   JOHN BROOKS, *Showing Off in America*

10. Many people are married to people **who** *have been married to other people* **who** *are now married to still others to* **whom** *the first parties may not have been married* but *to* **whom** *somebody has likely been married.*

    LIONEL TIGER, "Omnigamy: The New Kinship System"

Life

One of my favorite possessions, **which** *I picked up a few years ago at a flea market,* is a copy of the December 21, 1942, issue of *Life.* At $1.00, it cost me ten times what it would have cost my mother, **who** *graduated from high school that year,* or my father, **who** *was soon to enlist in the Navy.* Recently, as my generation has begun to face the possibility of a peacetime draft registration **that** *would include both sexes,* I have found that my issue of *Life,* once no more than a period piece, has gained a timely poignance. In its portrayal of a nation obsessed with war, and with the roles men and women should play in war, it suggests a number of disturbing comparisons with our present situation.

The sacrifices necessary to war pervade not only most of the articles but many of the advertisements in *Life*'s 1942 Christmas issue. "Please don't call long distance *this* Christmas!" Bell Telephone requests. "It may be the 'holiday season'—but war needs the wires." An ad for the United States Rubber Company portrays a young mother explaining to her infant son that his father has been lent to his country "so that in the years to come, young mothers everywhere . . . will be able to say 'Merry Christmas' to their sons." The magazine's cover story, "Lonely Wife," is a photo-essay **whose** *text offers advice to wives of servicemen.* Move into a smaller place, but make sure "your husband is the master when he returns on furlough." Take an evening course in camouflage. "Volunteer work is another good outlet." The males **who** *remain at home* are "wolves" to be kept "at bay"; in one photograph pretty Joan, the Lonely Wife, enterprisingly keeps a potential wolf's hands occupied by having him help wind her knitting yarn. Another photo, of five women playing cards, is captioned: "Company of other women, of little interest when husbands are around, is now appreciated by Joan." She is last pictured in church kneeling in solitary prayer before a war shrine, beseeching the Lord "to take into thine own hand both him and the cause wherein his country sends him."

Life's vision of a nation united in war—so different from the only American war I remember, Vietnam, *during* **which** *my older brother's registration as a conscientious objector brought me nothing but relief,* is also that of a society comfortably and securely stratified according to what we now popularly call role-models. An ad for the New Haven Railroad shows a soldier in his berth contemplating "a dog named Shucks, or Spot, or Barnacle Bill. The pretty girl **who** *writes so often* . . . that gray-haired man, so proud and awkward at the station . . . the mother **who** *knit the socks he'll wear soon.*" One of the few light-hearted articles in *Life*'s Christmas issue is a feature on Las Vegas gamblers, **which** *straightfacedly observes,* "Keno is a woman's game. Like old-fashioned lotto or moviehouse bingo, it requires little intelligence."

MARY JO SALTER, "Annie, Don't Get Your Gun"

Chapter 4: THE SUBORDINATE CLAUSE pages 89–98

The Subordinate Clause: Combinations

1. People often write obscurely **because** *they have never taken the trouble to learn to write clearly.*

   W. SOMERSET MAUGHAM, *The Summing Up*

2. **As** *the twentieth century approaches its end,* the conviction grows that many other things are ending too.

   CHRISTOPHER LASCH, *The Culture of Narcissism*

3. A. Hopkins Parker was living in a fool's paradise, **wherever** *he was.*

   JOHN KNOWLES, *A Separate Peace*

4. **Insofar as** *we are aware of these contradictions,* this disorder among our statements is itself a source of tension.
S. I. HAYAKAWA, *Language in Thought and Action*

5. A married woman doesn't dare reveal her bare head **lest** *it rouse the lust of strange men.*
ISAAC BASHEVIS SINGER, "Yochna and Shmelke"

6. The Japanese believed fireflies to be transformed from decaying grasses, **while** *glowworms were said to arise from bamboo roots.*
HOWARD ENSIGN EVANS, "In Defense of Magic: The Story of Fireflies"

7. Ellen felt her eyes brighten **as** *she leaned over the cooking pots to gather them together.*
ELIZABETH MADOX ROBERTS, *The Time of Man*

8. On one of these Saturdays, **although** *it was sunny,* Father put on his derby.
CLARENCE DAY, "A Holiday with Father"

9. **When** *the spring rains and mounting sun begin to tint the meadow grass,* **when** *the alewives run up the streams,* **when** *the blackbirds and the spring frogs sing their full chorus,* then the snipe arrives at night on the south wind.
EDWARD HOWE FORBUSH, *Birds of Massachusetts and Other New England States*

10. Pilings passed alongside **while** *the old man guided us out with ease.*
STUDENT WRITER

11. The people I respect most behave **as if** *they were immortal and society was eternal.*
E. M. FORSTER, "What I Believe"

12. **When** *I walked up to the end of one trench* its proprietor, a tan man, looked at me **while** *the other soldier continued to regard the sky.*
A. J. LIEBLING, "The Shape of War"

13. **Unless** *there is some exceptionally strong biological necessity for sleep,* natural selection would have evolved beasts that sleep not.
CARL SAGAN, *The Dragons of Eden*

14. **If** *Thoreau had merely left us an account of a man's life in the woods* or **if** *he had simply retreated to the woods and there recorded his complaints about society,* or **even if** *he had contrived to include both records in one essay, Walden* would probably not have lived a hundred years.
E. B. WHITE, "A Slight Sound at Evening"

15. **When** *the people's representatives have sought to govern* **as if** *they had inherited the royal prerogatives,* they soon produced the same evils which men had complained about under royal government.
WALTER LIPPMANN, *The Good Society*

Jody

In a mid-afternoon of spring, the little boy Jody walked martially along the brush-lined road toward his home ranch. Banging his knee against the golden lard bucket he used for school lunch, he contrived a good bass drum, **while** *his tongue fluttered sharply against his teeth to fill in snare drums and occasional trumpets.* Some time back the other members of the squad that walked so smartly from the school had turned into the various little canyons and taken the wagon roads to their own home ranches. Now Jody marched seemingly alone, with high-lifted knees and pounding feet; but behind him there was a phantom army with great flags and swords, silent but deadly.

JOHN STEINBECK, "The Red Pony"

The World's Biggest Membrane

Viewed from the distance of the moon, the astonishing thing about the earth, catching the breath, is that it is alive. The photographs show the dry, pounded surface of the moon in the foreground, dead as an old bone. Aloft, floating free beneath the moist, gleaming membrane of the bright blue sky, is the rising earth, the only exuberant thing in this part of the cosmos. **If** *you could look long enough,* you would see the swirling of the great drifts of white cloud, covering and uncovering the half-hidden masses of land. **If** *you had been looking for a very long, geologic time,* you could have seen the continents themselves in motion, drifting apart on their crustal plates, held afloat by the fire beneath. It has the organized, self-contained look of a live creature, full of information, marvelously skilled in handling the sun.

LEWIS THOMAS, "The World's Biggest Membrane"

The Subordinate Clause: Creations

1. **As** *I opened the door to the engine house,* hundreds of thoughts ran through my head.

   STUDENT WRITER

2. Childbirth is painful **because** *the evolution of the human skull has been spectacularly fast and recent.*

   CARL SAGAN, *The Dragons of Eden*

3. I have noticed that most men, **when** *they enter a barber shop and must wait their turn,* drop into a chair and pick up a magazine.

   E. B. WHITE, "The Sea and the Wind That Blows"

4. **Where** *the parties directly responsible do not work out an adjustment,* public officials intervene.

   WALTER LIPPMANN, *The Phantom Public*

5. He had **such** a long and dull evening **that** *he smoked two extra cigars.*

   CLARENCE DAY, "Father Is Firm with His Ailments"

6. **Even if** *family, friends, and movies should fail,* there is still the radio or television to fill the void.

   ANNE MORROW LINDBERGH, *Gift from the Sea*

7. **If** *there had been a cliff handy,* I would have been tempted to jump from it.

   DONALD HALL, *String Too Short to Be Saved*

8. Even the smallest boys, **unless** *fruit claimed them,* brought little pieces of wood and threw them in.

   WILLIAM GOLDING, *Lord of the Flies*

9. **When** *in Faulkner's* Light in August *Percy Grimm pulls the trigger of the black, blunt-nosed automatic and puts that tight, pretty little pattern of slugs in the top of the overturned table behind which Joe Christmas cowers,* our trigger finger tenses, **even while,** *at the same time, with a strange joy of release and justice satisfied, we feel those same slugs in our heart.*

   ROBERT PENN WARREN, "Why Do We Read Fiction?"

10. **While** *awaiting a call,* an Indian may occasionally emerge for air, **unless** *the lobby is* **so** *crowded* **that** *he might lose his place to a transient who does not understand the house rules.*

A. J. LIEBLING, "The Jollity Building"

Something Happened

The brakes gave way **just as** *the loaded Coca-Cola truck began its descent of the final hill leading into the village.* **As** *the truck careened wildly,* the driver fought for control. Near the bottom of the hill, he lost the battle. The truck snapped into a field, jumping a stone wall and flinging bottles in every direction, **as if** *trying to lighten the load and lessen the coming impact.* In a few seconds, it rested quietly on its side among the daisies, near a small white chapel in the center of my home town, where nothing ever happens.

Before *the dust settled,* people began emerging from their nearby homes. Like bees drawn to honey, they gathered, children, grandparents, employees, and housewives, nearly the entire village population. They hovered near the accident, forming into colonies, a few darting back and forth from group to group, buzzing with excitement **as** *they compared notes.*

STUDENT WRITER

The Subordinate Clause: Sentence Acrobatics

1. There is a brilliant statement of Freud's that in the Middle Ages people withdrew to a monastery, **whereas** *in modern times they become nervous.*

WALTER LIPPMANN, *Drift and Mastery*

2. **If** *every competition is,* **as** *the behaviorists insist, just an echo of the spermatozoids' race for their place under the sun,* the Olympic Games could be regarded as a somewhat gigantic insemination.

JOSEPH BRODSKY, "Playing Games"

3. Prior to 1909, **when,** at the urging of Charles Evans Hughes, then governor, *the legislators made the practice of the bookmaking trade a misdemeanor,* the bookies of New York formed an honorable and highly respected guild.

A. J. LIEBLING, "Turf and Gridiron"

4. The scuba diver's first rule is never dive alone, **so that, if** *your equipment gives out or* **if** *you become panicky, your buddy can share his gear with you or calm you down.*

STUDENT WRITER

5. **If** *you are lucky enough to have lived in Paris as a young man,* then **wherever** *you go for the rest of your life,* it stays with you, for Paris is a moveable feast.

ERNEST HEMINGWAY, *A Moveable Feast*

6. The paradox of Japan, thirty-five years after it was left shattered and desolate by the Second World War, is that its swift emergence as an economic superpower has **so** overwhelmed it with plenty **that** *it is not unlike some heir to sudden huge wealth* who, rather than feeling elated, is embarrassed, bewildered, and somewhat lonely **as** *he tries to adjust to the shock of affluence.*

ROBERT SHAPLEN, "Letter from Tokyo"

7. Late one evening when I was lying on my bed fully dressed, brooding about my laziness, neglected work, and lack of will power, I got the signal that I was wanted on the pay telephone downstairs.
[*Note:* In this sentence, **when** functions as a relative.]

ISAAC BASHEVIS SINGER, "The Joke"

8. **If** *the absolute consistency of styles in any given year in the past now seems a bit baffling,* it is not, **as** *a good many people think,* **because** *fashion was once a conspiracy,* with designers, editors, and department-store buyers all closeted in a back room at Maxim's deciding how women should dress.
HOLLY BRUBACH, "America the Comfortable"

9. **Although** *technological advances since 1925 have been prodigious,* and **although** *science news magazines are springing up like toadstools,* the American public appears to be **as** badly informed about the real nature of science **as** *it ever was.*
NILES ELDREDGE, "Creationism Isn't Science"

10. In Brazil, where prisoners are hooded **so that** *they cannot see their captors,* an American minister nevertheless had a face-to-face encounter with Luis Miranda Filho, the most vicious of his tormentors, who ceased administering electric shock for a minute, knelt before his victim, and threatened to kill him **if** *he did not cooperate.*
[*Note:* In this sentence, **where** functions as a relative.]
JERI LABER, "The Torturers"

The End of Modernism

In the past thirty years, vanguard art seems to have lost its "political" role. At the same time, **although** *we still have lots of art*—a stream of it, feeding an apparently insatiable market and providing endless opportunities for argument, exegesis, and comparison—painting and sculpture have ceased to act with the urgency that was once part of the modernist contract. They change, but their changing no longer seems **as** important **as** *it did in 1900, or 1930, or even 1960.* **When** *one speaks of the end of modernism,* one does not invoke a sudden historical terminus. Histories do not break off clean, like a glass rod; they fray, stretch, and come undone, like rope. There was no specific year in which the Renaissance ended; but it did end, **although** *culture is still permeated with the active remnants of Renaissance thought.*
ROBERT HUGHES, *The Shock of the New*

Chapter 5: REVIEW OF CHAPTERS 2, 3, 4 pages 99–105

Fenway Park

Fenway Park, in Boston, is a lyric little bandbox of a ballpark. Everything is painted green and seems in curiously sharp focus, like the inside of an old-fashioned peeping-type Easter egg. It was built in 1912 and rebuilt in 1934, and offers, as do most Boston artifacts, a compromise between Man's Euclidean determinations and Nature's beguiling irregularities. Its right field is one of the deepest in the American League, while its left field is the shortest; the high left-field wall, three hundred and fifteen feet from home plate along the foul line, virtually thrusts its surface at right-handed hitters.
JOHN UPDIKE, "Hub Fans Bid Kid Adieu"

Monkey Business

Squirrel monkeys with "gothic" facial markings have a kind of ritual or display which they perform when greeting one another. The males bare their teeth, rattle the bars of their cage, utter a high-pitched squeak, which is possibly terrifying to squirrel monkeys, and lift their legs to exhibit an erect penis. While such behavior would border on impoliteness at many contemporary social gatherings, it is a fairly elaborate act and serves to maintain dominance hierarchies in squirrel-monkey communities.

CARL SAGAN, *The Dragons of Eden*

Review of Chapters 2, 3, 4: Sentence Acrobatics

1. A provincial city **which** *becomes overnight the capital of a great nation* is not like a boom town, **because** *it has no ebullience.*

   A. J. LIEBLING, "A Man Falling Downstairs"

2. It was one of those motels **that** *give you a two-by-four towel to dry a three-by-five body.*

   STUDENT WRITER

3. Born in Tupelo, Mississippi, he was an only child **whose** *parents scraped along on odd jobs* **until** *the family moved to Memphis* **when** *Elvis was eleven.*

   JAY COCKS, "Last Stop on the Mystery Train"

4. The appellations "socialist" and "communist," though much used, sound extreme. Like the cry of "wolf," **moreover,** they have been overdone.

   JOHN KENNETH GALBRAITH, *Economics and the Art of Controversy*

5. She wore a knit sweater-suit of hard, bright blue **which neither** *sagged* **nor** *pulled,* **but** gave her admirable figure the wooden perfection of a model in a store window.

   SALLY BENSON, "Home Atmosphere"

6. A cardinal rule for the designers of commercial nuclear power plants is that all systems essential to safety must be installed in duplicate, at least, **so that even if** *some of the apparatus fails there will always be enough extra equipment to keep the plant under control.*

   DANIEL FORD, *Three Mile Island: Thirty Seconds to Meltdown*

7. One night **when** *there was to be a grand display of fireworks in the Bois,* Mother insisted on going, **so** *after dinner they drove out there in their evening clothes,* **and** both of them enjoyed it immensely **until** *it came time to go back* **and** they found that they could not get a carriage.

   CLARENCE DAY, "Father's Methods of Courtship"

8. In fact fireflies are **neither** flies **nor** bugs **nor** worms, **but** soft-bodied beetles called Lampyridae, a name based on an old Greek word **that** *also evolved into our word "lamp."*

   HOWARD ENSIGN EVANS, "In Defense of Magic: The Story of Fireflies"

9. The boy—a stocky, sharp-eyed, talkative towhead of about twelve—was exuberantly grateful, **but** the old man, **whose** *face was seamed and yellow,* feebly crawled into the back seat **and** slumped there silently.

   TRUMAN CAPOTE, *In Cold Blood*

10. **When** *the day comes for the first grass-cutting,* the mower starts, stops, starts, sends out a cloud of smoke, **and** has to go into the shop, **where** *it is diagnosed as needing professional attention,* is tagged, **and** takes its place in an endless line of machines, **while** *we get in touch with a neighbor,* **who** *is in command of a sickle.*

    KATINKA LOESER, "Taking Care"

Monument Valley

Because all Navajo dwellings face east, our camp faced east—toward the rising sun and the rising moon and across a limitless expanse of tawny desert, that ancient sea, framed by the towering nearby twin pinnacles called The Mittens. We began to feel the magic even before the sun was fully down. It occurred when a diminutive wraith of a Navajo girl wearing a long, dark, velvet dress gleaming with silver ornaments drifted silently by, herding a flock of ghostly sheep to a waterhole somewhere. A bell on one of the rams tinkled faintly, and then its music was lost in the soft rustle of the night wind, leaving us with an impression that perhaps we had really seen nothing at all.

JOHN V. YOUNG, "When the Full Moon Shines Its Magic Light over Monument Valley"

America the Comfortable

When fashion began in the seventies to appropriate plain clothes—the dutiful, sensibly planned sportswear that has historically been the American garment industry's mainstay—American style finally came of age. This is the way of dressing we know best, and, whether or not it looks especially attractive, it's comfortable, and we're comfortable with the idea of it. The idea is essentially a moral one—a matter of ethics, aesthetics aside. The religion may have been lost along the way, but the Puritan sensibility instilled to this day in many Americans from birth holds our material desires in check. Objects—a chair, a spoon, a shoe—are defined by the function they perform, and any detail that doesn't serve that function is frivolous, mere trimming. The beauty of a Shaker chair is in its integrity. Good prose must be pared down, stripped of decoration, if it's to follow the plainspoken example set by *The Elements of Style*. Elegance is, to the American way of thinking, a little austere.

HOLLY BRUBACH, "America the Comfortable"

Chapter 6: THE FOUR ELEMENTS OF STYLE pages 119–130

The Four Elements of Style: Combinations

1. The sun was coming over the ridge now, glaring on the whitewash of the houses and barns, making the wet grass blaze softly.

   JOHN STEINBECK, "The Red Pony"

2. The early Hebrew world must have been polydemonistic, fearful of every phenomenon.

   ABRAM LEON SACHAR, *A History of the Jews*

3. The bull was hooking wildly, jumping like a trout, all four feet off the ground.

   ERNEST HEMINGWAY, "The Undefeated"

4. While most olfactory processing is in the limbic system, some occurs in the neocortex.

   CARL SAGAN, *The Dragons of Eden*

5. I stood on the balcony that summer afternoon in my long gaberdine, a velvet cap over my red hair, with two disheveled sidelocks, waiting for something more to happen.

   ISAAC BASHEVIS SINGER, "The Betrayer of Israel"

6. That constitutional advance—the end of literary censorship—has been accepted.

CHARLES REMBAR, "For Sale: Freedom of Speech"

7. Young artists, primed by art schools' often starry-eyed vision of the modernist past, are faced with a market voracious for new styles and new looks.

CARTER RATCLIFF, "Art Stars for the Eighties"

8. My wife, inviting me to sample her very first soufflé, accidentally dropped a spoonful of it on my foot, fracturing several small bones.

WOODY ALLEN, "My Philosophy"

9. He sat and stared at the sea, which appeared all surface and twinkle, far shallower than the spirit of man.

HENRY JAMES, "The Middle Years"

10. The public, in accordance with a well-established convention, listens respectfully to these forecasts but does not believe them.

JOHN KENNETH GALBRAITH, *Economics and the Art of Controversy*

11. During my last two years of high school, I worked as a maintenance man, one of two, at a motel in Portland, Maine, my home town.

STUDENT WRITER

12. The Marine Biological Laboratory in Woods Hole is a paradigm, a human institution possessed of a life of its own, self-regenerating, touched all around by human meddle but constantly improved, embellished by it.

LEWIS THOMAS, "The MBL"

13. Wash was there to meet him, unchanged: still gaunt, still ageless, with his pale, questioning gaze, his air diffident, a little servile, a little familiar.

WILLIAM FAULKNER, "Wash"

14. During the three centuries following the fourteenth, history was virtually a genealogy of nobility, devoted to tracing dynastic lines and family connections and infused by the idea of the noble as a superior person.

BARBARA W. TUCHMAN, *A Distant Mirror: The Calamitous 14th Century*

15. The mornings are the pleasantest times in the apartment, exhaustion having set in, the sated mosquitoes at rest on ceiling and walls, sleeping it off, the room a swirl of tortured bedclothes and abandoned garments, the vines in their full leafiness filtering the hard light of day, the air conditioner silent at last, like the mosquitoes.

E. B. WHITE, "Will Strunk"

A Parable

Buddha told a parable in a sutra:

A man traveling across a field encountered a tiger. He fled, the tiger after him. Coming to a precipice, he caught hold of the root of a wild vine and swung himself down over the edge. The tiger sniffed at him from above. Trembling, the man looked down to where, far below, another tiger was waiting to eat him. Only the vine sustained him.

Two mice, one white and one black, little by little started to gnaw away the vine. The man saw a luscious strawberry near him. Grasping the vine with one hand, he plucked the strawberry with the other. How sweet it tasted!

PAUL REPS, *Zen Flesh, Zen Bones*

Midsummer

They would ride through the hot, dim woods that sultry, ominous August. From the hard ground, littered with spots of sifted sun, on the hills their horses would carry them in a minute to the hollows. There was something terrible about the hollows, deep-bottomed with decaying leaves, smelling of dead water and dark leafage and insufferable heat. The sound of the horses' feet was like a confused heartbeat on the swampy ground. They both felt it. They used to get off their horses, without having said a word, and helplessly submerge themselves in each other's arms, while the sweat ran down their backs under their shirts. They never talked there. They stood swaying together with their booted feet deep in the mulch, holding each other, hot and mystified in this green gloom. From far away in the upper meadows they could always hear the cicada reaching an unbearable, sharpened crescendo.

NANCY HALE, "Midsummer"

The Four Elements of Style: Creations

1. The men of the sardine fleet, **loaded with dough,** were in and out all afternoon.
   JOHN STEINBECK, *Cannery Row*
2. However **lonely or sad one may be,** one can exist alone.
   R. D. LAING, *The Divided Self*
3. The whole school seemed united behind the team—**everyone sitting close on the cold bleachers, uttering boisterous vows of victory.**
   STUDENT WRITER
4. The kitchen was **dank** and **cool,** with **the underwater smell of stone floors.**
   MOLLIE PANTER-DOWNES, "Pastoral at Mr. Piper's"
5. Working a typewriter by touch, like **riding a bicycle** or **strolling on a path,** is best done by not giving it a glancing thought.
   LEWIS THOMAS, "Autonomy"
6. He looked down at me, **benignant, profound.**
   WILLIAM FAULKNER, *The Sound and the Fury*
7. In **the living insect,** an additional element is needed to account for the working of the system: **some sort of nervous control.**
   HOWARD ENSIGN EVANS, "In Defense of Magic: The Story of Fireflies"
8. Like **a phonograph dropping a new LP,** she changes the subject.
   REX REED, *Do You Sleep in the Nude?*
9. The newcomer is a lady of about thirty, **with a long thin face and a commanding nose, and greenish eyes.**
   E. M. FORSTER, "Voltaire's Laboratory"
10. They listen, **anxious, their chests tight, cowering against the door.**
    VICTOR SERGE, *Men in Prison*

Bat-Chat

Bats are obliged to make sounds almost ceaselessly, to sense, by sonar, all the objects in their surroundings. They can spot with accuracy, on the wing, small insects, and they will home onto things they like with infallibility and speed. With such a system for the equivalent of glancing around, they must live in a world of ultrasonic bat-sound, most of it with an industrial, machinery sound. Still, they communicate with each other as well, by clicks and high pitched greetings. More over, they have been heard to produce, while hanging at rest upside down in the depths of woods, strange, solitary, and lovely bell-like notes.

LEWIS THOMAS, "The Music of *This* Sphere"

The Four Elements of Style: Analyzing Levels of Structure

1. 1 He would stand there,
    2 hatless and tanned,
    2 chin down almost to his chest,
    2 his hands dug deep in the pockets of his handsome tweed topcoat.

JOHN O'HARA, "Are We Leaving Tomorrow?"

2. 2 Whether or not the clothes make the person,
  1 they do make the movement:
  1 people walk down the street, sit in a chair, or illustrate conversation with gestures in ways that change from one era to the next.

HOLLY BRUBACH, "Designer Dancing"

3. 1 A force that would not be important in the Libyan theater, / , might be strong enough to upset the whole balance of strength in Tunisia,
    2/ where the armies were relatively large
    2 where battalions were still considered important units.

A. J. LIEBLING, "Giraud Is Just a General"

4. 1 By this time they were on the bridge,
    2 crossing the shining water far below—
      3 that day an interesting slate blue,
        4 a color that wet stones sometimes are.

ALICE ADAMS, "Berkeley House"

5. 1 Mr. Whipple squeezed the Charmin like a man possessed,
    2 cackling softly,
    2 eyes closed,
    2 alone in the supermarket.

STUDENT WRITER

6. 1 He sat at the round wicker table and fondled his discovery:
    2 a half-woman, half-lion figurine made of terra-cotta,
      3 displaying thick lips and a flat nose and large breasts,
      3 with a slightly broken tail.

ALAN LELCHUK, "The Doctor's Holiday"

7. 1 Nancy held the cup in both hands,
    2 looking at us,
    2 making the sound,
      3 like there were two of them,
        4 one looking at us and the other making the sound.

WILLIAM FAULKNER, "That Evening Sun"

8. 2 By the time the murals were installed, / , in the Orangerie in Paris,
      3/ the following year
  1 Monet's reputation among critics and the public had suffered a reversal.

JEROME KLEIN, "The Strange Posthumous Career of Claude Monet"

9. 1 The hostess, / , walked toward them,
    2/ a fat woman in a green gown,
    2/ with thick strings of jewels on her exposed chest
    2 arms outstretched.

JERZY KOSINSKI, *Being There*

10. 1 The reformers exalted the rights of the state, the conservatives the rights of the indivividual;
1 the one doctrine became collectivism,
2 which ends in militarized despotism,
and
1 the other doctrine became *laissez faire,*
2 which meant at last that no one must do anything.

WALTER LIPPMANN, *The Good Society*

11. 1 On his feet were single-thong flip-flops,
2 which, / —showed his toes to be growing in separate directions.
3/ when he kicked them off—
4/ as he did in the car,
5/ to sit cross-legged on the bucket seat

PAUL THEROUX, "Yard Sale"

12. 2 In Tanzania,
3 south of the railway the Chinese have built from Dar-es-Salaam to the Zambian frontier,
3 north of the Mbungu country,
1 there lies the Selous Game Reserve,
2 named for the great hunter Frederick Selous,
2 established by the British during their mandatory rule of Tanganyika, and
2 now the biggest, wildest, and least-known animal sanctuary of all Africa.

JAN MORRIS, "Visions of Wilderness"

13. 1 All of the other guests had gone upstairs to bed,
and
1 the ladies, / , had turned their backs on Mr. Payson,
2/ having a last drink together
2 who, / , was resting stuporously with his chin fallen forward on the bulge of his shirt front,
3/ unaware of the affront
3 his eyes closed.

MARK SCHORER, "Portrait of Ladies"

14. 2 Having no hope of improving their lives in any of the ways that matter,
1 people have convinced themselves that what matters is psychic improvement:
2 getting in touch with their feelings,
2 eating health food,
2 taking lessons in ballet, or belly-dancing,
2 immersing themselves in the wisdom of the East,
2 jogging,
2 learning how to "relate,"
2 overcoming the "fear of pleasure."

CHRISTOPHER LASCH, *The Culture of Narcissism*

15. 1 Dr. Harrington, / , stood beside the gramophone,
2/ tall and thin in his white flannels
2 singing with wide open mouth,
2 his eyes comically upturned towards the low cabin ceiling;
1 his white flannel arm was round Miss Paine's waist.

CONRAD AIKEN, "Bring! Bring!"

Sky-Change

The sky was really changing now, fast; it was coming on to storm, or I didn't know signs. Before it had been mostly sunlight, with only a few cloud shadows moving across fast in a wind that didn't get to the ground, and looking like burnt patches on the eastern hills where there was little snow. Now it was mostly shadow, with just gleams of sunlight breaking through and shining for a moment on all the men and horses in the street, making the guns and metal parts of the harness wink and lighting up the big sign on Davies' store and the sagging, white veranda of the inn. And the wind was down to earth and continual, flapping the men's garments and blowing out the horses' tails like plumes. The smoke from houses where supper had been started was lining straight out to the east and flawing down, not up. It was a heavy wind with a damp, chill feel to it, like comes before snow, and strong enough so it wuthered under the arcade and sometimes whistled, the kind of wind that even now makes me think of Nevada quicker than anything else I know. Out at the end of the street, where it merged into the road to the pass, the look of the mountains had changed too. Before they had been big and shining, so you didn't notice the clouds much. Now they were dark and crouched down, looking heavier but not nearly so high, and it was the clouds that did matter, coming up so thick and high you had to look at them instead of the mountains. And they weren't firm, spring clouds, with shapes, or the deep, blue-black kind that mean a quick, hard rain, but thick, shapeless and gray-white, like dense steam, shifting so rapidly and with so little outline that you more felt than saw them changing.

WALTER VAN TILBURG CLARK, *The Ox-Bow Incident*

Chapter 7: THE PREPOSITIONAL PHRASE pages 142–154

The Prepositional Phrase: Combinations

1. **After** *the extinction of the dinosaurs,* mammals moved into daytime ecological niches.

   CARL SAGAN, *The Dragons of Eden*

2. A sickly light, **like** *yellow tinfoil,* was slanting over the high walls into the jail yard.

   GEORGE ORWELL, "A Hanging"

3. The publisher and the ungrateful candidate had a resounding argument later **at** *a dinner party* given **by** *John Erskine.*

   A. J. LIEBLING, "The Boy in the Pistachio Shirt"

4. **Thanks to** *my former job in the saloon,* I had valuable contacts in vital supply centers.

   E. B. WHITE, "The Years of Wonder"

5. **With** *his cap,* Dick slapped the snow from his dark blue ski-suit **before** *going outside.*

   F. SCOTT FITZGERALD, *Tender Is the Night*

6. We violate probability, **by** *our nature.*

   LEWIS THOMAS, "On Probability and Possibility"

7. Time went on, **without** *much improvement on my part.*
CLARENCE DAY, "Father Teaches Me to Be Prompt"

8. Shostakovich makes this setting a violent railing against fate, **with** *screaming unisons* **in** *the winds and sudden snaps and snarls* **from** *the percussion.*
NICHOLAS KENYON, "Testimony"

9. It was an affirmation, a moral victory paid for **by** *innumerable defeats,* **by** *abominable terrors,* **by** *abominable satisfactions.*
JOSEPH CONRAD, *Heart of Darkness*

10. They came slowly up the road **through** *the colorless dawn* **like** *shadows left behind* **by** *the night.*
ERSKINE CALDWELL, "Man and Woman"

11. The entire station was uncomfortable to sit in, **with** *its broken mosaic tile walls, scummy and mostly empty gum machines, and greasy fluorescent lamps that filled the tomb-like station* **with** *cold light.*
STUDENT WRITER

12. The steelworkers' strike is still perching **over** *the doorway of No. 10* **like** *some large black bird that will not go away.*
MOLLIE PANTER-DOWNES, "Letter from London"

13. **Despite** *Mr. Kaplan's distressing diction, his wayward grammar, his outlandish spelling,* Mr. Parkhill was determined to treat him exactly as he treated every other pupil.
LEO ROSTEN, "Mr. K*A*P*L*A*N and the Hobo"

14. **By** *changing the language of art,* you affect the modes of thought; and **by** *changing thought,* you change life.
ROBERT HUGHES, *The Shock of the New*

15. **In** *the moonlight,* the child
Shone blue and flat, **like** *the fresco*
Of *a cherub painted high*
Across *the dome* **of** *a cathedral ceiling.*
DAVID ST. JOHN, "Until the Sea Is Dead," *The New Yorker*

Technology

Technology, Barry Commoner has pointed out, has broken free **of** *the cycles* **of** *nature.* Energy-intensive technology has shifted people **from** *soap* **to** *detergents,* **from** *natural* **to** *synthetic fibers,* **from** *wood* **to** *plastic,* **from** *soil husbandry and land care* **to** *fertilizer* **as** *the means* **of** *increasing agricultural production;* and the spread **of** *synthetic chemicals* has grown **beyond** *measure.* **In** *the West,* technology has shifted people **toward** *a new order.*
HAROLD HAYES, "A Conversation with Garrett Hardin"

Dr. Broad

In *gown and mortarboard,* Dr. Broad entered the classroom **on** *the hour,* opened his notebook, and read aloud, slowly pacing **between** *door and window.* A dozen heads, including two immaculate Sikh turbans, bent earnestly to take down what he said. Nut-brown and nearly bald, **like** *a healthy monk,* he read **in** *an even tone* **at** *an even but slightly too rapid rate.* **In** *the course* **of** *the three terms* he would take up **in** *turn* Descartes, Spinoza, Locke, Hume, Leibniz, Kant, and Hegel. He gave an account **of** *each thinker's life and work,* an exposition **of** *his principal arguments,* and an analysis **of** *where he had gone wrong.* He was, **in** *effect,* dictating his own critical history **of** *modern philosophy,* and anyone who could keep up **with** *him* would possess it. I could almost do it but not quite.

ROBERT FITZGERALD, "The Third Kind of Knowledge"

The Prepositional Phrase: Creations

1. 2 **In** *the sunshine* **of** *a cloudless day,*
   1 a military parade had been in progress.

   JERZY KOSINSKI, *Being There*

2. 1 The United States, / , must employ secret agents.
   2/ **like** *every other government*

   WALTER LIPPMANN, "To Ourselves Be True"

3. 1 Father and Margaret were united **by** *the intense interest they both took* **in** *cooking.*

   CLARENCE DAY, "Father Thumps on the Floor"

4. 1 Definitions, / , tell us nothing about things.
   2/ **contrary to** *popular opinions*

   S. I. HAYAKAWA, *Language in Thought and Action*

5. 2 **Despite** *my anxiety,*
   1 I was aware of the ridiculousness of my situation.

   ISAAC BASHEVIS SINGER, "Brother Beetle"

6. 2 **With** *a last desperate glance* **at** *Rosemary* **from** *the golden corners* **of** *his eyes,*
   1 he went out.

   F. SCOTT FITZGERALD, *Tender Is the Night*

7. 2 **In** *the daytime,*
   2 **in** *the hot mornings,*
   1 these [outboard] motors made a petulant, irritable sound;
   2 **at** *night,*
   2 **in** *the still evening* when the afterglow lit the water,
   1 they whined about one's ears **like** *mosquitoes.*

   E. B. WHITE, "Once More to the Lake"

8. 1 I remember **with** *pleasure* the warm sun coming **through** *the window* **of** *our cabin,*
   2 warming the fruits **in** *the bowl* **on** *the table* and making the kitchen smell **like** *an orchard.*

   STUDENT WRITER

9. 1 His shoulders were very broad,
   2 **like** *those* **of** *a weight lifter,*
   and
   1 his arms were thickly knotted **with** *muscles.*

   BILL BARICH, *Laughing in the Hills*

10. 1 These notions will affect everything **from** *Federal policies* **on** *unemployment and inflation* **to** *new styles* **of** *housing and social issues.*

    LUCY KOMISAR, "Where Feminism Will Lead"

Super-Cat City

Imagine that you are strolling **through** *a super-cat city* **at** *night.* **Over** *yonder* is the business quarter, its evening shops blazing **with** *jewels.* The great stockyards lie **to** *the east* where you hear those sad sounds: that low mooing **as of** *innumerable herds,* waiting slaughter. Beyond lie the silent aquariums and the crates **of** *fresh mice.* (They raise mice **instead of** *hens* **in** *super-cat land.*) **To** *the west* is a beautiful but weirdly bacchanalian park, **with** *long groves of catnip,* where young super-cats have their fling, and where a few crazed catnip addicts live on till they die, unable to break off their strangely undignified orgies. And here where you stand is the sumptuous residence district. Houses **with** *spacious grounds* everywhere: no densely packed buildings. The streets have been swept up—or lapped up—until they are spotless. Not a scrap **of** *paper* is lying around anywhere: no rubbish, no dust. Few **of** *the pavements* are left bare, as ours are, and those few are polished: the rest have deep soft velvet carpets. No footfalls are heard.

CLARENCE DAY, *This Simian World*

The Prepositional Phrase: Sentence Acrobatics

Note: To help you see how these writers chose to combine the sentences, their versions are presented here in terms of levels of structure, with key **prepositional phrases** highlighted.

1. 1 Something or other lay in wait for him,
   2 **amid** *the twists and the turns of the months and the years,*
   2 **like** *a crouching beast in the jungle.*
   HENRY JAMES, "The Beast in the Jungle"

2. 2 **Instead of** *punishing her child or insulting her,*
   1 Mrs. Allen listened to her daughter's story.
   STUDENT WRITER

3. 1 Jesus was in the kitchen,
   2 sitting behind the stove,
   2 **with** *his razor scar on his black face* **like** *a piece of dirty string.*
   WILLIAM FAULKNER, "That Evening Sun"

4. 2 **Besides** *the prestige of military command second to the King,*
   1 the Constableship had lucrative perquisites attached to the business of assembling the armed forces.
   BARBARA W. TUCHMAN, *A Distant Mirror: The Calamitous 14th Century*

5. 2 **According to** *the linguistic school currently on top,*
   1 human beings are all born **with** *a genetic endowment* **for** *recognizing and formulating language.*
   LEWIS THOMAS, "Information"

6. 1 **From** *the side* he's **like** *the buffalo on the U.S. nickel,*
   2 shaggy and blunt-snouted,
   2 **with** *the small clenched eyes and the defiant but insane look of a species once dominant,*
   3 now threatened **with** *extinction.*
   MARGARET ATWOOD, *Surfacing*

7. 1 The public **in respect to** *a railroad strike* may be the farmers whom the railroads serve;
   1 the public **in respect to** *an agricultural tariff* may include the very railroad men who were on strike.
   WALTER LIPPMANN, *The Phantom Public*

8. 2 **Like** *so many successful guerrillas* **in** *the war* **between** *the sexes,*
   1 Georgia O'Keeffe seems to have been equipped early **with** *the immutable sense of who she was and a fairly clear understanding that she would be required to prove it.*

JOAN DIDION, "Georgia O'Keeffe"

9. 1 Animals know their environment **by** *direct experience only;*
   1 man crystallizes his knowledge and his feelings **in** *phonetic representation;*
   1 **by** *written symbols* he accumulates knowledge and passes it on to further generations of men.

S. I. HAYAKAWA, *Language in Thought and Action*

10. 2 **During** *the whole of a dull, dark, and soundless day* **in** *the autumn of the year,*
    2 when the clouds hung oppressively low in the heavens,
    1 I had been passing alone, / , and at length found myself, / / , **within** *view of the melancholy House of Usher.*
    2/ **on** *horseback,*
    2/ **through** *a singularly dreary tract of country*
    2/ / as the shades of the evening drew on

EDGAR ALLAN POE, "The Fall of the House of Usher"

Fighto

He was a foot long **from** *head* **to** *toe* and was covered **with** *a clear wet slimy film.* His only limbs were two powerful hind legs to propel him and two small forelegs to help him keep his balance. We called the beast "Fighto" **because of** *his size and stature.* He was the only creature **on** *earth* that could be so beautiful and so ugly **at** *the same time.*

His two eyes were **like** *tiny marbles* **with** *a thick layer* **of** *skin stretched over them.* He had no eyelids, just a transparent protective cover **over** *his eyes* **like** *a pair* **of** *soft-lens contacts.* The two pureys rested **atop** *his massive head* **like** *a pair* **of** *ball bearings* **on** *a lump* **of** *molded clay.*

His nostrils protruded **like** *his eyes* but, **unlike** *them,* were hollow **instead of** *crystalline.* His skin had a rough leathery texture, even though it felt **like** *a mixture* **of** *unsolidified Jello and Vaseline petroleum jelly.* It had little bumps that gave way when you touched them and returned **to** *their original state* when you removed your hand.

His forelegs were small and seemed to have no use at all other than to hold him upright. His hind legs were large, **with** *three toes,* and held enough concentrated power to propel him three feet or more **in** *a single bound.* His body was beautifully streamlined, **like** *a well-designed car,* but it had an aura **of** *pure ugliness* **about** *it.* All in all, he was **like** *a miniature monster* **on** *the "Creature Double Feature."*

The aroma he carried was the odor **of** *his habitat,* a permeating stench **of** *the swamp,* sticky, musty, and damp. He made little or no sound except when he swished **through** *the tall wet grass,* attempting to elude our grasp, or when he bumped **into** *the walls* **of** *the bathtub* where he had been held captive **after** *his apprehension.* The gentle giant had a dark green-brown complexion that glistened when the light hit it.

That fantastic beast was something **from** *another world.* He was the giant monster **from** *the miniature world* **of** *the swamp,* a world few if any **of** *us* ever know. He was **from** *the world* **of** *bull mummichogs and man-eating foliage.* He lived **in** *a universe* where tiny things were big and big things were unrecognizable. He was ugly **in** *our overgrown universe* but beautiful **in** *his own right place.*

STUDENT WRITER

Chapter 8: THE VERBAL PHRASE pages 165–178

The Verbal Phrase: Combinations

A. Infinitive phrases

1. **To avoid** *the sin of being bareheaded,* he covered his skull with both hands.
ISAAC BASHEVIS SINGER, "Yochna and Shmelke"

2. He used to beg in court at the age of six **to have** *his father set free.*
JACK KEROUAC, *On the Road*

3. **To avoid** *dependence on any single country,* the Iraqis deliberately diversified their foreign connections in both development and sales.
JOSEPH KRAFT, "Letter from Baghdad"

4. **To mark** *the occasion on this night,* they were wearing collars and neckties.
A. J. LIEBLING, "Westbound Tanker"

5. He got out at the nearest Elevated station, **to take** *a train for the office,* with the air of a man who had thoroughly wasted the morning.
CLARENCE DAY, "My Father Enters the Church"

B. Participial phrases

1. **Looking** *for clues to his personality,* I found that Mr. Vincent would celebrate his seventy-sixth birthday in a few weeks.
STUDENT WRITER

2. His far-flung cane, **used** *as a divining-rod at the last crossroads,* had brought him hither.
THEODORE DREISER, "The Lost Phoebe"

3. He stalked up and down a few feet, **smiling** *as his wooden spoon delivered mouthfuls,* **veering** *back and forth on his toes,* **stalking** *with youthful gait again for a moment.*
DONALD HALL, "Ezra Pound"

4. And this letter to Monroe Rosenblatt, **written** *in her mind time and time again,* was of importance.
ARTHUR KOBER, "Letter from the Bronx"

5. **Unbalanced** *with rage,* I got to the exit just as an attendant brought in a carton **containing** *two white kittens.*
KATINKA LOESER, "Taking Care"

6. Every round was like a tiny concentration of high-velocity wind, **making** *the bodies wince and shiver.*
MICHAEL HERR, *Dispatches*

7. **Placing** *his fist just under Goldworm's sternum,* he hugged sharply, **causing** *a side order of bean curd to rocket out of the victim's trachea and carom off the hat rack.*
WOODY ALLEN, "A Giant Step for Mankind"

8. Roger Dewey and Daryl Freed were sitting on the floor in earnest conversation, **bobbing** *heads at each other like plastic birds* **dipping** *for water.*
ANN BEATTIE, "Friends"

9. **Asked** *to write,* they would sit for minutes on end, **staring** *at the paper.*
JOHN HOLT, "How Teachers Make Children Hate Reading"

10. We caught two bass, **hauling** *them in briskly as though they were mackerel,* **pulling** *them over the side of the boat in a businesslike manner without any landing net, and* **stunning** *them with a blow to the back of the head.*

E. B. WHITE, "Once More to the Lake"

Peer Tutoring

In most academic settings we write mainly **to be** *judged.* In real life we write mainly **to be** *understood.* Peer criticism helps students experience writing as a real activity in this sense, because in writing peer critiques, tutors write for three audiences whose demands they must try to balance and satisfy. **To help** *the author whose work they are criticizing,* they must be clear and tactful. **To satisfy** *their own integrity,* they must be honest and truthful. And **to meet** *the standards of the final arbiter,* the teacher, who will evaluate and grade their critical writing, they must be thorough in details as well as tactful, helpful, and truthful. Peer criticism is the hardest writing most students will ever do.

KENNETH A. BRUFFEE, "Two Related Issues in Peer Tutoring"

Peace Corps

In the early hours of a cold October morning in 1960, presidential candidate John F. Kennedy stood on the steps of the University of Michigan's student union. **Addressing** *some 10,000 students,* he asked: "How many of you are willing to spend ten years in Africa or Latin America or Asia working for the U.S. and working for freedom?" A few days later, some Michigan students sent Kennedy a list of several hundred volunteers. From this spontaneous challenge and response was born a federal agency that, for a decade, enjoyed unprecedented popularity: the Peace Corps. **Bolstered** *in Congress by such liberal Democratic stalwarts as Senators Hubert H. Humphrey of Minnesota and Richard L. Neuberger of Oregon,* the Peace Corps was a burst of idealism in an age when idealism was respectable. Today the Peace Corps is racked by conflicting ideologies from within and lack of federal support from without. Aside from learning to live with a drastically reduced budget, the corps faces an arsenal of questions about its status as a government agency, its purpose, and, most important, its viability as an aid program in the 1980s.

MICHAEL A. LERNER, "Peace Corps Imperiled"

The Verbal Phrase: Creations

1. 1 He raked the lawn with his fingers,
   2 **pulling** *out a handful of dry grass.*

JOHN CHEEVER, "The Happiest Days"

2. 2 **To bring** *about what they have decreed,*
   1 the gods use the desires and strivings of men.

PHILLIP EDWARDS, "The Spanish Tragedy"

3. 2 **Startled** *by the roar of a lawnmower,*
   1 I tumbled out of the hammock,
   2 **vowing** *revenge on my energetic neighbor.*

STUDENT WRITER

4. 1 A divided drove of branded cattle passed the windows,
   2 **lowing,**
   2 **slouching** *by on padded hoofs,*
   2 **whisking** *their tails slowly on their clotted bony croups.*

JAMES JOYCE, *Ulysses*

5. 2 On the fine day that eventually dawned,
1 he fled down to the steerage,
2 **pursued** *by the fear that a squall might spoil the weather.*

KAY BOYLE, "Kroy Wen"

6. 2 **To prove** *that he was all man,*
1 General Patton had to augment his battle costume with a pearl-handled revolver.

HAROLD ROSENBERG, *Discovering the Present*

7. 2 **Dignified** *in his fine clothes,*
3 with their fine accessories,
1 he was yet swayed and driven as an animal.

F. SCOTT FITZGERALD, *Tender Is the Night*

8. 1 He plunged along with his tiny camera,
2 **stepping** *over bodies,*
and
1 I followed,
2 **trying** *to take notes.*

HUNTER S. THOMPSON, "The Kentucky Derby Is Decadent and Depraved"

9. 2 **To live** *openly,*
1 one must first have a framework of open living—
2 a political framework very different from anything that now exists on the international level.

E. B. WHITE, "Unity"

10. 2 **Viewed** *from a suitable height,*
1 the aggregating clusters of medical scientists in the bright sunlight of the boardwalk at Atlantic City, /, have the look of assemblages of social insects.
2/ **swarmed** *there from everywhere for annual meetings*

LEWIS THOMAS, "On Societies as Organisms"

Independence Days

My Fourths of July all run together, a parade of twilights where I sit expectantly on grassy hillsides **waiting** *for enough darkness for the first big rocket;* where little children, the hot, white glow of sparklers against their half-thrilled, half-frightened faces, spin their magic sticks into hoops of fire and toss them, **dying,** as high as they can. Late arrivals pick their way through the tangle of seated forms, **bending** *over now and then as they look for the faces of friends in the fading light.* Then there is the great whoosh, and the crowd is frozen in the brilliance of the first cascade of stars and roars its delight at a bang that makes the hillside tremble.

This has always been for me among the most pleasant of our patriotic tribal rituals. For on those evenings I and all the others with me on the grass become willing figures in one of those freckled old cover illustrations by Norman Rockwell, good, clean Americans all, **open-mouthed** *at the booming of the rockets,* **exhilarated** *by the thunder of the explosions,* **warmed** *by the shower of red, white, and blue sparks that drip to the ground in the finale's huge firework flag.* **Stirred** *by the incendiary symbolism of an old liberation,* we march ragtag home to inaudible fifes and drums.

LOUDON WAINWRIGHT, "A Changing Patriotism"

The Verbal Phrase: Sentence Acrobatics

Note: To help you see how these writers chose to combine the sentences, their versions are presented here in terms of levels of structure, with **verbal phrases** highlighted.

1. 1 The whole point of the Ralegh story is that a man's cloak was frequently the most valuable part of his wardrobe,
   2 **costing** *hundreds of pounds.*
   ELIZABETH BURTON, *The Pageant of Elizabethan England*

2. 2 **To launch** *this concern,*
   1 the Count spent a couple of weeks **promoting** *a bookmaker* **known** *as Boat-race Harry.*
   A. J. LIEBLING, "The Jollity Building"

3. 2 **Viewing** *his weakness in bargaining power,*
   1 the worker was never in doubt as to the appropriate solution.
   JOHN KENNETH GALBRAITH, *Economics and the Art of Controversy*

4. 2 **To keep** *a nuclear reactor operating smoothly and under control,*
   1 a number of systems, subsystems, components, structures, and people have to work together in a coordinated and reliable way.
   DANIEL FORD, *Three Mile Island: Thirty Minutes to Meltdown*

5. 1 Freed and T.W. walked out of the living room,
   2 **clowning,**
   2 with arms around each other's waists,
   2 **swaying** *their hips with all the grace of cows* **walking** *on ice.*
   ANN BEATTIE, "Friends"

6. 2 On the date our Constitution was adopted,
   1 in most states a man had to own a certain amount of property **in order to vote** and a greater amount of property **in order to hold office.**
   CHARLES REMBAR, "For Sale: Freedom of Speech"

7. 1 Her legs, / , resembled a child's tiny legs **burdened** *under an immense winter coat* as they carried her delicately across the dance floor.
   2/ **buried** *beneath the volume of three petticoats*
   STUDENT WRITER

8. 1 They'd seen him **rushing** *eagerly down the winter streets,*
   2 **bareheaded,**
   2 **carrying** *his books to the pool hall, or*
   2 **climbing** *trees* **to get** *into the attics of buddies where he spent days* **reading** *or* **hiding** *from the law.*
   JACK KEROUAC, *On the Road*

9. 2 **Watching** *television,*
   1 you'd think we lived at bay,
   2 in total jeopardy,
   3 **surrounded** *on all sides by human-seeking germs,*
   3 **shielded** *against infection and death only by a chemical technology that enables us to keep killing them off.*
   LEWIS THOMAS, "Germs"

10. 1 We had been having an unseasonable spell of weather—
   2 hot, close days,
   3 with the fog shutting in every night,

4 **scaling** *for a few hours at midday,*
4 *then* **creeping** *back again at dark,*
4 **drifting** *in first over the trees on the point,*
4 *then suddenly* **blowing** *across the fields,*
4 **blotting** *out the world and* **taking** *possession of houses, men, and animals.*

E. B. WHITE, "Death of a Pig"

Once More to the Lake

We went fishing the first morning. I felt the same damp moss **covering** *the worms in the bait can,* and saw the dragonfly alight on the tip of my rod as it hovered a few inches from the surface of the water. It was the arrival of this fly that convinced me beyond any doubt that everything was as it always had been, that the years were a mirage and there had been no years. The small waves were the same, **chucking** *the rowboat under the chin as we fished at anchor,* and the boat was the same boat, the same color green and the ribs broken in the same places, and under the floorboards the same fresh-water leavings and débris—the dead hellgrammite, the wisps of moss, the rusty discarded fishhook, the dried blood from yesterday's catch. We stared silently at the tips of our rods, at the dragonflies that came and went. I lowered the tip of mine into the water, tentatively, *pensively* **dislodging** *the fly,* which darted two feet away, poised, darted two feet back, and came to rest again a little farther up the rod. There had been no years between the ducking of this dragonfly and the other one—the one that was part of memory. I looked at the boy, who was silently watching his fly, and it was my hands that held his rod, my eyes watching. I felt dizzy and didn't know which rod I was at the end of.

We caught two bass, **hauling** *them in briskly as though they were mackerel,* **pulling** *them over the side of the boat in a businesslike manner without any landing net, and* **stunning** *them with a blow on the back of the head.* When we got back for a swim before lunch, the lake was exactly where we had left it, the same number of inches from the dock, and there was only the merest suggestion of a breeze. This seemed an utterly enchanted sea, this lake you could leave to its own devices for a few hours and come back to, and find that it had not stirred, this constant and trustworthy body of water. In the shallows, the dark, water-soaked sticks and twigs, smooth and old, were undulating in clusters on the bottom against the clean ribbed sand, and the track of the mussel was plain. A school of minnows swam by, each minnow with its small individual shadow, **doubling** *the attendance,* so clear and sharp in the sunlight. Some of the other campers were in swimming, along the shore, one of them with a cake of soap, and the water felt thin and clear and unsubstantial. Over the years there had been this person with the cake of soap, this cultist, and here he was. There had been no years.

E. B. WHITE, "Once More to the Lake"

Chapter 9: APPOSITIVES AND ADJECTIVE PHRASES pages 190–200

Appositives and Adjective Phrases: Combinations

1. **Quick to learn through sight and sound,** today's student often experiences difficulty in reading and writing.

GORE VIDAL, "French Letters: Theories of the New Novel"

2. The circadian rhythm, **the daily cycling of physiological functions,** is known to go back at least to animals as humble as mollusks.

CARL SAGAN, *The Dragons of Eden*

3. The president of the Boat Club, **Tom Smith,** was the coach.

ALLAN SEAGER, "The Joys of Sport at Oxford"

4. **Pig-eyed and jowly,** he seemed to be enjoying himself.

STUDENT WRITER

5. This is what freedom means: **to be able to be a human being first.**

ERIC HOFFER, "What America Means to Me"

6. They walked along, **two continents of experience and feeling, unable to communicate.**

WILLIAM GOLDING, *Lord of the Flies*

7. Two kinds of person are consoling in a dangerous time: **those who are completely courageous, and those who are more frightened than you are.**

A. J. LIEBLING, "The Knockdown: Paris Postscript"

8. He was a young man, **lean, fair, and morose,** with lanky hair and a shuffling gait.

JOSEPH CONRAD, *Heart of Darkness*

9. James Caan is almost the definition of a "gritty" actor—**rough skin, jabbing movements, nervous tics, nervous sweat.**

PAULINE KAEL, "Safes and Snouts"

10. The work of Purcell's most widely known today is his opera ***Dido and Aeneas,*** with libretto by Nahum Tate.

DONALD GREENE, *The Age of Exuberance*

11. There was a bathhouse in the town, **an aluminum lean-to with a hot spring piped into a shallow concrete pool,** and because of the hot baths the town attracted old people, **believers in cures and the restorative power of desolation, eighty- and ninety-year-old couples who moved around the desert in campers.**

JOAN DIDION, *Play It as It Lays*

12. My friend, **Knud Swenson, the pianist,** has told me all about Scandinavians and fish.

LOUISE BOGAN, "Conversation Piece"

13. This is a snail shell, **round, full, and glossy as a horse chestnut.**

ANNE MORROW LINDBERGH, *Gift from the Sea*

14. Bridget, **the waitress, an awkward girl whose mouth dropped wide open in crises,** went to answer the bell.

CLARENCE DAY, "Father Among the Potted Palms"

15. Every year sees megalopolis, **the urban smear that is staining the entire American northeast and blurring city boundaries everywhere,** relentlessly on its way to ecumenopolis, or a totally urbanized world, according to planner Constantinos Doxiadis.

ADA LOUISE HUXTABLE, "The World of the Absurd"

Khrushchev

Russia weighs its words. When a new edition of Russia's most widely used dictionary was published during Khrushchev's era, it contained a single significant change from the previous edition. "Khrushch," **a kind of beetle,** was no longer described as "deleterious to agriculture."

GEORGE WILL, "Reaping the Whirlwind"

Sakyamuni Descending from the Mountain

Sakyamuni is erect, ecstatic, half-dead, his cloak a drooping wing. Without the wind's help, he would never reach the valley below. He is puppetlike, **skin and bone.** The bald bump on his head seems to exert a spiritual pull, keeping him upright in the helpful push of the wind. Where did he get that bump? On the mountaintop. It is itself a miniature mountain of enlightenment to come. No human head can contain or bury in its bony casing the bliss of what Sakyamuni knows already.

ALEXANDER ELIOT, "The Brush of Legends"

Appositives and Adjective Phrases: Creations

1. 1 She crossed the wide street—
   2 **a slim, solitary figure** in **the darkness.**

YUKIO MISHIMA, "Swaddling Clothes"

2. 2 **Iris-necked and pink-footed,**
   1 the pigeons ran about picking up seeds.

OSCAR WILDE, *The Picture of Dorian Gray*

3. 1 Is man what he seems to the astronomer,
   2 **a tiny lump of impure carbon and water impotently crawling on a small and unimportant planet?**

BERTRAND RUSSELL, *A History of Western Philosophy*

4. 1 A lovely hand, / , tentatively rose.
   2/ **almost too thin to be seen**

HERBERT KOHL, *36 Children*

5. 1 The tree was tremendous,
   2 **an irate, steely black steeple beside the river.**

JOHN KNOWLES, *A Separate Peace*

6. 1 Three young hoodlums from Brooklyn drifted in,
   2 **wooden-faced,**
   2 **hands-in-pockets,**
   2 **stylized as a ballet.**

WILLIAM S. BURROUGHS, *Junkie*

7. 1 It is a difficult lesson to learn today—
   2 **to leave one's friends and family and deliberately practice the art of solitude for an hour or a day or a week.**

ANNE MORROW LINDBERGH, *Gift from the Sea*

8. 1 I walked over to the TV set and turned it on to a dead channel—
   2 **white noise at maximum decibels,**
      3 **a fine sound for sleeping,**
      3 **a powerful continuous hiss to drown out everything strange.**

HUNTER S. THOMPSON, *Fear and Loathing in Las Vegas*

9. 1 Two girls, / , came and sat on my right.
   2/ **one of them with pert buckteeth and eyes as black as vest buttons,**
   2/ **the other with white skin and flesh-colored hair,**
      3/ like an underdeveloped photograph of a redhead

JOHN UPDIKE, "Hub Fans Bid Kid Adieu"

10. 1 Too many moralists begin with a dislike of reality:
    2 **a dislike of men as they are.**

CLARENCE DAY, *This Simian World*

Polynesia

There is one fragment of the Pacific the American believes he knows well: **Polynesia.** He may not be quite certain of Sumatra and Mindanao or the difference between a *prau* and a gin pahit, but Polynesia he knows. This is the South Seas, Paradise, the Sunny Isles. It is a place of soft winds, surfboards and outriggers, the pink bulk of the Royal Hawaiian Hotel, the scent of flowers. It is a place where beachcombers, **defiantly drunk but still white and superior,** watch their *vahines* swim in the waves. In some haunting subtle way a vision of Polynesia creeps into the knowledge of all Americans, **a vision flawless and jeweled.** In Polynesia the defects of America are magically eliminated. The place is warm and sunny. It glows.

EUGENE BURDICK, *The Blue of Capricorn*

Appositives and Adjective Phrases: Sentence Acrobatics

Note: To help you see how these writers chose to combine the sentences, their versions are presented here in terms of levels of structure, with **appositives** and **adjective phrases** highlighted.

1. 1 She looked back at him,
    2 **erect,**
    2 her face like a strained flag.

WILLIAM FAULKNER, "A Rose for Emily"

2. 1 The only anadromous (/) fish that still persists in any quantity is the steelhead,
    2/ **"running upward," in Greek**
    2 a **subspecies of rainbow trout.**

BILL BARICH, "Steelhead"

3. 2 **Patient, cold, and callous,**
    2 our hands wrapped in socks,
    1 we waited to snowball the cats.

DYLAN THOMAS, *Quite Early One Morning*

4. 1 Faith, / , is a stiffening process,
    2/ to my mind
    2 **a sort of mental starch,**
        3 which ought to be applied as sparingly as possible.

E. M. FORSTER, "What I Believe"

5. 1 The nights were beautiful, heavy, starry—
    2 **those summer nights when you feel surrounded by all the warmth and primitive fervor of life.**

VICTOR SERGE, *Men in Prison*

6. 1 There was a speck above the island,
    2 **a figure dropping swiftly beneath a parachute,**
    2 **a figure that hung with dangling limbs.**

WILLIAM GOLDING, *Lord of the Flies*

7. 1 Elder Robert J. Theobold, / , is twenty-eight years old,
    2/ **pastor of what was until October 12, 1968, the Friendly Bible Apostolic Church in Port Hueneme, California**
    2 born and bred in San Jose,
    2 **a native Californian whose memory stream could encompass only the boom years.**

JOAN DIDION, "Notes Toward a Dreampolitik"

8. 2 On the Rolling Stones' album ***Let It Bleed,***
1 the song **"You Can't Always Get What You Want"** features lead singer **Mick Jagger** backed by the London Philharmonic Choir.
[*Note:* The appositives in this sentence are *bound* modifiers.]

STUDENT WRITER

9. 1 Patients who have had prefrontal lobotomies have been described as losing a "continuing sense of self"—
2 **the feeling that I am a particular individual with some control over my life and circumstances,**
2 **the "me-ness" of me,**
2 **the uniqueness of the individual.**

CARL SAGAN, *The Dragons of Eden*

10. 2 When Yochna turned twelve,
1 she was besieged by marriage brokers offering matches,
but
1 her father, / , brought her a groom from Trisk,
2/ **Reb Piniele**
2 **a yeshiva student, / , who studied seventeen hours a day.**
3/ **an orphan**

ISAAC BASHEVIS SINGER, "Yochna and Shmelke"

Write On!

According to one UCLA woman, "The only reason for going to the bathroom is to read the graffiti." Her confession jokingly refers to the many amusing, hastily scrawled sayings on the school's restroom walls, yet her fascination with graffiti also suggests something more than a taste for light reading. The dictionary defines graffito (**the singular form of the word,** derived from *graffio,* **Italian for "a scratch"**) as simply "an inscription, slogan, drawing, etc., crudely scratched or scribbled on a wall or other public surface." But a more penetrating definition of graffiti is possible, **one that helps explain the young woman's compulsion.** As a ubiquitous form of popular "literature," graffiti provide the reader with brief insights, **tiny peepholes,** into the minds of individuals who write not only for themselves, but for all of us. Their graffiti, scrawled on the walls and stalls, reveal four levels of social adjustment: **hostility, anguish, cynicism, and humor.**

STUDENT WRITER

Chapter 10: REVIEW OF CHAPTERS 7, 8, 9 pages 201–208

Rock of Ages

Alcatraz Island is covered with flowers now: orange and yellow nasturtiums, geraniums, sweet grass, blue iris, black-eyed Susans. Candytuft springs up through the cracked concrete in the exercise yard. Ice plant carpets the rusting catwalks. "WARNING! KEEP OFF! U.S. PROPERTY," the sign still reads, big and yellow and visible for perhaps a quarter of a mile, but since March 21, 1963, the day they took the last thirty or so men off the island and sent them back to prisons less expensive to maintain, the warning has been only *pro forma,* the gun turrets empty, the cell blocks abandoned. It is not an unpleasant place to be, out there on Alcatraz with only the flowers and the wind and a bell buoy moaning and the tide surging through the Golden Gate, but to like a place like that you have to want a moat.

JOAN DIDION, "Rock of Ages"

The Kool-Aid Wino

When I was a child I had a friend who became a Kool-Aid wino as the result of a rupture. He was a member of a very large and poor German family. All the older children in the family had to work in the fields during the summer, picking beans for two-and-one-half cents a pound to keep the family going. Everyone worked except my friend who couldn't because he was ruptured. There was no money for an operation. There wasn't even enough money to buy him a truss. So he stayed home and became a Kool-Aid wino.

RICHARD BRAUTIGAN, *Trout Fishing in America*

Review of Chapters 7, 8, 9: Sentence Acrobatics

Note: To help you see how these writers chose to combine the sentences, their versions are presented here in terms of levels of structure, with key **prepositional phrases, verbal phrases, appositives,** and **adjective phrases** highlighted.

1. 1 The Thames, / , had submerged the lower part of the landing stair.
 2/ **rain-pitted,**
 2/ **high and sullen under a leaden sky**

ELIZABETH BURTON, *The Pageant of Elizabethan England*

2. 2 **In order to help** *mentally retarded or physically handicapped children,*
 1 one must have patience, sympathy, and maturity.

STUDENT WRITER

3. 1 He was only a little boy,
 2 **ten years old,**
 2 **with** *hair* **like** *dusty yellow grass and* **with** *shy polite gray eyes and* **with** *a mouth that worked when he thought.*

JOHN STEINBECK, "The Red Pony"

4. 1 We continue to share **with** *our remotest ancestors* the most tangled and evasive attitudes **about** *death,*
 2 **despite** *the great distance we have come* **in** *understanding some of the profound aspects of biology.*

LEWIS THOMAS, "The Long Habit"

5. 1 The friars were an element of daily life,
 2 **scorned yet venerated and feared** *because they might, / , have the key to salvation.*
 3/ after all

BARBARA W. TUCHMAN, *A Distant Mirror: The Calamitous 14th Century*

6. 1 The sociable country postman, / , had just given him a small parcel which he took out with him,
 2/ **passing** *through the garden*
 2 **leaving** *the hotel to the right and* **creeping** *to a bench he had already haunted,*
 3 **a safe recess in the cliff.**

HENRY JAMES, "The Middle Years"

7. 1 My father, / , reluctantly put away pen and paper **on** *his lectern.*
 2/ **a small man,**
 2/ **frail,**
 2/ **wearing** *a long robe and* **with** *a velvet skullcap* **above** *his high forehead,*
 2/ his eyes blue, and
 2/ his beard red

ISAAC BASHEVIS SINGER, "The Betrayer of Israel"

8. 1 Then, / , he looked down at the rotted overturned log,
    2/ **standing** *beside Sam in the gloom of the dying afternoon*
    2 **gutted and scored** *with claw marks and, / , the print of the enormous warped two-toed foot.*
        3/ **In** *the wet earth beside it*

WILLIAM FAULKNER, "The Bear"

9. 2 **Lecherous,**
    2 **truculent,**
    2 **irrational,**
    2 **cruel,**
    2 **conniving,**
    2 **excitable,**
    2 **dreaming** *about lascivious heavens while hypocritically enforcing oppressive legal codes:*
  1 the stereotype of the Moslem is only partially softened **by** *a Kahlil Gibran* who puts it **into** *sentimental doggerel* or **by** *a Rudolph Valentino* who does it **with** *zest and good humor.*

HARVEY COX, "Understanding Islam"

10. 1 Their voices rang out and then died away,
    2 **leaving** *the street hot, empty, and silent,*
        3 **except for** *the thin sound of some country music* **drifting** *along* **like** *an old dog's leash* **trailing** *in the dust.*

DANIEL MENAKER, "I Spy"

Home-Coming

On the day before Thanksgiving, toward the end of the afternoon, having motored all day, I arrived home and lit a fire in the living room. The birch logs took hold briskly. About three minutes later, not to be outdone, the chimney itself caught fire. I became aware of this development rather slowly. Rocking contentedly in my chair, enjoying the stupor that follows a day on the road, I thought I heard the dull, fluttering roar of a chimney swift, a sound we who live in this house are thoroughly accustomed to. Then I realized that there would be no bird in residence in my chimney at this season of the year, and a glance up the flue made it perfectly plain that, after twenty-two years of my tenure, the place was at last afire.

E. B. WHITE, "Home-Coming"

Beer Can

This seems to be an era of gratuitous inventions and negative improvements. Consider the beer can. It was beautiful—as beautiful as the clothespin, as inevitable as the wine bottle, as dignified and reassuring as the fire hydrant. A tranquil cylinder of delightfully resonant metal, it could be opened in an instant, requiring only the application of a handy gadget freely dispensed by every grocer. Who can forget the small, symmetrical thrill of those two triangular punctures, the dainty *pffff*, the little crest of suds that foamed eagerly in the exultation of release? Now we are given, instead, a top beetling with an ugly, shmoo-shaped "tab," which, after fiercely resisting the tugging, bleeding fingers of the thirsty man, threatens his lips with a dangerous and hideous hole. However, we have discovered a way to thwart Progress, usually so unthwartable. *Turn the beer can upside down and open the bottom.* The bottom is still the way the top used to be. True, this operation gives the beer an unsettling jolt, and the sight of a consistently inverted beer can might make people edgy, not to say queasy. But the latter difficulty could be eliminated if manufacturers would design cans that looked the same whichever end was up, like playing cards. What we need is Progress with an escape hatch.

JOHN UPDIKE, "Beer Can"

Chapter 11: THE ABSOLUTE PHRASE pages 218–230

The Absolute Phrase: Combinations

1. **Luncheon over,** Dick returned to his villa.
F. SCOTT FITZGERALD, *Tender Is the Night*

2. Other firemen rushed around, **each intent on his own assignment.**
STUDENT WRITER

3. He looked good coming through the fog, **the edges of his body softened by mist, the contours hidden in smoke.**
BILL BARICH, *Laughing in the Hills*

4. **His hands hanging naturally at his sides,** the general waited to be seated.
F. SCOTT FITZGERALD, *Tender Is the Night*

5. A woman in a turquoise-blue bathing suit was rising out of blue waves, **her mouth in an unnaturally wide smile.**
ANN BEATTIE, "A Vintage Thunderbird"

6. It is a splendid vision: **technology the king, Jayne Mansfield the queen.**
E. B. WHITE, "Coon Tree"

7. He wore his full-dress uniform, ***with* the heavy braided white cap pulled down rakishly over one cold gray eye.**
JAMES THURBER, "The Secret Life of Walter Mitty"

8. **His mouth dry, his heart down,** Nick reeled in.
ERNEST HEMINGWAY, "Big Two-Hearted River" (Part II)

9. After the yard sale, they made themselves scarce—**Floyd Senior to his Boston apartment and his flight attendant, Edith to the verge of a nervous breakdown in Cuttyhunk.**
PAUL THEROUX, "Yard Sale"

10. Her face was distorted with age—**her nose a little crooked, her cheekbones prominent and one higher than the other, her eyes sunk into the sockets, her forehead large.**
DAVID PLANTE, "This Strange Country"

11. Was Spinelli trying to say that all life was represented here in his antipasto, ***with* the black olives an unbearable reminder of mortality?**
WOODY ALLEN, "Fabrizio's: Criticism and Response"

12. **My train to leave in ten minutes,** I paced the platform nervously.
STUDENT WRITER

13. Grown people frowned at the three girls on the curbside, **two with their coats draped over their heads, the collars framing the eyebrows like nuns' habits, black garters showing where they bit the tops of brown stockings that barely covered the knees, angry faces knotted like dark cauliflowers.**
TONI MORRISON, *The Bluest Eye*

14. By the end of the novel, **every possibility of a nontragic solution of the affair exhausted,** the two men—**themselves on the verge of destruction**—are destined to be reunited over the corpse of this woman.
SIMON O. LESSER, "Saint and Sinner: Dostoevsky's *Idiot*"

15. Clark McCormack had seemed to Everett the center of a vast social network, the pivot for dozens of acquaintances, all of whom were constantly calling or dropping by the Deke house: **one to bring Clark the stolen stencil for a mimeographed midterm; another to drop off a box of Glenn Miller records in anticipation of a party; others,** usually extraordinarily pretty girls, **to leave their convertibles for Clark to use.**

JOAN DIDION, *Run River*

Superstar

In Andy Warhol's new loft studio "The Factory" Viva leaned against the whitewashed plaster wall, **her cotton-candy hair bright blonde under the spotlights.** Her fine-boned face and attenuated body were reminiscent of sepia-tinted photographs, found in an attic trunk, of actresses of the early 1930s. She was wearing an Edwardian velvet coat, a white matelassé blouse, and tapered black slacks. "Do I look OK?" she asked Paul Morrissey, Warhol's technical director. "Like a star," he replied grandly.

BARBARA L. GOLDSMITH, "La Dolce Viva"

The Hunter

It was all over though. The big cat lay tangled in the first willows, **his head and shoulder raised against the red stems, his legs reaching and his back arched downward,** in the caricature of a leap, but loose and motionless. The great, yellow eyes glared balefully up through the willows at the rock fort on top of the south wall. The mouth was a little open, **the tongue hanging down from it behind the fangs.** The blood was still dripping from the tongue into the red stain it had already made in the snow. High behind the shoulder, the black pelt was wet too, and one place farther down, on the ribs. Standing there, looking at it, Harold felt compassion for the long, wicked beauty rendered motionless, and even a little shame that it should have passed so hard.

WALTER VAN TILBURG CLARK, *The Track of the Cat*

The Absolute Phrase: Creations

1. 1 He ran, / , deep in the great sweep of men flying across the fields
   2/ bayonet **fixed**

TONI MORRISON, *Sula*

2. 1 Mitchell sat there unblinking,
   2 the dimmed bulb on his table **the only illumination in the place.**

A. J. LIEBLING, "Destination: United Kingdom"

3. 1 Her features were thick,
   2 **her jaw heavy,**
   2 **her whole figure repellently powerful.**

JOHN COLLIER, "Wet Sunday"

4. 1 The sewing room was large and light,
   2 the sun often **streaming through the high windows,**
   3 its rays **intensifying the whiteness of the walls and the monotony of the regulation dress.**

EMMA GOLDMAN, *Living My Life*

5. 1 Against the wall there were two bunks,
   2 **one above the other.**

STUDENT WRITER

6. 1 The oyster eaters, / , stood around the tables opening or eating or awaiting new supplies.
 2/ some of them **with gloves** and all of them **with knives**
 CALVIN TRILLIN, "A Stag Oyster Eat Below the Canal"

7. 2 With nothing else **to do,**
 1 I began pacing around and around our cell.
 STUDENT WRITER

8. 1 Temple leaned around the door,
 2 past his dim shape,
 2 her face **wan as a small ghost in the refracted light from the dining room.**
 WILLIAM FAULKNER, *Sanctuary*

9. 1 It was a peasant's face,
 2 **the cheeks hollow under the high cheekbones,**
 2 **the beard stubbled,**
 2 **the eyes shaded by the heavy brows,**
 2 **big hands holding the rifle,**
 2 **heavy boots showing beneath the folds of the blanket cape.**
 ERNEST HEMINGWAY, *For Whom the Bell Tolls*

10. 1 After a little while Mr. Gatz opened the door and came out,
 2 his mouth **ajar,**
 2 his face **flushed slightly,**
 2 his eyes **leaking isolated and unpunctual tears.**
 F. SCOTT FITZGERALD, *The Great Gatsby*

Komodo Dragon

There are today a few remaining large reptiles on Earth, the most striking of which is the Komodo dragon of Indonesia: cold-blooded, not very bright, but a predator exhibiting a chilling fixity of purpose. With immense patience, it will stalk a sleeping deer or boar, then suddenly slash a hind leg and hang on until the prey bleeds to death. Prey is tracked by scent, and a hunting dragon lumbers and sashays, **head down, its forked tongue flicking over the ground for chemical traces.** The largest adults weigh about 135 kilograms (300 pounds), are three meters (about ten feet) long, and live perhaps to be centenarians. To protect its eggs, the dragon digs trenches from two to as much as nine meters (almost thirty feet) deep—probably a defense against egg-eating mammals (and themselves: Adults are known occasionally to stalk a nest-hole, waiting for the newly hatched young to emerge and provide a little delicacy for lunch). As another clear adaptation to predators, the dragon hatchlings live in trees.

CARL SAGAN, *The Dragons of Eden*

The Absolute Phrase: Sentence Acrobatics

Note: To help you see how these writers chose to combine the sentences, their versions are presented here in terms of levels of structure, with **absolute phrases** highlighted.

1. 1 He stops for a moment and rubs his mustache,
 2 **his pensive expression an odd contrast to the aloha shirt he's wearing.**
 STUDENT WRITER

2. 1 She talked fast and fluently,
 2 moving about a lot on the chair arm,
 2 **her legs kicking straight as if hammered on the knee,**
 2 **her head jerking to restore invisible strands of hair,**
 2 **her thumbs bending and straightening.**
 KINGSLEY AMIS, *Lucky Jim*

3\. 1 Evolution is still an infinitely long and tedious biologic game,
2 ***with* only the winners staying at the table,**
but
1 the rules are beginning to look more flexible.

LEWIS THOMAS, "The Lives of a Cell"

4\. 1 "Here in the corner you turn flat," he said,
2 demonstrating a quick spin on the heel with knees bent,
3 **his right shoulder down,**
4 acting as a pivot.

PENELOPE GILLIATT, "In Trust"

5\. 1 She was dressed to play golf,
and
1 I remember thinking she looked like a good illustration,
2 **her chin raised a little jauntily,**
2 **her hair the color of an autumn leaf,**
2 **her face the same brown tint as the fingerless glove on her knee.**

F. SCOTT FITZGERALD, *The Great Gatsby*

6\. 2 At the corner of Serpukhovskaya,
1 we kissed and then got into separate taxis—
2 **I to spend an evening at home,**
2 **she to begin another chapter of her violent, complex life.**

ANDREA LEE, *Russian Journal*

7\. 1 Zurito sat there,
2 **his feet in the box-stirrups,**
2 **his great legs in the buckskin-covered armor gripping the horse,**
2 **the reins in his left hand,**
2 **the long pic held in his right hand,**
2 **his broad hat well down over his eyes to shade them from the lights,**
2 watching the distant door of the toril.

ERNEST HEMINGWAY, "The Undefeated"

8\. 2 Silently,
1 in a dream she had come to him after her death,
2 **her wasted body within its loose brown graveclothes giving off an odor of wax and rosewood,**
2 **her breath, / , mute,**
3/ that had bent upon him
3 reproachful,
3 a faint odor of wetted ashes.

JAMES JOYCE, *Ulysses*

9\. 1 Temple was sitting on the bed,
2 **her legs tucked under her,**
2 erect,
2 **her hands lying in her lap,**
2 **her hat tilted on the back of her head.**
1 She looked quite small,
2 **her very attitude an outrage to muscle and tissue of more than seventeen and more compatible with eight or ten,**
3 **her elbows close to her sides,**
3 **her face turned toward the door against which a chair was wedged.**

WILLIAM FAULKNER, *Sanctuary*

10. 2 As her little bird body revealed itself on the scene,
3 either immobile in trembling mystery or tense in the incredible arc which was her lift,
4 **her instep stretched ahead in an arch never before seen,**
4 **the tiny bones of her hands in ceaseless vibration,**
4 **her face radiant,**
4 **diamonds glittering under her dark hair,**
4 **her little waist encased in silk,**
4 **the great tutu balancing, quickening, and flashing over her beating, flashing, quivering legs,**
1 every man and woman sat forward,
1 every pulse quickened.

AGNES DE MILLE, *Dance to the Piper*

Eighty-Yard Run

The pass was high and wide and he jumped for it, feeling it slap flatly against his hands, as he shook his hips to throw off the halfback who was diving at him. The center floated by, **his hands desperately brushing Darling's knee** as Darling picked his feet up high and delicately ran over a blocker and an opposing linesman in a jumble on the ground near the scrimmage line. He had ten yards in the clear and picked up speed, breathing easily, feeling his thigh pads rising and falling against his legs, listening to the sound of cleats behind him, pulling away from them, watching the other backs heading him off toward the sideline, **the whole picture,** the men closing in on him, the blockers fighting for position, the ground he had to cross, **all suddenly clear in his head,** for the first time in his life not a meaningless confusion of men, sounds, speed. He smiled a little to himself as he ran, holding the ball lightly in front of him with his two hands, **his knees pumping high, his hips twisting in the almost girlish run of a back in a broken field.** The first halfback came at him and he fed him his leg, then swung at the last moment, took the shock of the man's shoulder without breaking stride, ran right through him, **his cleats biting securely into the turf.** There was only the safety man now, coming warily at him, **his arms crooked, hands spread.** Darling tucked the ball in, spurted at him, driving hard, hurling himself along, **all two hundred pounds bunched into controlled attack.** He was sure he was going to get past the safety man. Without thought, **his arms and legs working beautifully together,** he headed right for the safety man, stiff-armed him, feeling blood spurt instantaneously from the man's nose onto his hand, seeing his face go awry, **head turned, mouth pulled to one side.** He pivoted away, keeping the arm locked, dropping the safety man as he ran easily toward the goal line, **with the drumming of cleats diminishing behind him.**

IRWIN SHAW, "The Eighty-Yard Run"

Chapter 12: NOUN SUBSTITUTES pages 245–255

Noun Substitutes: Combinations

1. **Reserving** *judgments* is a matter of infinite hope.

F. SCOTT FITZGERALD, *The Great Gatsby*

2. **The fact that** *few people feel terribly discontented with their lot* is a plausible explanation of the highly nonrevolutionary mood of the moment.

JOHN KENNETH GALBRAITH, *Economics and the Art of Controversy*

3. He knew **where** *everything was when he wanted it.*
   JOHN STEINBECK, *Cannery Row*

4. **To design** *a highway to minimize ambiguity, error and accidents* increases everyone's sense of security.
   ROBERT SOMMER, *Tight Places*

5. He told her **that** *she should finish high school,* and **that** *afterward she would have a scholarship waiting for her.*
   WINTHROP SARGEANT, "Presence"

6. **Whether** *the Elizabethans cheated like mad at cards and dice at home* is hard to say.
   ELIZABETH BURTON, *The Pageant of Elizabethan England*

7. Other writers then began to echo Simmons's suggestions—**that** *women could support themselves by their* **cooking.**
   STUDENT WRITER

8. She didn't know **what to make** *of the man.*
   CLARENCE DAY, "Father's Methods of Courtship"

9. **The fact that** *these issues matter to the political system* means **that** *all the principal institutions and actors in the system are part of the budget process.*
   W. BOWMAN CUTTER, "The Battle of the Budget"

10. **Correcting** *the overestimated Consumer Price Index* will slow down the inflationary spiral.
    STUDENT WRITER

11. Our civic education does not even begin to tell the voter **how** *he can reduce the maze of public affairs to some intelligible form.*
    WALTER LIPPMANN, *The Phantom Public*

12. Basically the family has fulfilled three social functions—**to provide** *a basic labor force,* **to transmit** *property,* and **to educate and train** *children* not only into an accepted social pattern but also in the work skills upon which their future subsistence would depend.
    J. H. PLUMB, *In the Light of History*

13. For one shameless moment Mr. Parkhill wondered **whether** *he could reconcile it with his conscience* if he did promote Mr. Kaplan to Advanced Grammar and Civics.
    LEO ROSTEN,
    "The Rather Baffling Case of H*Y*M*A*N* K*A*P*L*A*N"

14. The end, nonetheless, was **that what** *he had expected failed to come to him.*
    HENRY JAMES, "The Beast in the Jungle"

15. **To couple** *the concept of freedom to breed with the belief* **that** *everyone born has an equal right to the commons* is **to lock** *the world into a tragic course of action.*
    GARRETT HARDIN, "The Tragedy of the Commons"

Barriers

People feel safer behind some kind of physical barrier. If a social situation is in any way threatening, then there is an immediate urge to set up such a barricade. For a tiny child faced with a stranger, the problem is usually solved by **hiding** *behind its mother's body* and **peeping** *out at the intruder* to see **what** *he or she will do next.* If the mother's body is not available, then a chair or some other piece of solid furniture will do. If the stranger insists on **coming** *closer,* then the peeping face must be hidden too. If the insensitive intruder continues to approach despite these obvious signals of fear, then there is nothing for it but **to scream or flee.**

DESMOND MORRIS, *Manwatching: A Field Guide to Human Behavior*

Brotherly Love

Whenever Harold got hurt, which was perhaps rather often, the important thing to do was **to choke** *him.* If we had tried **to comfort** *him first, his wails would have brought Mother up on the run. We also had found by experience* **that** *it was a great mistake* **to choke** *him in silence,* because that silence itself would make Mother suspect **that** *something dreadful had happened.* Consequently, while **choking** *our indignant little brother,* we had to make joyful sounds. This must have given us the appearance of peculiarly hard-hearted fiends.

CLARENCE DAY, "Mother Shows Us Off"

Noun Substitutes: Creations

1. One simple, unrefuted fact about radioactive substances is **that** *scientists do not agree about the "safe" amount.*

   E. B. WHITE, "Sootfall and Fallout"

2. A century from now our great-grandchildren may marvel at **how** *little we knew about fireflies.*

   HOWARD ENSIGN EVANS, "In Defense of Magic: The Story of Fireflies"

3. I went to bed still trying to figure out **whether** *they had framed me with some amateur theatricals.*

   A. J. LIEBLING, "Non Angeli Sed Angli"

4. **Driving** *alone* gave me a chance **to think** about **what** *my answers might be.*

   STUDENT WRITER

5. I vowed **that** *my child would never know want.*

   ISAAC BASHEVIS SINGER, "Fate"

6. We need only a single case as an example of **what to avoid.**

   NORMAN COUSINS, "The Physician in Literature"

7. **To fight** *on horseback or foot wearing 55 pounds of plate armor,* **to crash** *in collision with an opponent at full gallop* while holding horizontal an eighteen-foot lance half the length of an average telephone pole, **to give and receive** *blows with sword or battle-ax* that could cleave a skull or slice off a limb at a stroke, **to spend** *half of life in the saddle* through all weathers and for days at a time, was not a weakling's work.

   BARBARA TUCHMAN, *A Distant Mirror: The Calamitous 14th Century*

8. **Whatever** *sum we spent last year* was only discovered after we'd spent it, and nobody can be sure **what** *next year's bill will be.*

   LEWIS THOMAS, "Your Very Good Health"

9. **Baking** *bread,* **weaving** *cloth,* **putting** *up preserves,* **teaching** and **singing** *to children,* must have been far more nourishing than **being** *the family chauffeur* or **shopping** *at super-markets,* or **doing** *housework with mechanical aids.*

   ANNE MORROW LINDBERGH, *Gift from the Sea*

10. **The fact that** *there is still a great deal of libel litigation* does not mean **that** *the press is hampered more now than* formerly.

    CHARLES REMBAR, "For Sale: Freedom of Speech"

News and Views

The newspaper is the only mass medium which acts as a daily source of detailed information about the world. Unlike the electronic media, which afford only brief profiles of news events, the newspaper covers a wide array of news stories with supplemental facts and background information. Because newspapers have such great potential for **relating** *information to the public,* mass communication researchers have been investigating **what** *they call "the agenda-setting influence of the press."* The agenda-setting theory attempts **to explain how** *newspapers,* by **highlighting** *particular events, influence the reader's perception of* **what** *is important in the world.* The basic premise is **that** *certain readers will consider an event important simply because it is in the newspaper.* The press then has the effect of **setting** *an agenda of "important" issues* for people **to think** *about and* **discuss.** As communications specialist Bernard Cohen has noted, "The press may not be successful much of the time in **telling** *people* **what to think,** but it is stunningly successful in **telling** *its readers* **what to think** *about."*

STUDENT WRITER

Noun Substitutes: Sentence Acrobatics

Note: To help you see how these writers chose to combine the sentences, their versions are presented here in terms of levels of structure, with **noun substitutes** highlighted.

1. 2 Once we have cast another group in the role of the enemy,
1 we know **that** *they are to be distrusted—*
2 **that** *they are evil incarnate.*
[*Note:* In this sentence, the **that**-*clause* at level 2 functions as an appositive.]
JEROME D. FRANK, *Law and the Modern Mind*

2. 1 **To live** *for the moment* is the prevailing passion—
2 **to live** *for yourself,*
3 not for your predecessors or posterity.
[*Note:* In this sentence, the **infinitive phrase** at level 2 functions as an appositive.]
CHRISTOPHER LASCH, *The Culture of Narcissism*

3. 2 Whenever he gave any money to Mother,
1 he asked her **what** *it was for* and made a note of it in his pocket notebook.
CLARENCE DAY, "Father and His Hard-Rocking Ship"

4. 1 I knew **that** *I had to move forward and continue on,*
for
1 **to turn** *back now* would be **making** *a decision* I would regret for the rest of my life.
STUDENT WRITER

5. 1 **What** *I am trying to do* is **to add** *together those elements, / , which I suppose* **to be** *the forces of off-campus history.*
2/ some horrible,
2/ some merely funny,
2/ but all significant
WILLIAM GOLDING, "Fable"

6. 1 **Brushing** *our teeth with Colgate toothpaste* becomes a dramatic and timely **warding off** *of terrible personal calamities,*
2 like **getting** *fired or* **losing** *one's girlfriend.*
S. I. HAYAKAWA, *Language in Thought and Action*

7. 1 Profits are now appraised not by the standards of **whether** *they are earned, deserved, or subject to the nine-point rule of possession,* but by the evidence of **whether** *they are favorable for economic performance.*

JOHN KENNETH GALBRAITH, *Economics and the Art of Controversy*

8. 1 I am fairly certain **that** *she is the only member of the American Academy of Arts and Letters, / , who has thwarted an attempted rape by* **staging** *a fit of* **sneezing.**
2/ male or female

JOHN HERSEY, "Lillian Hellman"

9. 2 "There is no boon in nature,"
1 one of the new philosophers had written harshly in the first years of the industrial cities.
1 Nevertheless, / , a sparse mercy had persisted,
2/ through war, famine, and death
2 like a mutation whose time had not yet come.
[Note the **direct quotation** in the first sentence.]

LOREN EISELEY, *The Unexpected Universe*

10. 1 I think man's gradual, creeping contamination of the planet, *his* **sending** *up of dust into the air,* his strontium additive in our bones, his discharge of industrial poisons into rivers that once flowed clear, *his* **mixing** *of chemicals with fog on the east wind* add up to a fantasy of such grotesque proportions as to make everything said on the subject seem pale and anemic by contrast.

E. B. WHITE, "Sootfall and Fallout"

Mr. Gatsby

Already it was deep summer on roadhouse roofs and in front of wayside garages, where new red gas-pumps sat out in pools of light, and when I reached my estate at West Egg I ran the car under its shed and sat for a while on an abandoned grass roller in the yard. The wind had blown off, leaving a loud, bright night, with wings beating in the trees and a persistent organ sound as the full bellows of the earth blew the frogs full of life. The silhouette of a moving cat wavered across the moonlight, and, turning my head to watch it, I saw **that** *I was not alone*— fifty feet away a figure had emerged from the shadow of my neighbor's mansion and was standing with his hands in his pockets regarding the silver pepper of the stars. Something in his leisurely movements and the secure position of his feet upon the lawn suggested **that** *it was Mr. Gatsby himself,* come out to determine **what** *share was his of our local heavens.*

I decided **to call** *to him.* Miss Baker had mentioned him at dinner, and that would do for an introduction. But I didn't call to him, for he gave a sudden intimation **that** *he was content to be alone*—he stretched out his arms toward the dark water in a curious way, and, far as I was from him, I could have sworn *he was trembling.** Involuntarily I glanced seaward—and distinguished nothing except a single green light, minute and far away, that might have been the end of a dock. When I looked once more for Gatsby he had vanished, and I was alone again in the unquiet darkness.

F. SCOTT FITZGERALD, *The Great Gatsby*

* a **that**-*clause* with **that** deleted

Chapter 13: RECOMBINING SENTENCES pages 268–280

Recombining Sentences: Recombinations

1. There lies the root of the matter.
   WALTER LIPPMANN, "The American Idea"

2. **It** was perfectly clear to me **what** *I ought to do.*
   GEORGE ORWELL, "Shooting an Elephant"

3. **It** is difficult **to overestimate** *the degree to which the invention of cellular respiration released the forces of living organisms.*
   GEORGE WALD, "The Origin of Life"

4. Over on Main Street sounded a man's voice, laughing.
   SHERWOOD ANDERSON, *Winesburg, Ohio*

5. **It** is a truth universally acknowledged **that** *a single man in possession of a good fortune must be in want of a wife.*
   JANE AUSTEN, *Pride and Prejudice*

6. "You have ideas; **what** you need **is** money," he said.
   STUDENT WRITER

7. **It was** a large mirror **that** climbed the wall in scrolls almost to the ceiling.
   LOUISE BOGAN, "Conversation Piece"

8. **What** both of us were too dumb to understand **was** that although great passions may be possible without actually liking each other, marriages aren't.
   A. ALVAREZ, *Life After Marriage*

9. **It was** Nietzsche **who** was to have the most decisive influence on de Chirico.
   JOHN ASHBERY, "Metaphysical Magic"

10. **It is** the leisure time, community organization, and specialization of labor in the first cities **that** permitted the emergence of the arts and technologies we think of as the hallmarks of civilization.
    CARL SAGAN, *The Dragons of Eden*

11. **There** is nothing more important for a narcissist than a smooth surface.
    JOSEPH BRODSKY, "Playing Games"

12. **There are** some people **who** cannot resist the desire to get into a cage with wild beasts and be mangled.
    HENRY MILLER, *Tropic of Cancer*

13. **There** were four men sitting at one of the tables, drinking coffee.
    STUDENT WRITER

14. **There is** nothing in the teachings of Jesus or St. Francis **that** justifies us in thinking that the opinions of fifty-one percent of a group are better than the opinions of forty-nine percent.
    WALTER LIPPMANN, "Why Should the Majority Rule?"

15. **There are** no universal geniuses; **there are** only universal fools.
    THOMAS SZASZ, *Heresies*

16. Biological evolution **has been accompanied by** increasing complexity.
    CARL SAGAN, *The Dragons of Eden*

17. Prison fixtures **are being installed** in the restrooms of city parks.
ROBERT SOMMER, *Tight Places*

18. English-usage guilt-feelings **have not** yet **been** noticeably **eased by** the work of linguistic scientists, parallel to the work **done by** the psychiatrists.
MARTIN JOOS, *The Five Clocks*

19. Attempts **were made by** prominent Iranians to organize political support for Bani-Sadr.
SHAUL BAKHASH, "The Day of the Mullahs"

20. The issue of women in combat **is made** problematic **by** the increasingly narrow definition of combat and the increasingly technological aspects of war.
MARY JO SALTER, "Annie, Don't Get Your Gun"

A Note on the English Character

There are national faults as **there are** national diseases, and perhaps one can draw a parallel between them. **It** has always impressed me **that** *the national diseases of England should be cancer and consumption*—slow, insidious, pretending to be something else; while the diseases proper to the South should be cholera and plague, which strike at a man when he is perfectly well and may leave him a corpse by evening. Mr. and Mrs. John Dashwood are moral consumptives. They collapse gradually without realizing what the disease is. **There** is nothing dramatic or violent about their sin. You cannot call them villains.

E. M. FORSTER, "Notes on the English Character"

Pros and Cons

There is nothing new about prisoners doing some honest work. As long ago as the early nineteenth century, industry **was seen** as the inmate's ticket to moral redemption, and wardens **were judged** by their bottom lines. By 1828 Sing Sing claimed to be economically self-sufficient by virtue of stonecutting, blacksmithing, and other activities. Private companies, however, sought to limit the competition from so much cheap labor. During the Depression, Congress came to the companies' aid by severely curtailing the right to sell **prison-made** goods across state lines. Work programs began to shut down. Many of those legal barriers remain, but prison industries are making a comeback for both sociological and financial reasons.

BENNETT H. BEACH, "Doing Business Behind Bars"

Small Town, U.S.A.

To grow up in a small town is to have not a number but a name and rank that **are known** to everybody, and a history too. It is to understand not how Edgar Lee Masters wrote *Spoon River Anthology,* but how he got his material, how he came to know the secret lives of so many so well. A small town rearing consists, by and large, of getting to know and **to be known by** everybody, and to feel that intimate communal familiarity as both affectionate support and unrelenting intrusion; the flight from intimacy to the city's anonymity **has** often **been impelled primarily by** a craving for privacy. The bonding that occurs when one's very history is community property is formidable and, to certain temperaments, oppressive. **It is** that bonding, that sense of utterly being of and belonging to a place, **that** makes most true small-towners more suspicious than city folk of strangers.

FRANK TRIPPETT, "Small Town, U.S.A."

Recombining Sentences: Acrobatics

Note: To help you see how these writers chose to combine the sentences, their versions are presented here in terms of levels of structure, with **recombining patterns** highlighted.

1. 1 **It** overlooks a staggering amount of basic research **to say** *that modern medicine began with the era of antibiotics.* [**it**-*inversion*]

LEWIS THOMAS, "The Planning of Science"

2. 1 **It is not known whether** *Debbie was a good student or not,* [**it**-*inversion,* passive]

for

1 she worked such long hours after school that she had little time left for studying.

STUDENT WRITER

3. 1 **It is** this smothering coat **that** needs constantly **to be stripped off,** [**it**-*cleft,* passive]

2 in life as well as in relationships.

ANNE MORROW LINDBERGH, *Gift from the Sea*

4. 1 **It is taken for granted by** everyone **that** *where labor* **is involved** *or where farmers* **are concerned there will** *always* **be** *a row.* [**it**-*inversion,* passive, **there**-*pattern*]

JOHN KENNETH GALBRAITH, *Economics and the Art of Controversy*

5. 1 **It** was vain **to pretend** *that she was an old friend,* [**it**-*inversion*]

for

1 all the communities were wanting,

2 in spite of which **it was** as an old friend **that** he saw she would have suited him. [**it**-*cleft* plus inversion]

HENRY JAMES, "The Beast in the Jungle"

6. 1 **There is** no precise time **recorded** when a majority of Americans looked up and decided that their government had ceased to be a friend and helper and had become a hindrance. [**there**-*pattern,* passive]

HUGH SIDEY, "When a Fed Was a Friend"

7. 1 Some things that happen to us **can't be borne,** [passive]

2 with the paradoxical result that we carry them on our backs the rest of our lives.

ANTHONY BRANDT, "Rite of Passage"

8. 2 In the Eden metaphor,

1 **there is** no evidence of murder before the Fall. [**there**-*pattern*]

But

1 those fractured skulls of bipeds not on the evolutionary line to man may be evidence that our ancestors killed, / , many manlike mammals.

2/ even in Eden

CARL SAGAN, *The Dragons of Eden*

9. 1 The futurist ethos **expressed by** Marinetti before World War I, / , supplied the oratorical framework for Mussolini's rise to power and set the stage for his appearance. [passive]

2/ with its cult of speed, male potency, antifeminism, and violent struggle

ROBERT HUGHES, *The Shock of the New*

10. 1 **It** is true **that** *the atomic bomb* **had been perfected** *only after Germany* **had been eliminated** *from the war,* and **that** *Japan was the only possible proving ground for the bomb as an actual weapon.* [**it**-*inversion,* passive]
2 Nevertheless,
1 **there were** many both in Japan and elsewhere in the Orient **who** would think that we had been willing to use a weapon of this terribleness against Japan when we might not have been willing to use it against a white enemy. [**there**-*cleft*]

NORBERT WIENER, *I Am a Mathematician*

Laying Waste

It has been apparent for quite some time now **that** *humankind is systematically fouling its own habitat,* littering its natural household with lethal debris that endangers life itself. Modern chemical industries spew out great masses of waste every day, some of it deadly beyond measure. The simplest way to dispose of those residues, of course, is to discharge them directly into the environment—to spill the vapors out into the atmosphere, to pour the liquids into nearby bodies of water, to dump the solids onto empty parcels of land. Because such methods **are** so widely **used,** we often take a certain comfort from the thought that many of the most hazardous of these wastes—chemical solvents, toxic substances, radioactive materials—**are sealed** away in underground dump sites, where **it is assumed that** *they stew impotently in their own juices for a few years and gradually lose their bite.*

We call this process "disposal," but it is a dangerously inapt word in many ways. To dispose means to get rid of, to discard, to do away with; and that is exactly what we find **it** hard **to do.** The chemicals we bury beneath our feet are among the best-built products of our shoddy age, tough chains of molecules that will not easily degrade or break down. Time has little effect on them. The sun will not purify them. All the waters in the world will not dissolve them or wash them clean. To store them in the ground, then, is to inject them into the body of the earth itself, where they can seep to the surface or bleed through the walls of their subterranean pits into the underground waterways on which all life depends.

It is sometimes difficult **to find** *the right words for describing this situation—* the right notes for sounding a general alarm—because the vocabularies and images on which we must draw for the purpose are so remote from everyday human experience. The chemicals leaking into our living spaces have long laboratory names that defy pronunciation and sound as sanitary as the ingredients in toothpaste. Their power to do harm **is** often **expressed** in fractions so minute (one part per billion, say, can be a dangerous dosage) that the mind does not know what to make of them. They **have been deposited** in so many dump sites throughout the country that a map identifying their locations would look like an explosion of dots. How, then, is one to convey the nature of the problem? How is one to organize all of those odd statistics, all of those technical details, into a story?

Every now and then an incident occurs in one of those places on the map, places with names like Minamata and Grassy Narrows, Seveso and the Love Canal. They are eruptions, angry boils on the surface of an infected earth, but they allow a story **to be told** because they involve manageable numbers of people, casualty figures that fall within the range of the normal human imagination, plots that **can be followed.**

KAI T. ERIKSON, "Laying Waste"

Chapter 14: REVIEW OF CHAPTERS 11, 12, 13 pages 281–289

Crazy Thoughts

My father was fair, his sidelocks dark, his beard red like tobacco. He had a short nose and blue eyes. A strange thought occurred to me—that he resembled the czar whose picture hung in our cheder. I knew well enough that a comparison like that was a sacrilege. The czar was a vicious man, and my father was pious and a rabbi. But my brain was full of crazy thoughts. If people knew what I was thinking, they would put me in prison. My parents would disown me. I would be excommunicated like the philosopher Spinoza, of whom my father spoke at the Purim dinner. That heretic had denied God. He said that the world was not created but had existed for eternity.

ISAAC BASHEVIS SINGER, "Guests on a Winter Night"

Three Heresies

A. In the classic tale about the emperor's finely woven clothes, a child discovers that the emperor is unclothed. That makes him a naked emperor. But, for modern man, the point of this story should be not that the emperor is naked, but that he is a liar.

B. The less a person understands another, the greater is his urge to classify him—in terms of nationality, religion, occupation, or psychiatric status. Intimate acquaintance with another person renders such classification quite unnecessary. Categorizing and classifying people is a means not of knowing them better, but of making sure that we will not know them too well. In short, classifying another person renders intimate acquaintance with him quite unnecessary—and impossible.

C. In intimate and lasting human relations, psychological autonomy and physical proximity vary inversely. Those who foolishly want to maximize both—for example, in marriage or friendship—will have neither; whereas those who wisely are satisfied with one or the other, or some of each sometimes—as married people used to be and as friends now tend to be—may have one or the other or sometimes some of each.

THOMAS SZASZ, *Heresies*

Review of Chapters 11, 12, 13: Sentence Acrobatics

Note: To help you see how these writers chose to combine the sentences, their versions are presented here in terms of levels of structure, with **absolute phrases, noun substitutes,** and **recombining patterns** highlighted.

1. 1 **There** are two great identical snakes on a Levantine libation vase of around 2000 B.C.,
   2 coiled around each other in a double helix,
   3 representing the original generation of life.

LEWIS THOMAS, "Some Biomythology"

2. 1 A sea of faces, / , ringed around us,
   2/ **some hostile,**
   2/ **some amused**
   and
   1 in the center, / , **stood a magnificent blonde—**
   2/ facing us
   2 stark naked.

RALPH ELLISON, *Invisible Man*

3. 2 Wherever technologies are producing changes not adequately **matched by** changes in social institutions,
1 **there** are people under strain and tension.
S. I. HAYAKAWA, *Language in Thought and Action*

4. 1 **That** *rote learning is the wrong way to teach reading* **was recognized** more than seventy years ago.
BRUNO BETTELHEIM AND KAREN ZELAN, *On Learning to Read: The Child's Fascination with Meaning*

5. 1 The separation or lateralization of cortical functions **was discovered** on **brain-damaged** individuals.
1 **It** is, / , important **to demonstrate that** *the conclusions apply to normal humans.*
2/ however
CARL SAGAN, *The Dragons of Eden*

6. 1 The Gallup polls are reports of **what** *people are thinking.*
But
1 **that** *a plurality of the people* **sampled** *in the poll think one way* has no bearing upon **whether** *it is sound public policy.*
WALTER LIPPMANN, *The Public Philosophy*

7. 2 Into the dark, smoky restaurant,
3 smelling of the rich raw foods on the buffet,
1 **slid Nicole's sky-blue suit** like a stray segment of the weather outside.
F. SCOTT FITZGERALD, *Tender Is the Night*

8. 1 He stood with his arms folded,
2 **a cat in each sleeve,**
2 resembling the Prophet Muhammad,
3 who, / , when he preached from the tallest minaret in Mecca **was seen** to carry his white cat, // , asleep in the sleeve of his robe.
4/ it **is written**
4// whom he called Muezza
KATINKA LOESER, "Taking Care"

9. 1 The beach sounds are jazzy,
2 **percussion fixing the mode—**
3 **the surf cracking and booming in the distance,**
3 **a little nearer dropped barbells clanking,**
3 **steel gym rings, / , ringing,**
4/ flung together
3 **palm fronds rustling above me,**
4 like steel brushes washing over a snare drum,
3 **troupes of sandals splatting and shuffling on the sandy cement,**
4 **their beat varying,**
5 **syncopation emerging and disappearing with changing paces.**
STUDENT WRITER*

10. 1 He had uttered a mad wish **that** *he himself might remain young, and the portrait grow old;* **that** *his own beauty might be untarnished, and the face on the canvas bear the burden of his passions and his sins;* **that** *the painted*

* This amazingly acrobatic sentence was created by a student of Francis Christensen's.

image might **be seared** *with the lines of suffering and thought, and* **that** *he might keep all the delicate bloom and loveliness of his then just conscious boyhood.*

OSCAR WILDE, *The Picture of Dorian Gray*

Some Self-Analysis

I have long wondered just what my strength was as a writer. I am often filled with tremendous enthusiasm for a subject, yet my writing about it will seem a sorry attempt. Above all, I possess a driving sincerity—that prime virtue of any creative worker. I write only what I believe to be the absolute truth—even if I must ruin the theme in doing so. In this respect I feel far superior to those glib people in my classes who often garner better grades than I do. They are too often pitiful frauds—artificial—insincere. They have a line that works. They do not write from the depths of their hearts. Nothing of theirs was ever born of pain. Many an incoherent yet sincere piece of writing has outlived the polished product.

THEODORE ROETHKE, *On the Poet and His Craft*

The Undefeated

Alone in the center of the ring the bull stood, still fixed. Fuentes, tall, flat-backed, walking toward him arrogantly, his arms spread out, the two slim, red sticks, one in each hand, held by the fingers, points straight forward. Fuentes walked forward. Back of him and to one side was a peon with a cape. The bull looked at him and was no longer fixed.

His eyes watched Fuentes, now standing still. Now he leaned back, calling to him. Fuentes twitched the two banderillos and the light on the steel points caught the bull's eye.

His tail went up and he charged.

He came straight, his eyes on the man. Fuentes stood still, leaning back, the banderillos pointing forward. As the bull lowered his head to hook, Fuentes leaned backward, his arms came together and rose, his two hands touching, the banderillos two descending red lines, and leaning forward drove the points into the bull's shoulder, leaning far in over the bull's horns and pivoting on the two upright sticks, his legs tight together, his body curving to one side to let the bull pass.

"Olé!" from the crowd.

The bull was hooking wildly, jumping like a trout, all four feet off the ground. The red shaft of the banderillos tossed as he jumped.

ERNEST HEMINGWAY, "The Undefeated," *The Short Stories of Ernest Hemingway*

INDEX